To the Real Heroes in the War against The Real Terrors.
To all those fighting Heart Disease, Cancer, Stroke,
Obesity, Diabetes, Alzheimer's, COPD (Emphysema),
Hypertension, AIDS, etc., The Aging Syndrome & Death

Published by Forever Young Books.

Special Quantity Pricing for bulk purchases for Bookstores, Classes,
Study   Groups,   or   Support   Groups   are   available.   Inquire   at
orders@foreveryoungbooks.com

ISBN-10: 0978602102
ISBN-13: 978-0978602109

Library of Congress Control Number: 2011926197

Visit any Websites below to get your FREE $99 Lifesaving Elixxir Newsletter
subscription for 6 months with your receipt. Also get latest Updates & News.

http://www.Immortalism.com
http://www.Elixxirprogram.com
http://www.Elixxir.com
http://www.ElixxirSociety.com
http://www.NoMoreDying.com

Table of Contents

Cure Disease, Old Age & Death

Join the Movement.

Sign Our Demand.

It may save your life.

- 9/11 killed about 3,000 people. A One-Time Tragedy.
- Heart Disease kills about 616,000 Americans — much more than half a million — each year. Over 205 times the U.S. deaths in 9/11.
- Cancer kills over half a million Americans each year. Around 563,000. That's 190 times 9/11.
- Stroke kills 136,000 Americans in one year. 45 times 9/11.
- Heart Disease, Cancer, and Stroke kill over 1.3 million Americans each year. Total U.S. Deaths from Terror-Diseases: more than 2 million Americans exterminated each year. Prematurely. Brutally. Needlessly.

Over 2 Million Dead from Diseases Every Year.
667 Times 9/11.
In One Year. **Every Year**.

Bush and the U.S. response to 9/11?

A blank check for the Pentagon's "War Against Terror" to replace the blank check for The Cold War. Invasions of Iraq and Afghanistan. Military disasters with no end in sight. Wars which the majority of Americans want to end.

The cost so far of the so-called "War Against Terror"?

Just the Iraq War alone has a pricetag so far of **$3 trillion!** (Best estimate by Nobel Laureate Joseph Stiglitz) Yes, that's 3,000 billion dollars right there.

The U.S. government's response to the more than 2 million Americans slaughtered by cancer, heart disease, stroke and other top killer-diseases ... each and every year?

Drop Dead!

Just as Science is on the verge of revolutionary breakthroughs. New lifesaving treatments. Even downright cures. The Bush-Cheney regime for five years stopped the increase in the National Institutes of Health's (NIH) research budget and started axing it. Just when stem cell research and the mapped genome offer real hope of new treatments and cures, Bush-Cheney banned all federal funding for stem cell research. Washington's death-meting cuts made the NIH lose 17% of its buying power.

Therefore **We The People....**

in pursuit of our inalienable rights to Life, Liberty and Happiness, and in light of the Wall Street bailouts which we the taxpayers were forced to pay for, hereby Demand and Order the U.S. Congress and the White House to provide immediately...

$888 BILLION for a

WAR AGAINST DISEASE, OLD AGE & DEATH (D.O.D.™)

to

1. **SAVE as many of the over 2 MILLION AMERICANS who will be KILLED *This* and *Every Year* by Heart Disease, Cancer, Stroke, Obesity, Emphysema, Alzheimer's, Diabetes, Pneumonia, Kidney & Liver diseases, Osteoporosis, AIDS, Parkinson's, Spinal Cord Injury, Septicemia and other major terrors;**

2. **RESCUE Americans fighting life-threatening illnesses from financial hardship or bankruptcy by giving them EMERGENCY FINANCIAL AID for unemployment, disability, health care, longterm nursing care, Medicare before retirement age, and the option of early retirement;**

3. **INCREASE RESEARCH FUNDING DRAMATICALLY to discover new and better Preventions, Treatments and CURES for Heart Disease, Cancer, Stroke, Obesity, Alzheimer's and all major killers;**

   Our War Against Disease, Old Age & Death will fund a *new scientific paradigm* which views heart disease, cancer, stroke, diabetes, osteoporosis, Alzheimer's, obesity as Diseases of Aging, as Symptoms of The Aging Syndrome. In line with the 1974 act of Congress creating the National Institute on Aging.

   Anti-aging research is the most probable, the cheapest, and the fastest path to revolutionary treatments and cures for age-related diseases like heart disease, cancer, stroke, Alzheimer's, and obesity.

Anti-aging research is the most direct and obvious solution to our number one national security threat: our aging population.

79 million Americans from the boomer generation falling prey to costly chronic aging-related diseases is a dire threat to the U.S. health care system and to the U.S. economy.

We therefore demand $100 billion for the National Institutes of Health (NIH). Of this $100 billion, $25 billion must go to the National Institute on Aging (NIA). All other NIH institutes' budgets should be maintained or increased. $25 billion will go to support promising anti-disease anti-aging research labs and scientists around the world.

4. PREVENT CANCER, HEART DISEASE, STROKE, and all other top killers. Through funding, creating, or investing in scientific DIETARY or LIFESTYLE-CHANGE programs which are proven to (or are likely to) prevent or slash our risk for aging-correlated ailments like cancer, heart disease, stroke, obesity, hypertension, diabetes, Alzheimer's, osteoporosis.

To avoid waste and corruption, this $888 billion all-out War Against Disease, Old Age & Death will be administered by a new Department of Life which will be staffed and overseen by people from Nonprofits and Advocacy Organizations, national and local, established and new, organized by or serving people fighting life-threatening diseases and The Aging Syndrome.

Since most of these 2 million plus yearly deaths are premature, preventable, needless and tragic, We the People order the White House and the U.S. Congress to approve this $888 billion bailout with the utmost urgency and overriding priority since there are 667 times the number of 9/11 American fatalities being killed this year. This is not a one-time outrage. But an annual atrocity.

We the People are Sovereign. Therefore to disobey our Order is to be guilty of the most lethal and unforgivable High Crimes & Treason subject to Impeachment.

NAME _____

Signature _____

Mailing Address _____

_____

E-mail _____

Cell Phone _____ **Phone** _____

Profession/Job _____

Facebook _____

Twitter _____

Website _____

U.S. Citizen? _____ **Eligible to Vote?** _____ **Age** _____

___ **Please contact me! I can help more by**

   ___**Donations** ___**Volunteering**

Date Signed _____

PLEASE TAKE A MINUTE NOW
& GO TO http://www.NoMoreDying.com

Join thousands of Americans. SIGN THIS ORDER online to Congress and the White House.

IT MAY SAVE YOUR LIFE.

In submitting our final signatures for our Demand, we will only submit your name, address and signature. The other info is for us to authenticate your identity only, and to see how we can all work to spread the word on the net of our urgent life-saving Demand.

Foreword

Therefore choose life, that you and your descendants may live.
Deuteronomy 30:19

Y ou are going to grow old and die. Not because it is necessary. But because the powers that be have decided you
must. And they're betting on your going quietly into that
dark night.

Let me explain. For the first time in human history, we have
the tools to slow down, stop, or even reverse your biological aging.

With the successful mapping of the human genome, it is just
a matter of time.

Science can track down the handful of genes believed to control the human aging process, your aging process. As soon as we
identify these genes, we shall "modify" them to retard, stop, or
turn back the clock on your biological aging, and let you escape
death with an indefinitely-prolonged lifespan in which you are
"eternally" youthful, vigorous, and healthy.

200 Years Young? Ask The *New York Times*

Wishful thinking? Don't just take my word for it!

Recently, The *New York Times* ran a story on "Pushing Limits
of the Human Life Span." It covered a conference in Los Angeles
of a group of "eminent academic scientists who have reputations

to think of." The Times reported that this distinguished group of scientists agrees that science is on the verge of "significantly" extending the human lifespan. How significantly? Up "to 150, 200 or more years," is the group's consensus. The Times concluded: "The question no longer is 'Will it happen?' But rather 'When?'"

The cover of *Esquire*, the respected men's magazine, recently asked "CAN YOU LIVE FOREVER?" Inside was a special 12-page report including a meditation on "A World of Immortal Men" by Edward O. Wilson, the distinguished and renowned Harvard professor and intellectual. And what does Wilson, the recipient of the National Medal of Science and two-time Pulitzer Prize winner, think of our prospect for immortality? "I see no reason why humanity and the species as a whole cannot be immortal," the Harvard professor concludes.

Ask Dr. William Haseltine, founder of Human Genome Sciences and a former Harvard professor. Dr. Haseltine is considered brilliant even by his detractors and certainly no idle daydreamer. What does he think about the possibility of humans staying young for hundreds of years, indefinitely, even "forever"?

"I believe our generation is the first to be able to map a possible route to individual immortality," Dr. Haseltine has publicly stated. "This is the first time we can conceive of human immortality." He elaborates: *"If we can give you a resupply of those stem cells, we can keep you young as a mature adult...forever."* (italics added)

And you know what? No one's laughing. In fact, joining him in this conclusion is Dr. Ronald Klatz, President of the American Academy of Anti-Aging Medicine who declares flatly that "Human immortality is achievable by the year 2029."

Whether it's 2029 or later or earlier, cutting-edge scientists like Dr. Michael West, the founder of Geron and Advanced Cell Technologies, agree with Haseltine and Klatz in their basic conclusion that sooner or later, humans will become immortal.

In evolutionary time, it is five minutes to D-Day. Five minutes to our finally achieving humanity's most ancient dream: Freedom from Disease, Old Age & Death (D.O.D.™)

Why They Want You to Grow Old & Die

Yes, it's going to happen. But the question is, Will it happen in time for you?

It's a race against Time. It's a matter of life and death, literally. So you would think that your government is doing everything in its power to save your life, right?

Wrong!

Let me give you one cold, cruel fact. And if it does not stir you into anger and action, then you deserve to rot and die.

One Stealth B-2 bomber costs $2.2 billion. That is more than twice as much as the entire National Institute on Aging (NIA) budget for biological aging research, the most important thing the U.S. government is doing right now, bar none! (The Pentagon wanted to order 40 more Stealth bombers. That would have been 88 billion dollars right there.)

Anti-aging life-extension research can save not only you, but your spouse, your lover, your children, your parents, your best friends. And this manifesto shall explain why anti-aging life-extension research is also our best hope to save the planet from Global Warming and Biodiversity Loss.

But as a priority, anti-aging life-extension research ranks almost dead bottom for the U.S. government. And to a lesser or greater degree, it is also one of the lowest priorities for most governments in the world.

At a time when anti-aging breakthroughs (which can cure us of Killer-Diseases like Cancer, Heart Disease, Stroke, Diabetes, Alzheimer's) are imminent, only 4% of the most recent budget of the National Institutes of Health (NIH) went to the National Institute on Aging (NIA), the most important U.S. government agency as far as saving your life is concerned.

This is how much contempt the powers that be have for you.

You don't count; you're worth shit. In the government's calculations, you're disposable garbage! (The exact figures may change slightly from year to year, but the same situation remains.)

Listen to Richard Cutler, Ph.D., a distinguished gerontologist and a veteran of the NIA: *"The public ought to know that their government is not trying to cure aging."*

Why not? When most people fear growing old and dying more than anything else, and rightly so! Why not when an aging demographics is our biggest socio-political problem?

Because, Dr. Cutler answers, *"They're scared to death about the impact it might have upon the economy of the nation — too many old people around."*

In other words, the U.S. government is playing God. It has decided that you must grow old and die. For the good of the economy, of course.

By this monstrous coldblooded calculation, your aging, ailing parents should commit suicide as soon as possible. People with AIDS should check out too. After all, the anti-AIDS "cocktails" which can keep them alive are simply too expensive. Especially for all who desperately need it in poor Third World countries. Disabled or retarded people? Show them the exit! After all, they're all bad for the economy.

Who gave them the mandate to play God with our lives? Isn't this the kind of reasoning which eventually leads to the gas chambers of The Third Reich?

How can the powers that be be so cocksure that you won't flex your voting muscles and throw them bums out? How can they bank on your being so well-behaved, so passive, so submissive?

They can be so cocky because from day one you have been relentlessly, effectively, and subtly programmed with **The Death Ideology (Mortalism),** the belief system of The Death Society. The ideology that *turns our changeable biological condition into* *immutable ontological essence.* The ideology that *glorifies Aging and Death as "natural," "a part of life," "acts of God," "the keys to a better life," "closure," "fulfillment" and even "enlightenment." And last but not least, the ideology which worships surrender to Death as "heroism" or "martyrdom."*

Paradigms have consequences. The wrong paradigm will kill you. The right paradigm will save you.

The wrong paradigm — The Death Ideology or The Mortalist Paradigm — results in the U.S. government spending almost nothing on the only thing that really matters to your personal physical survival — basic anti-aging research.

The Death Ideology also explains why those Nasty Old Men in Washington (and they are still mostly men) could find at least 100 billion dollars for an anti-missile missile system, but cannot find any money for giving the American people universal health care or adequate retirement security.

The wrong ideology also explains why we have Extreme Capitalism, or the excesses of **"Globalization"** and the so-called **"New World Order."** These are all aliases for Mortalist Capitalism.

Globalization or "Market Capitalism" must be so harsh and punitive because it is nothing but Economic Puritanism in sheep's clothing.

<u>Economic Puritanism is the Mortalist superstition that because of humanity's "fall" we are "cursed" by a wrathful Yahweh in Genesis and are allowed to eat and live only by the sweat of our toil.</u> "...In the sweat of thy face shalt thou eat bread..." Genesis 3: 17-19. The other part of this "curse" is Mortality, the superstition that we must die because of "the fall." This superstition is still strong today, and it becomes a self-fulfilling prophecy for all those who believe in it. Its conclusive and merciless debunking is an important part of this manifesto.

The *"work ethic"* of "Globalization" and "The New World Order" *decrees that punitive toil is our end, not the means to our end.* This is the key to the puzzle as to why in this age of computers, automation, robots, and Internet, mortals are working harder than ever before — even in the richest societies.

Mortalist Work is designed to be excessive, compulsive, joyless and always punitive. It is still executing a 4,000 year "curse" — The Genesis Curse — hurled by Yahweh against all of humanity for all time because Eve screwed up by picking the wrong apple in the "garden." If you wonder why you or your loved ones or parents are working so irrationally hard, it is because of this Death Ideology programming written into that software called your brain. All mortals are still "doing hard time."

The aim of The Productivity Fetish in the so-called "global economy" is to deprive us of pleasure, fulfillment, and happiness. This is the essence and function of Economic Puritanism. Just as in the sexual realm, it is the fear that someone somewhere is having fun. (See "The Death Ideology," "The Genesis Curse: The Origin of the 'Work Ethic,' "Mortalist Capitalism & Its Discontents")

The Immortalist Manifesto not only criticizes the excesses of "Globalization" or "The New World Order," it also offers a **compelling new alternative.** It is the first and only attempt to present a new, viable, life-affirming worldview and paradigm as an answer to the ideology of Extreme Globalist Capitalism.

You will see why The Mortalist Paradigm (aka The Death Ideology) is as out of date as the earth-is-flat paradigm in the emerging Post-Mortalist Era we're already in, in The Elixxir Society that is coming. (We are already Post-Mortalist, not yet Immortalist.) You will understand how deadly the wrong paradigm is to you and society. And you will have the alternative in your hands: the Immortalist Paradigm, the Post-Mortalist Worldview.

You will understand why there are such rantings and ravings by Mortalism (and its chief apologist Mortalist Christianity i.e.

the Vatican, the Religious Right) against human cloning, stem-cell research, organ replacements, human genome mapping, bio-technology and nanotechnology (electronic circuits and devices built at molecular level), and more.

Why the Vatican and the Pope are still railing against in vitro fertilization which has given life to over 300,000 worldwide, and the joy of children and grandchildren to many more.

The Vatican and the old Mortalist Religions. They are against nonprocreative sex (Post-Mortal Sex) or nonsexual procreation (Post-Mortal Procreation). Of course they are! These are after all the unwitting herald of the fact that we are already in the early days of The Post-Mortalist Era.

Our brave new world is as unstoppable and irreversible as the new dawn. Just as the Vatican and its theologians and "ethicists" have failed to stop the Pill and the Condom, so too they are failing in their frenzied and shrill campaign to stop the emergence of The Post-Mortalist Era and a full-fledged Immortalist Era.

You will see that nothing makes more sense of the new mil-lennium we're in than this new paradigm and worldview. You will say Eureka! after you finish this book. The pieces of the puzzle will fall into place. It will suddenly all make sense. You will suddenly have at your command the language and analysis to describe your yearnings, frustrations, and hopes. You will possess a totally new paradigm which fits perfectly with the new world of biotech and nanotechnology that we're thrust into. Unlike others, you will be able to digest and assimilate and benefit.

And more importantly, this new Immortalist paradigm gives you the real possibility of literally saving your own life, and that of our planet from Global Warming.

Sooner or later, humans will no longer grow old and die. Sooner or later, humans will stay young and live forever. **But it must be sooner, not later, for you and me!**

For to miss this most momentous milestone of human history, this next step in evolution, by even a day is like missing by a million years!

This manifesto gives you a gameplan to prevent such an unmitigated tragedy. <u>Your fate, and that of the human species, is in your hands.</u>

Stay Young & Prosper!™

Elixxir

PART I
NO MORE DYING: *A PREVIEW*

1   Disease, Old Age and Death are no longer necessary or acceptable. We are either the last to grow old and die, or the first to stay young and live forever. We choose to be the first to stay young and live forever.

2   Our goal is simple: Kill Disease, Old Age and Death!

3   We demand that the conquest of Disease, Old Age and Death be the number one priority of every society on the planet.

4   We demand a dramatic increase in funding for research to cure Diseases like Heart Disease, Cancer, Stroke which kill 1.3 million just in the U.S. each year. Or about 70% of all deaths in most countries.

5   If trying to prevent the 3,000 killed by militant attacks on the World Trade Center and the Pentagon from happening again justifies 3 trillion for invading and occupying Iraq and Afghanistan, then preventing 2.2 million U.S. deaths each year from heart disease, cancer, stroke and other top killer diseases justifies a proportional increase in funding for Disease and Anti-Aging Research. The 2.2 million American deaths are a sure thing year-in and year-out. And it is a bigger threat than any war or "rogue state" — in fact it is more than all the deaths from all the wars waged by or participated in by the U.S., including the First and Second World Wars.

6   Since Science and Medicine already recognize them as "aging-related diseases," we demand that instead of plunking down all our funding on symptoms of Aging such as Heart Disease, Cancer, Stroke, Diabetes, Alzheimer's, we need to also invest in a new paradigm, an alternative strategy which seeks to cure aging-related diseases such as Cancer, Heart Disease, Stroke, Diabetes, Alzheimer's by funding anti-aging research which is probably the fastest and cheapest path to curing Heart Disease, Cancer, Stroke, Diabetes, Alzheimer's, and other top killer diseases.

7 As **an aging population and demographics is the Number One Threat to the economic security and future of the**

U.S., E.U., Japan and many other countries, we point out that the most direct and obvious solution to this problem is anti-aging research to keep the population biologically youthful, healthy and productive for as long as possible. This allows chronologically advanced people to keep producing and contributing to the economy. And since they stay healthy, they will not overburden and collapse health care systems with serious chronic and protracted diseases.

8   **Human Biological Aging is the master disease. Heart disease, cancer, stroke, diabetes, Alzheimer's and most, if not all, of our top killers-diseases are symptoms of The Aging Syndrome.** This is what scientists and physicians really mean when they describe such diseases as "aging-related" or "aging-correlated." But The Death Society we live in does not allow Science, Medicine and Research to go after the root cause of it all. Scientists, doctors and researchers are funded to go after symptoms of aging, but not aging, the master disease, itself.

9   This is an irrational strategy which is extremely frustrating and costly. If we can control or cure The Aging Syndrome, its symptoms will be prevented or disappear. Just as pneumonia and Kaposi's sarcoma in people with AIDS are symptoms of AIDS. We are not foolish enough to squander all our AIDS research budget on its many symptoms, but instead focus on curing, treating or preventing AIDS. We demand the same funding strategy for curing heart disease, cancer, and stroke and all major killer-diseases.

10 Mobilize Science and Medicine. Track down the human aging process. Control, retard and reverse it. And heart disease, cancer, stroke, diabetes, Alzheimer's and obesity will all disappear like smallpox and polio.

11 The rationale behind the Immortalist agenda: Humanity cannot be truly happy until it has banished Disease, Old Age and Death SM (D.O.D.).

12 The Death Ideology, the ideology which worships a change-able biological reality as ontological essence, must be over-thrown. This Mortalism which makes us submit and grovel to Disease, Old Age and Death must fall like the walls of Jericho.

13 *Accepting Disease, Old Age and Death is a perversion of our natural instinct for self-preservation. The only ones who are "not afraid" of Old Age and Death: the clinically depressed, the Haters of Life.*

14 We indict Disease, Old Age and Death as the root cause of all human misery, neurosis, and depression. As long as Old Age and Death exist, there can be no true happiness. We expose evil as the dance of mortals playing god. We convict the evil trinity of Disease, Old Age and Death for Crimes Against Humanity.

15 In the beginning was The Dream. The conquest of aging and death. The attainment of the elixir of youth. The advent of physical immortality. The Dream is about to come true.

16 In the not too distant future — in our lifetimes, we will no longer grow old or die, as humans have since time immemorial.

17 Humanity's epic struggle against Mortality is about to end with a decisive victory. Our weapons include diet, science, medicine, molecular biology, genetic engineering, cloning, artitificial intelligence, nanotechnology, whatever it takes. Success is inevitable.

18 Immortality is our **Evolutionary Destiny**.

19 The Bible foretold of its advent. "Behold, I show you a mystery: We shall not all sleep, but we shall all be changed.... in the twinkling of an eye...this corruption shall put on incorruption, and this mortal must put on immortality... (I Corinthians 15: 51-53).

20 The First Breakthrough in anti-aging and life-extension research has already happened. Yet most people do not know it.

21 Science has repeatedly proven there is an eating program which can keep us young, slim and sexy for life. It can dramatically slow our aging so we can stay young and healthy to 120 years or more. This breakthrough scientific program is also our best bet for preventing cancer, heart disease, stroke, hypertension, diabetes, osteoporosis, and Alzheimer's, without prohibitively expensive drugs and technology. And it can extend the maximum human lifespan of 120 by up to 50%, in vigor and health. How to transform this 100% scientific youth-extending program into la dolce vita (the sweet life)? Answer: The Elixxir Program™.

22 More anti-aging life-extension breakthroughs are coming soon. With the help of revolutionary advances in human genome mapping, diet, nutrition, preventive medicine, stem-cell research and cloning (of replacement organs), molecular biology, genetic engineering, nanotechnology (nanorobots cleaning up mess caused by aging at cellular level), we will stop the aging process dead in its tracks, soon.

The Elixxir Gameplan for Survival

23 Each breakthrough will give us mortals that most precious of all commodities — Time. Each breakthrough will allow us to stay around long enough to benefit from the next breakthrough.

24 Each breakthrough will take less and less time to arrive as progress in anti-aging life-extension research will become exponential. Average life expectancy will therefore quickly jump to 90, 100, 120 and beyond. The current "maximum" human lifespan of 120 years shall be greatly exceeded. (Anti-aging is life-extending. When you retard aging, you stretch lifespan.)

25 For the first time in history, we shall have an indefinitely-extended lifespan, and more importantly, an indefinitely-extended youthspan and healthspan.

26 If we stay around long enough, Virtual Immortality — a situation of de facto Immortality where we cannot die except by murder, accident or suicide — is ours.

27 Once Virtual Immortality is attained, Actual Immortality is a matter of time.

∞

We demand a Real War
against The Real Terrors.

9/11 killed around 3,000.

But every year, Heart Disease, Cancer,
Stroke kill 1.3 million in the U.S. alone.

∞

∞

We demand that the conquest of Disease, Old Age and Death (D.O.D.) be the Number One Priority of every society and government on the planet.

∞

28 <u>The Elixxir Gameplan.</u> **First, get on The Elixxir Program to stay young, healthy, and buy time. Second, create an ImmorTalist movement powerful enough to guarantee the anti-aging life-extension breakthroughs arrive in time for us and is available to all who desire it. Third, gain more years from each breakthrough until we can stay youthful, healthy, and slim for as long as we wish.**

29 Yes, given time, and assuming we don't let Global Warming destroy us, <u>it is inevitable that we shall conquer Disease, Old Age and Death (D.O.D.). But it is not inevitable that humanity's conquest of D.O.D. will come in time to save you or me. Only the greatest of all grassroots and mass movements will be able to maximize the chances that The Cure will come in time to save us, in our lifetime!</u>

30 This is what the **Techno-Utopians** in their polyannaish fantasies refuse to see. This is why they are **Pseudo-Immortalists**. For real immortalists operate with eyes wide open.

31 For the billions around the world struggling with a life-threatening illness like Heart Disease, Cancer or Stroke, the most potent movement to lobby for breakthrough drugs which can mimic the results of The Elixxir Program is absolutely a matter of life and death. There is no more higher priority or urgency.

32 If you are fighting a life-threatening disease, your best and perhaps only hope for a Cure in time to save you lies with the success of The ImmorTalist movement. Why? Because no other movement or party or church makes the Cure of Heart Disease, Cancer, Stroke or whatever disease you are suffering from its number one priority, bar none.

33 The Mortalist Era is dying, The Post-Mortalist Era is emerging. This is what all the controversy and debate over genome mapping, cloning, stem-cell research, organ replacements, in virtro fertilization, molecular biology, biotechnology and nanotechnology are all about.

34 The Human is evolving into the Superhuman, and we are its vanguard. We have seen the future, and it is us.

35 We are not yet immortals, but we have rejected Death — and are on our way. We are the "first fruits" of Immortality, and it is our mission to make it available to as many as possible.

36 We Immortalists do not care to be "mainstream." To be mainstream is to age and die in the "normal" way.

37 We Immortalists are inherently scandalous. <u>In The Death Society we live in, to openly desire to stay young forever is the biggest scandal.</u>

38 To desire to stay forever young is to be attacked by Death Ideologists as "narcissistic," "immature," "irresponsible," "bimbo," even "queer." These epithets have always been thrown at women and gays by the powers that be. We embrace them as great Immortalist virtues.

39 We Immortalists are notorious rule-breakers. The ultimate rule: you must grow old and die. We spit on the ultimate rule.

40 Our Immortalist gameplan for success in life is to outlast the competition.

41 Even "Sir" Nathan Meyer Rothschild glimpsed the wisdom of our strategy when he reportedly said, "I've got to keep breathing. It'll be my worst business mistake if I don't."

42 <u>Our goal is physical immortality, not financial immortality.</u>

43 Anti-Aging Research is the shortest, cheapest and fastest route to a Cure for Heart Disease, Cancer, Stroke, Obesity, Diabetes, Parkinson's and Alzheimer's.

∞

**Anti-Aging Research is the
shortest, cheapest and fastest route
to a Cure for Heart Disease,
Cancer, Stroke, Obesity,
Diabetes, Parkinson's and Alzheimer's.**

∞

• This is because, as Science and Medicine recognize, they are all "aging-related diseases." Or Diseases of Aging.

• Yet The Death Society refuses to invest any real money on anti-aging research. The most likely path to a Cure to save you in time from one of the aging-related killers.

• Why? Because the Mortalist regimes' Death Ideology believes they are allowed to go after the symptoms of aging only, but they dare not touch Aging, the master disease. Their Superstition is killing you and your loved ones.

How to Cure Cancer & Heart Disease: Beyond Mortalist Medicine

44 We expose Mortalist medicine as mere band-aid. It dares not go after the ultimate culprit — Old Age and Death. It only attacks their symptoms — heart attack, stroke, cancer, diabetes, or crippled immune system. We advocate Immortalist Medicine, which labors under no such superstition. It recognizes no sacred cows, no taboos. It dares to track down the root cause of all Disease.

45 A new strategy for conquering top killers such as cancer, heart disease, stroke, diabetes, Alzheimer's, and osteoporosis is desperately needed.

46 *Instead of trying to cure or treat each disease one by one, The Elixxir Society will tackle them all at once by targeting the overall problem of biological aging.*

47 This is because all these killer-diseases are aging-related. They increase in probability as we grow biologically older. Therefore if we greatly retard our rate of biological aging, we will greatly decrease our rate of falling prey to these ailments.

48 We shall triumph over Disease by curing Old Age and Death, not vice versa. Cancer, heart disease, stroke, malaria, AIDS

and all the other top killers will be conquered only when there is a **paradigm shift** from Mortalism to Immortalism.

49 Staying youthful biologically as we advance chronologically is the <u>most efficient and cost-effective way</u> to prevent these major afflictions which bring so much suffering, expense, and Death to humanity.

50 **We Immortalists fight against any cuts in government funding for research on cancers, heart disease, hypertension, stroke, diabetes, AIDS, Alzheimer's, Parkinson's and other top killer-diseases. At the same time, we demand an all-out drive (at the same level as the Pentagon budget) to discover, control, retard and reverse the causes of human biological aging, knowing that it promises to be the shortest route to a cure for Cancer, Heart Disease, Stroke, Obesity, Diabetes, Alzheimer's and other top killers.**

51 While not all of us will be afflicted by cancer or heart disease, all of us will surely grow old and die – unless we have a great historical movement which enshrines as our national and global priority the conquest of Old Age and Death and rescues us in time.

52 The Elixxir Society™ shall not rest until all the major afflictions of humankind are conquered. It shall not rest until the scourge of Disease is wiped off the face of the earth for all time. But it understands that even if the top diseases were all eradicated today, we will only add a few more years to lifespan, and will still grow old and die! So going after symptoms of Aging but not Aging itself means society will have all the same chronic problems and more arising from a population aging badly and lingering rudely.

53 This is why Immortalism rejects The Death Ideology's insistence that we should stop at curing diseases instead of seizing the momentum to march forward on that last mile to storm and overrun the evil fortress of Disease, Old Age and Death.

54 If your loved one has fallen prey to cancer, heart disease, AIDS, or any of the major killers, you owe it to their memory to support our War on D.O.D. (Disease, Old Age & Death) to eradicate that which killed your loved one.

55 Humans will no longer be plagued by chronic ailments from midlife on. The Elixxir Society demands not only greatly extended lifespan but also greatly extended healthspan. This will prevent our healthcare system from collapsing under the weight of caring for ever-increasing numbers of the biologically old who are surviving longer but suffering from chronic ailments, disability, or senility and in need of exorbitant medical or nursing home care.

56 *Ensuring that chronologically advanced people stay biologically young is the best way to guarantee the solvency of our health care system.*

57 AIDS will be a thing of the past.

58 The Elixxir Society™ will spare no effort or resource to eradicate this plague from our life, our planet. It will make the development of an AIDS vaccine a high priority. Any AIDS treatment that is available to the First World will be available to the Third World.

59 From 1997 to 2001, an estimated 438,000 persons in the U.S. alone died each year from diseases caused by smoking or exposure to secondhand smoke. (US Centers for Disease Control) This means 1.75 million Americans died of smoking-related causes in four short years. Worldwide, smoking-related deaths are estimated to now kill 6 million people. (WHO) And the U.S. Death Society, through its Commerce Department, pushes U.S. tobacco on poor Third World countries. The Tobacco Cartel is guilty of the most monstrous Crimes against Humanity. This pogrom is repeated year in and year out. And yet it's totally legal in The Death Societies which rule the world.

60 The Elixxir Society will not tolerate up to a quarter of its deaths being smoking-related. If the tobacco industry does not produce a safe cigarette, and if they keep pushing cigarettes on kids and poor Third World countries, then we shall be forced to put the tobacco industry on trial as the bloodiest mass murderers in world history. (China and the E.U. should follow the footsteps of American states and sue tobacco companies for reimbursement of the cost of caring for smoking-caused diseases such as lung cancer, heart disease, and emphysema.)

The Real Threat to the U.S. & Other 'Developed' Nations

61 *The biggest threat to the "national security" of all the affluent societies,* whether it's the United States, Japan, Germany, Great Britain, or Sweden, *is not the threat of foreign missiles but their aging populations.*

62 *There is <u>only one real direct solution: anti-aging breakthroughs</u> so that these graying populations can stay biologically youthful while advancing chronologically. If the chronologically advanced continue to be healthy and productive, they can boost the economy and safety net instead of collapsing them.*

63 Investing in anti-aging research is a matter of national survival. The choice facing affluent societies is either solve the aging demographics problem or perish.

64 The Forever Young Society will be the most productive society in all of history. This is because in The Death Society, productivity is limited to a few decades between young adulthood and late-middle-age (twenties to early sixties). It takes almost two decades to train a person for maximum productivity. But retirement is at 65 or earlier. Because of midlife ailments such as heart disease, high blood pressure, cancer, diabetes, arthritis, and obesity, productivity declines in a Death Society like the U.S. soon after a person turns thirty.

We shall triumph over Cancer and Heart Disease
by curing Old Age and Death, not vice versa.

65 In The Forever Young Society (aka The Elixxir Society), it will still take the same amount of time to train someone. But since lifespan in the Forever Young Society will be at least 120, and since most will be in vibrant health for almost all of this span, productivity can continue until one is 100 years old or more. This is at the very least eight decades of productivity in The Forever Young Society compared to four in The Death Society.

66 In the U.S. workers will have at least twice as many productive years to pay into Social Security or pension plans. In European countries workers will have twice as much time to pay into their social welfare systems and their pensions. This is the way to guarantee that social welfare states will not collapse but instead thrive, and that the next generation and the next will continue to draw benefits.

Beyond Retirement-Unto-Death

67 *Instead of Retirement-Until-Death, we will have Serial Mini-Retirements (sabbaticals) starting as early as our thirties. After every ten years of work, we will get a year or two off.*

68 We Immortalists refuse to sacrifice our youth and prime on the altar of mindless and endless toil until 65. We will not burn ourselves out or squander our lives to hoard filthy lucre. We're more interested in making a life than making a living.

69 *Much of life in a limited-lifespan (Mortalist) society is wrecked by the need to fearfully and obsessively save up for retirement.* Mortalists deny and deprive themselves all throughout their adult life — they simply do not live! — so that they can have a little "nest egg" in retirement. Why do they get so frantic and neurotic about saving for retirement? It's because they expect to be sick, decrepit and senile in their "golden years." And they're terrified that they'll have no money to retain some dignity. This fear will disappear in The Elixxir Society where basic economic security is guaranteed.

70 When we know we are not going to be bedridden, senile, or old, when we know we can continue working past 65 at a good job, then we will be freed from the need to hoard for retirement. And life will be a hundred times more fulfilling and fun.

70A *Social Security in the U.S. will not collapse. The Elixxir Society will not only preserve Social Security payments, it will increase them. This is the way to fix it.*

71 The truth is this: even if absolutely nothing is done about Social Security, it will remain fully solvent until the year 2034. After that, if nothing is done, it will still be capable of paying up to 75% of what it owes retirees well into the next century.

72 Social Security will be there to fund all of our happy Mini-Retirements or sabbaticals in The Elixxir Society. (Unless we let the U.S. government steal $13 billion here and there from our Social Security surplus to fund costly little wars of absolutely no strategic importance.)

73 People will not want to retire at 65 if they are going to live up to 100 and beyond in good health and youthful vigor. Once they return from a Mini-Retirement, they will rejoin the work force and pump more money into the Social Security System.

Lifelong Financial Security

74 *Financial security is guaranteed not only in our later years but all throughout life — this is the ironclad guarantee of The Forever Young Society.*

75 In Elixxir's Forever Young Society, we may not be as rich as Bill Gates, but we will never have to worry about health insurance, poverty, retirement, hunger, homelessness. If we fall, there will be a strong net to catch us.

76 It's better than what's left of The American Dream — winning the lottery.

Beyond GNP & GDP

77 In The Elixxir Society, the ALE (Average Life Expectancy) and the HLE (Healthy Life Expectancy, the number of years one can expect to remain healthy) are more important than the GNP (Gross National Product) and the GDP (Gross Domestic Product). This is because the ALE or HLE is the best overall indicator of how close a society is to The Forever Young Society.

78 If ALE or HLE is high across the demographic spectrum, it usually means there is good, affordable, universally available health care, high literacy/good education, high levels of employment, a good safety net for hard times, and a nutritionally adequate diet.

The solution: anti-aging breakthroughs so the population can stay biologically youthful while advancing chronologically, continuing to be healthy and productive, boosting the economy and safety net instead of collapsing them.

79 The Elixxir Society does not judge itself based on the size or growth of its GNP or GDP (Gross Domestic Product). This is the pathological obsession of The Death Society where GNP is an end in itself. As the poor and middle-class in Third World and even First World nations know, even a GDP growth of 8% a year is irrelevant and worthless if it goes only to a tiny elite of the filthy rich.

80 We ImmorTalists are more interested in Quality of Life than "Standard of Living."

81 *Productivity (the amount a worker produces in one hour) is a Mortalist obsession. Immortalists (not to mention Immortals) see no reason to obsess about what they produce in each hour of an "eternal" existence of hundreds of years or more.*

∞

**The biggest threat to the 'national security'
of the United States, Japan, Germany,
Great Britain or Sweden is not foreign
missiles but their graying population.**

∞

82 A person with a healthy lifespan of a hundred years will always be more productive than one with a lifespan of 75 years, up to half of which are hobbled by chronic ailments and ill health.

83 *In The Elixxir Society, productivity is a means to our end. It is life-affirming, not merely market-enhancing, or capital-increasing. We Immortalists demand that productivity serves humans, and not vice versa.*

84 In The Forever Young Society, productivity is the way to conquer D.O.D. (Disease, Old Age and Death), to ensure that the Mortal shall put on Immortality.

85 An all-out mobilization for the War Against Disease, Old Age and Death will achieve the same great jump in productivity and output as the U.S. experienced during the Second World War. More. Much more. And Bonus: anti-aging labs and industries are clean and green, and will not add to Global Warming; the Anti-Aging Biotech Economy will not produce and peddle weapons of mass destruction in overkill quantities like the Military-Industrial Complex; nor will it profit from mass murder of mortals and hold hostage Homo Sapiens and Planet Earth itself.

The End of Failure

86 In The Elixxir Society, a 40-year-old no longer suffers a midlife crisis. After all, he still has at least eighty more years. If he does not like his current work or career, he can return to school and retrain for another one.

87 With time on our side, failure is impossible. One has time to try different jobs or careers in life. There will be no more regrets. No more agonizing over "What if I make the wrong choice in my career?" If you make the wrong choice, there is more than enough time to fix it.

88 For twenty years one can be a computer programmer. Then an artist for the next twenty-five. Then one can go back to school for one's third career. Or, one can be a carpenter in the first thirty years. A doctor in the second thirty years. And an investment banker after that.

89 *In our Immortalist future, we will all live multiple lives and perform multiple personas. Only a Mortalist fool will want to live one life, one persona at a time.*

90 Just as in our work, so too there will be no more failure in our personal lives. There will be no more need to sacrifice family for career — or career for family — since there will be more than enough time for both. Life will no longer be an either-or proposition. For the first time in human history, we can have it all.

91 Leisure time will be so generous it is inconceivable to us now. Even the humblest clerk will enjoy generous paid vacations. No more burnouts in the office or factory floor.

92 *Robotics will free The Elixxir Society from routine, repetitive, noncreative work and make it so much more efficient and productive than Mortalist Society. By using robotics to increase wealth shared by all, humanity will be able to liberate itself from the drudgery of unfulfilling work, and free to keep the work it enjoys.*

A New Deal for Women

93 Menopause will be a thing of the past. Since they can still bear children in what used to be "old age," women will no longer feel the pressure of the biological clock. In The Elixxir Society, women will not need to rush into marriage and raise children since they can do that into their nineties. Women can concentrate on their careers just as much as men if they choose.

94 Without the biological clock ticking away, women can have all that life has to offer. A new world will open up. Then and only then is total emancipation for women possible.

Real Pro-Family

95 Mothers and fathers will have all the time in the world to play with their children as they grow up. Instead of seeing the spouse as the other wage-earner, people will have all the quality time they need to keep their marriages evergreen. This is just one reason The Elixxir Society will be the most pro-family in all of human history.

96 The family will no longer be ravaged by Aging or be broken up by Death. Children can expect their parents to be around - indefinitely. Parents will get to see their grandchildren's children.

97 Our psyches will no longer be traumatized in childhood or early adulthood by the deaths of grandparents or parents. What a difference it will make in people's emotional and psychological development and in their lifelong happiness.

98 Adult children will not have to worry that senility will turn their parents into strangers and dependents. We won't have to worry that we'll be devastated by the expenses of nursing homes or of caring for our elderly parents at home. Nor will we need to feel guilty about not being able to care for our parents as our parents will be perfectly able to take care of themselves.

∞

We Immortalists are more interested in Quality of Life than 'Standard of Living.'

In The Elixxir Society, the ALE (Average Life Expectancy) and the HLE (Healthy Life Expectancy) are more important than the GNP (Gross National Product) and GDP (Gross Domestic Product).

∞

99 "Elderly" people will remain as youthful, fit and vigorous as anyone in the prime of life. Unlike Mortalist Society in which a longer life merely means a longer period of ugliness, obesity, decline, or senility, the scientific breakthroughs will extend the prime and productive years.

100 There is nothing more anti-family than the scorched-earth Extreme Capitalism of "market globalism" or The New World Order. Reigning in the U.S. and dominating the world, this ideology and its ruthless and insatiable demands are the true destroyer of the family. (Nope, it's not liberals, homosexuals, or "secular humanism"!)

Time for True Love

101 If you are unlucky in your first marriage, there is more than enough time for a second. And the best part is you do not enter it physically diminished by the ravages of time. No, you plunge into it in your prime. With a full head of hair. With perfect muscle tone. Youthful skin. No high blood pressure. No heart condition. No diabetes. No hemorrhoids. You go into it as a youth of twenty-five — healthy, vigorous, and beautiful.

102 There will be more than enough time to find our true love. And when we find her or him, our body will not have betrayed us. It will give us no small pleasure to be able to hold our own against sons and daughters who may be thirty to fifty years younger.

103 Sex will no longer be a quickie. Sex will be more loving, tender, blissful, beautiful, and, yes, more pleasurable than we ever imagined possible. Freed from the shadow of Death — and diseases like AIDS, sex will be radically different from the harried, guilt-ridden, repetitive, and compulsive variety we know.

∞

If you are unlucky in your first marriage, there is more than enough time for a second.

With Time on our side, failure is impossible.

∞

104 We will no longer use it to alleviate our anxiety or to appease our compulsion. We will not use it to possess, to denigrate, or to objectify. We will learn intimacy, tenderness and real commitment.

105 We will not use sex to "score" — to chalk up points in our quest for Immortality. We will learn to give pleasure and to receive it. We will expand our repertoire and explore the boundless possibilities. We will savor, experiment and linger.

A Population Explosion?

106 Contrary to the alarmist fear sowed by Mortalist propagandists, Immortality — virtual or actual — will not bring about a nightmarish population explosion. In fact, world population will inevitably stabilize in The Immortalist Era. And this will be good for quality of life in the Third World, and *good for the ecosystem.*

107 First, children will no longer serve as our surrogate immortality (since we can take the direct route). Nor would they be our retirement security (as they still are in poor countries without pension systems). So people will not feel compelled to have so many or any children.

108 Secondly, since women can have children way into what is presently "old age," they will not be in a hurry to have them.

109 We have seen the above phenomenon in the affluent nations. As people in the West and Japan live longer and have more retirement security, they have dramatically less children, to the point of zero or even negative population growth.

110 Thirdly, access to The "Elixir" Technology will be contingent on our practicing family planning and using contraception to avoid overburdening the earth and destroy-

ing our own future. The right to the "elixir" comes with
responsibility.

Why Mortals Are Not Green

111 *Mortals with a lifespan of eighty or less make bad environmentalists.*

112 They claim to care what happens to the earth a hundred years
from now. But they don't. Because they don't expect to be
around.

113 The Elixxir Society will be the first in history to live in har-
mony with its environment. For the first time, we will truly
(not just intellectually) understand the need to preserve the
ozone layer and rain forests, recycle our garbage and to protect our endangered species. Why? Because we know we will
be alive in the future. So if the ozone layer is depleted, we will
fry. If we do not recycle, we will be forced to live on a stink-
ing pile of garbage.

114 The old and disastrous Mortalist belief that God has given the
human race "dominion" over the earth — to plunder and pol-
lute as it pleases — will be rejected once and for all.

Why Fat Is Not Green

115 *Fat is bad for our ecosystem. One cannot be Fat and Green.*

116 A fat person feeds more. He needs more cattle, poultry, and
pigs slaughtered. He is more likely to drive a bigger car which
spews out more carbon monoxide. A fat person is more likely
to suffer heart disease, stroke, cancer, or diabetes. She or he
strains our health-care system much more than a slim person.

117 Fat is not only ugly, it's lethal. Not only for the individual,
but for the planet.

118 *The Immortalist Body Type is ultra-slim/boyish/
     girlish/androgynous/low-fat/forever. It also happens to be the
     best body type for the ecosystem.*

119 So long as it is derived from eating optimum calories, this
     slim body type is more likely to stay youthful, to be long-
     lived, much less likely to die of heart disease and cancer. It
     is vastly more efficient and less taxing on the planet. It needs
     less fuel (food) to maintain itself. It takes up less space in
     cars, buses and planes, not to mention houses. And, most im-
     portantly, it is very easy on our health care system. Not to
     mention the eye.

120 Less is more. Minimalism is the Immortalist aesthetics.

121 Since it is good for society and the ecosystem, The Immortal-
     ist Body Type must be encouraged in the Post-Mortalist Era.
     It will be given tax breaks. This will also encourage fat people
     to shed their weight.

122 We reject the big fat lies of The Fat Lobby.

123 Fat is deadly and oh so Mortalist.

124 We want to be slim — always. We spit on getting fat, ugly,
     and old.

The Beautiful Civilization

125 People in The Elixxir Society™ will no longer have to spend
     most of their lives struggling with their weight. We will main-
     tain our ideal weight throughout life.

126 This is because our bodies will stay young. And young bodies
     are slim sexy bodies. As we enhance and eventually replace
     our primitive carbon-based body (mere Mortalist hardware),
     we can look forward to banishing overweight and obesity.

127 The Elixxir Era will be the most beautiful in human history.
     No more obesity. No more wrinkles. No more potbellies. No

more sagging faces. No more cellulite. No more double chins. No more stretch marks. No more spider veins. No more liver spots.

128 People will look exactly as they wish. Cosmetic surgery will become inexpensive, routine and completely safe. If the barn needs painting, we shall paint it.

129 Physical height, weight, and looks will be made to order. People who want to grow taller or shorter — safely — can do so long after puberty. It will be as routine as playing with hair colors, makeups, makeovers, or Internet personas.

The Politics of Joy

130 The Elixxir Society will pay for a facelift or its equivalent by age forty. A free facelift by forty? Sounds ridiculous to The Death Ideology — and its governments. But if government is not in the business of Death but in that of delivering happiness, then why not! A free facelift at 40 is exactly what The Elixxir Society will offer us.

131 Yes, The Immortalist Government believes in and practices The Politics of Joy. It will put Happiness at the top of its agenda. It has the levitas of anything-is-possible youth, not the *gravitas* of Nasty Old Men. It would rather spend to make its citizens happy than flush $60 billion down the toilet on Reagan's demented "Star Wars." Or countless billions each year on corporate welfare and subsidies for the filthy rich and Big Business, or on reckless, needless military adventures.

132 The Elixxir Society is always closer to Happiness than The Death Society. This is because only when we have freed ourselves from Aging and Death's bondage can we be truly happy. The Immortalist life, even short of Immortality, produces more happiness than the "happiest" Mortal life. This is because it is plugged into the eternal, most ancient, most glorious quest, and

in doing so attains more meaning, purpose, and direction than is possible in the wretched Mortalist existence.

An Immortalist Golden Age

133 *We will no longer be driven by Death; we will be seduced by Life.* An unprecedented golden age for art and culture will descend upon us. People will have all the time in the world to read, write and think. They will have time to dance and see dance. Time to watch films and make films. Time to paint. To sculpt. Time to dream up new art forms and make great art.

134 A new kind of film, literature, media coverage, art will emerge. No longer will they treat every human life as either a "tragedy" or a "farce."

135 No longer will everything from The Book of Job to Oscar Wilde's Dorian Gray be forced to attach a Mortalist ending to it.

136 Filmmakers, journalists, authors, and artists will realize that "tragedies" and "farces" are Mortalist Art, designed as cautionary tales about "hubris" or mocking tales about the ridiculousness of human "dignity." Aspiring to becoming as the gods will only bring retribution and downfall, we are incessantly programmed in Mortalist Art and Media. The great man is really comic if not pathetic under the surface, we are told. Every story is Mortalist set-piece, Mortalist propaganda. When the "fall" of the great is announced, the gallery bursts into applause on cue. When the great slips on a banana peel, the gallery emits peals of derisive laughter.

137 Immortalist Art does not preach. It does not try to conform every human life into the predictable and didactic "tragedy" or "farce" structure. It sees that every life, especially a long and challenging one, will have its ups and downs. That, a life without "scandal" is not worth living. That with the advent of the long-lived Immortalist lifespan, there is always a second

act, and a third, and a fourth. That Immortalists do not judge every setback or mistake as "failure" or "character flaw." So an Immortalist always gives himself another chance unlike the self-flagellating, self-hating Mortalist.

138 Immortalist films, plays, literature and journalism will go beyond Mortalist "tragedies" and "farces" which are mere morality plays from the middle ages, tired and bankrupt strictures.

139 <u>Unlike The Death Society, The Elixxir Society values art and literature and encourages its blooming.</u> It will impose lower income taxes on artists and writers. Instead of its current disgraceful and malicious neglect, the National Endowment for the Arts will have as much funding as its European counterparts. More! European state funding for the arts will also greatly increase.

140 People will take up filmmaking and writing and art at sixty. With Old Age banished, the possibilities are endless.

141 Alienation, repression, and oppression — all symptoms of our mortality — will decrease in proportion to Death's diminishing.

142 **The old Mortalist superstitions shall all pass away. They will be crushed to the ground — never to rise again.** Never will they haunt, constrict, and terrify our lives again. Freedom from Death will make this inevitable.

143 **A new consciousness will emerge. Our worth will not be measured by how much we produce, how much we consume, how much money we make, or what our "net worth" is. Our worth will be measured instead by how long we stay young and how well we live.**

144 Instead of rampant boredom, depression, alcoholism, drug abuse, and chronic ailments, our lives will be revived, fired with excitement, meaning and purpose in The Elixxir Society.

Mobilizing to Conquer D.O.D.
(Disease, Old Age & Death)

145 To conquer Disease, Old Age and Death (D.O.D.) in time for
us, we will lobby for greatly-increased government and pharmaceutical funding for anti-aging and life-extension research,
choose leaders in government, the private sector, the European Union, and the United Nations who support such funding and who will make the conquest of D.O.D. the planet's
Number One Priority.

146 The Elixxir Society will boast of the best educational system
in human history. There will always be money for education
in The Elixxir Society. Our teachers will be well-paid and
well-respected.

147 In The Elixxir Society, we will rather spend too much than
too little on our schools and universities. It is, after all, our future. This is because a world-class educational system which
excels in Science and Technology is essential to produce the
breakthroughs which will let us triumph over D.O.D.

148 A teenager who excels in the sciences will gain more adula-
tion than a jock or pop star.

149 Our chronologically young will not waste time pumping up
their bodies with steroids. They will not morph into Rambos
and turn their schools into killing fields. They won't play god
because they will have real Immortality to look forward to.

Where Will The Elixir Come From?

150 We must leave no stone unturned to maximize the probability that the anti-aging and life-extension breakthroughs will
arrive in time to save us! The Elixxir Society will give you
every benefit of every doubt.

151 The good news. Such breakthroughs can come not only from the United States but also from countries with a developed scientific/medical research complex such as Japan, Germany, France, Great Britain, or Sweden.

152 Such breakthroughs can occur even in so-called "Third World" countries such as China (including Hong Kong and Taiwan) and even Cuba. In fact, such anti-aging life-extension breakthroughs can come from a single major pharmaceutical company committing itself to this goal.

153 In The Elixxir Society, Science and Technology is our front line. It must be sufficiently advanced to launch an all-out final offensive against our intractable foes — D.O.D. (Disease, Old Age and Death).

The Mark of The Elixxir Society

154 But how is Science and Technology in The Elixxir Society different from the U.S.? We all know that American Science and Technology was, until recently, second to none in the world.

155 *The distinguishing mark of The Elixxir Society's Science and Technology is its monomaniacal focus on the conquest of Disease, Old Age and Death. It systematically and relentlessly organizes and allocates its funds, its scientific and technological personnel and infrastructure towards humanity's ultimate goal — the eradication of D.O.D.*

Sword Into Plowshare

156 With the help of the government, the Military-Industrial Complex in the United States and other countries will retool into The Elixxir Complex in The ImmorTalist Era.

∞

No more obesity.
No more wrinkles.
No more potbellies.
No more sagging faces.
No more cellulite. No more double chins.
No more stretch marks.
No more spider veins.
No more liver spots. No more crow feet.
NO MORE AGING!

∞

157 Instead of bombers, The Elixxir Complex will build safer and better civilian planes, ultra-safe high-speed trains, and provide first-class scientists and laboratories for The Final Offensive against Disease, Old Age and Death. This complex will be provided with incentives to jump into youth-preservation life-extension research.

158 More jobs will be created in this conversion to The Elixxir Society than we ever dream possible. They will be good jobs — with livable pay, health insurance, job security, and Serial Mini-Retirements. And they will be protected against the perennial recessions and depressions of U.S. Imposed Global Mortalist Capitalism.

159 Anti-aging and lifespan-extension research and laboratories will never lack funding in The Elixxir Society. Neither will basic research in the basic sciences. They will be the bedrock of The Elixxir Complex. They will be as well-funded as the Pentagon used to be during the Cold War.

160 In addition to scientists and researchers, our educational system will produce the personnel, management, theories, and strategies needed to reorganize society from Death-submitting to Life-affirming. We shall finally turn our sword into plowshare.

161 Instead of the arms race, there will be a Life race. A final sprint for "the elixir." One to decide which society, which nation, which scientists will be awarded the everlasting glory of giving mortals The Breakthrough/s to slow, stop, and reverse the aging process. Much more glory here than in the Olympics. Instead of the politics of Mutually-Assured Destruction, the politics of All-Out Life.

162 Who will be the most advanced in innovating social and political structures for The Elixxir Society? Which country will solve the riddle of human biological aging for humanity and go down in history for all eternity? If love of country is a factor in this race for The Breakthroughs, so be it. It is better to

channel nationalism into the pursuit of Life than into a frenzy of Death.

163 **In The Elixxir Society, the fruits of antiaging youth-and-life-extension research must not and shall not be the captive of any drug company, no matter how big, rich or powerful.** Nor can the public interest in saving tens of millions of lives each year around the world allow such life-saving fruits to be patented or the resulting medicines sold for a king's ransom to gouge the citizenry.

163A Just as society cannot allow firemen or policemen to refuse to protect or save you unless you can pay them, so too The Elixxir Society shall no longer allow drug companies to extort from seriously ill or dying people. If we nationalize banks or the entire banking or financial sector to prevent its collapse, then surely it must be a million times more imperative for us to nationalize or even expropriate drug companies if they refuse to make anti-aging youth-preserving life-saving medicines available to those who must have them or die.

163B In the crumbling U.S. Death Society, and its economic clones, the system has no qualms about letting the drug companies pig out on their profits and no reservations about letting millions of citizens without health insurance or wealth die a premature and brutal death. To make sure such Systemic Homicides and Crimes against Humanity be banished forever, anti-aging youth-preservation and life-extension research must be and shall be funded by the immortalist government and its fruits and patents held in public trust by the state for all to share. Anti-aging Youth-Extension breakthroughs must remain in the public domain. Such life-saving interventions must be priced on a sliding-scale and/or mostly paid for by society's universal health care system so that anyone who wishes to avail of it, or is in need of it, shall get it.

Our Common Enemy

164 *The Elixxir Society is not against the rich, just the Mortalist rich who use their wealth to serve The Death Ideology (which is ultimately lethal even for them) and to condemn us to Death.*

165 A number of the wealthy are closet Immortalists and will join us. We will embrace them. But the enormous and ever-growing inequality between the rich and the poor in Mortalist Society must be addressed and the gap closed. To assume that when the anti-aging life-extending drugs arrive, those who cannot afford it will docilely allow the tiny elite who can afford it to enjoy staying young and living an indefinitely-extended healthy lifespan in peace and quiet is a big assumption. It is one thing for the masses to accept being unable to afford cancer drugs when the rich are also dying of cancer. But when the rich are no longer dying of cancer, or heart disease, or stroke, and when on top of this the rich manage to stay offensively young and live as long as Methuselah, then the masses' eyes will be opened and they will see that they are indeed The Have Nots. It is a safe wager that the masses' response will be very different and very hostile. Then their fatalism will be raised to ImmorTalist consciousness and rage. And the huge anti-globalization protests will pale in comparison to the Have-Nots' total resistance to Capitalist Death Society.

166 <u>Money is merely a way of keeping score for mortals so they can argue their case for immortality before the gods.</u> <u>There are better ways of keeping score.</u>

167 The rich will realize it is not in their interest to have a situation where desperate people can violently snatch from them their most precious asset: Virtual Immortality. So they will be forced to narrow the obscene gap between themselves and the rest of society.

168 *Everyone and anyone who wants the "elixir" will be able to afford it in The Elixxir Society. The "elixir" will be (and*

should be) priced on a sliding scale — according to your income, wealth, and financial ability.

169 The rich and powerful will see that - for their own protection and social stability — everyone should be given an equal stake in the "elixir" medication or technology. *Poor mortals with nothing to lose will not be nice to rich immortals with everything to lose.* To level the playing field, they will wield The *Threat of Apocalyptic Violence.*

170 The affluent nations will see that, to avoid "terrorism" (effective inexpensive low-tech guerilla war by poor individuals, groups or nations) or a tidal wave of "illegal" immigration — the emerging nations must all have access to The Breakthroughs.

171 Death is no respecter of ideological persuasion. Ronald Reagan's greatest enemy was not Communism; it was Alzheimer's (a symptom of The Aging Syndrome). Fidel Castro's most fearsome nemesis is not Capitalism; it is Mortality.

172 The final War against Disease, Old Age and Death shall enlist from all classes and nations. Our climactic battle against the grave shall cut across national boundaries, class, gender, race, ethnic origin, and sexual orientation. If anything can override primitive nationalism and patriotism, if anything can foster international solidarity, it is our common cause against D.O.D.

Immortalist Human Rights

173 Basic human rights — enshrined in the Constitution — must include first and foremost **Freedom from Disease, Old Age and Death (D.O.D.)**. The Immortalist State is sworn to do everything in its power to help us stay young and live as long as possible, and to ensure an optimal quality of life. After the anti-aging life-extension breakthroughs come, Freedom from Aging and Death requires that the government make the

"elixir" available to everyone who desires it — and deliver the best quality of life in history.

174 In The Elixxir Society, human rights must include the right to food, shelter, health care, education, and a decent quality of life. This is enshrined in its Constitution. Unemployment, no universal health insurance, starvation wages, job and retirement insecurity, pitting workers against workers in a race to the bottom, homelessness, infant mortality, hunger, malnutrition and poverty in the midst of plenty, criminal and murderous maldistribution of wealth, and last but not least, premature Disease, Aging and Death, all these will be relics of our Mortalist past.

175 Economic security throughout life will be a basic Immortalist human right.

176 War will be banished for all time. After indefinitely-extended-lifespan (Virtual Immortality) is attained, starting a war will be a crime against humanity. Nations will learn to compete in other ways.

177 We will be amazed at how quickly these "unsolvable" or "intractable" problems can be solved when the people demand it and the political will exists.

No to Coolie Labor

178 Business will prosper as never before. The markets will be truly free of unfair competition by cartel multinational corporations. The Elixxir Society will have a quality of life unprecedented in human history. But this will be achieved with foresight and stewardship — without raping our ecosystem.

179 **The industrialized nations will not sink to the wage level and working conditions of the Third World. Instead, they will lift the emerging economies to their wage level and working conditions.**

180 Life-affirming jobs will be created. Life-centered productivity will increase dramatically and our quality of life will skyrocket. Unemployment, layoffs and downsizings will be virtually unheard of. And crime will drop to almost zero.

Do-It-Yourself-ism Equals Death

181 We Immortalists are strong individualists. Only a strong individualist can defy The Death Society and reject its command to decay and decompose at the appointed time. But we are also realists: we understand that only as a community can we conquer Old Age and Death. Even God needs his Trinity.

182 There will always be government. The question is whether we are its slaves or its master. Whether it is Mortalist or Immortalist. Our prospects for "eternal" youth and life are not promising until the Immortalist worldview is enshrined in our laws and our government.

183 If we are talking about really stopping the biological aging process and radically lengthening the maximum human lifespan of 120 and not just adding a few years here and there, then we have to admit that individual efforts — no matter how disciplined or rigorous — will not save us from the darkness.

184 Just as one person cannot make it to the moon, so too we cannot greatly extend lifespan through individual effort and diligence alone. To stop Aging and Death in our lifetime, we need to lobby for an effort similar to the Apollo program which put the first human on the moon, ahead of schedule.

185 The do-it-yourself approach to Immortality has failed. We Immortalists know that we need government to conquer Aging and Death. We know that neither cosmetic surgery nor great makeup nor regular workouts can save us. Neither can vitamin and mineral supplementation, not even the right diet. 120, 140, even 160 years is not enough.

186 It is crucial that government comes up with the anti-aging life-extension breakthroughs - or makes it available to who-ever wants it. Otherwise we will have a situation analogous to that of AIDS where the life-saving anti-HIV drug "cocktails" have been so expensive that most people with AIDS or HIV in the world simply cannot afford them. But since aging af-flicts not only a minority but everyone, such a situation will be explosive.

Why a Movement?

187 <u>We need the greatest movement in all of history to usher in the next stage of our human evolution, to transform us from mortals into immortals.</u>

188 The agenda of The Immortalist Movement is simple - Abol-ish Aging and Death.

189 Why a mass movement instead of a debating society? *Be-cause a movement is the fastest way to change the paradigm of our society from that of The Death Ideology to that of The Immortalist Worldview. And this paradigm shift is essential if The Immortalist Breakthroughs are to arrive in time to rescue you and me.*

190 *The ImmorTalist Movement is Radical Immortalist. It de-mands a basic solution to the problem of mortality. We are not interested in halfway or band-aid measures. Our solution goes to the root cause of humanity's oldest problem. And we will accept no compromise.*

Our Short-Term Demands & Goals

191 We choose to invest in The ImmorTalist Movement - our vehicle for Immortality. We choose to endow it with our time,

energy, talents, and money. For without a movement, we know we will surely perish.

192 The Elixxir Movement is your best bet for Immortality. It is not Pseudo-Immortalism; it is Scientific ImmorTalism which is not based on faith in the "inevitability" of a hi-tech rescue just in the nick of time. **We are also the only ImmorTalists who understand the essential role to be played by a potent political ImmorTalist movement in the achieving of our goals.**

193 **Our Short-Term Demands & Goals**

1. Wage an All-Out War Against **Heart Disease, Cancer, Stroke, Obesity, Alzheimer's, Diabetes, AIDS, and all the other major killer-diseases** which exterminate more than 2 million people annually just in the U.S. alone, and tens of millions more worldwide each year. (This means The War Against The Real Terrors will be the government's Number One Funding Priority and will be funded at least as adequately as **the needless, reckless, disastrous wars in Iraq and Afghanistan** which **have turned the U.S. and EU into magnets for attacks**.) (Sign Demand in front of book.)

2. **Guarantee Financial Security and Support for People Fighting Life-Threatening Diseases** such as Heart Disease, Cancer, and Stroke. They are the real everyday heroes. Mortalist governments have scurried to bailout Wall Street, Investment Banks, Hedge Funds, the car industry. The Death Society has given the biggest tax breaks to the richest under cover of a few crumbs to the rest of us. It has lavished corporate welfare, billion-dollar tax-loopholes, and risk-free capitalism to Big Business. An ImmorTalist Movement, Party and State promise instead to bail out the real heroes: People struggling with cancer, heart disease, stroke, diabetes, Alzheimer's, etc, killers, as well as their overburdened loved ones and families. We need to give them paid leaves of absence, paid sick days, extended unemployment benefits, disability benefits, Medi-

care and Medicaid to fund new promising treatments, including dietary interventions which could prevent or even reverse killers such as heart disease, hypertension, diabetes, cancer, stroke, Alzheimer's, or osteoporosis.

3. **Make Anti-Aging Research a Top Priority.** Save the 76 million boomers in the U.S. and in all other countries so that they will continue to lead healthy, vigorous, and productive lives. Create a new research strategy and paradigm to cure cancer, heart disease, stroke, Alzheimer's, osteoporosis, diabetes, obesity and other Aging-Related ailments. If cancer, heart disease, stroke, Alzheimer's, osteoporosis, obesity, etc., are Aging-Related and Aging-Correlated diseases, as Science and Medicine agree they are, then Anti-Aging Research which sees them as *symptoms* of a Master Disease Syndrome (our human biological aging) may lead us to life-saving treatments or cures faster and more cheaply.

4. **Support Scientific Dietary Intervention to Prevent or Alleviate Heart Disease, Cancer, Stroke, Obesity, Diabetes, Alzheimer's, Osteoporosis, etc. Top Killers.** There is already an impeccable scientific, proven, tested eating program recognized by science and medicine as capable of slashing our risks for all the top killers above. At the same time, it dramatically slows down our biological aging and greatly extends the maximum lifespan. It is a program such as The Elixxir Program™. The Elixxir Society will do everything possible to educate its people on this proven and powerful anti-heart disease, anti-cancer, anti-stroke, anti-hypertension, anti-diabetes, anti-Alzheimer's eating program which is already available and affordable. And The Elixxir Society and State shall do everything in its power to invest in or fund such a program. Its goal is training and teaching as large a part of the population as voluntarily wish to be on such a program in order to greatly decrease the incidence of expensive diseases such as cancer, stroke, heart failure, and Alzheimer's, and to

slash costs for its health care system and maintain its long-term viability.

5 Respond to Global Warming, Biodiversity Collapse, Mass Extinctions. Unlike in The Death Society, global warming, biodiversity collapse, and mass species extinctions will be top priorities for The ImmorTalist Movement, Party and Society. And it will not be empty rhetoric. We demand that it be backed up by government budgets and the signing and implementation of the Convention on Biological Diversity (CBD) by the U.S. and the Vatican, and the creation of nature preserves and oceanic sanctuaries around the world.

194 **Our short-term goals means that anyone who wants to cure top killers like cancer, heart disease, stroke, diabetes, Alzheimer's, AIDS, osteoporosis, spinal cord injuries and Parkinson's has great reasons to support the ImmorTalist Movement and The ImmorTalist Party.** Agreement with our goals to eradicate all the top killer-diseases should be more than enough reason to support us. **You don't have to wish to live indefinitely to support us, or to vote for us.** No ImmorTalist Party or State is going to force anyone to live forever. Rest assured. But to continue supporting the established Mortalist parties — for which curing Cancer, Heart Disease, Stroke, and other killers is at the bottom of their funding priorities — is to collude in our own deaths.

195 **Slowing Your Aging by Half, Preventing Cancer, Heart Disease, Stroke, or an Average Lifespan of 100 is Already Possible!** But the Legal Drugs Industry and The Death Society are not interested in telling you. It is a scandal, crime, and outrage that the public has not been educated more on this youth-extending, health-preserving, and lifespan-extending eating program. The Elixxir Program is based on this scientific anti-aging program. It is an adaptation designed to make it possible for anyone to benefit from its anti-aging benefits and to thrive in a 21st century lifestyle. It is the only scien-

tific way to buy more time, to recharge your batteries, for the healthy and vital life you desire and deserve.

196 <u>This kind of ImmorTalist Dietary Intervention is so much cheaper than triple-bypass surgery, a heart transplant, chemo-therapy, intensive care, a long-term hospitalization or nursing home care. It is less expensive than many of the drugs from the pharmaceutical industry which are saddled with serious side-effects.</u>

197 An anti-aging intervention which dramatically slashes our risk of heart disease, cancer, stroke, diabetes, Alzheimer's, osteoporosis etc Aging-Related killers without side effects. A health-preserving intervention which is all-natural based on everyday foods, and does not ban any food category. Proven by decades of controlled experiments and studies published in prestigious peer-reviewed scientific journals. **This is about as close as we have come so far to the silver bullet against disease and the elixir for eternal youth.**

198 But The Drug Industry is not eager to publicize this. It dis-misses this eating program as "too difficult" since it makes more money peddling us drugs which neither prevent nor cure, but leave us in the purgatory of a chronically ailing state, so as to require longterm or lifetime medication — the better for its bottom line. It promotes drugs laden with side effects for hypertension, heart attacks and strokes which have much less of a proven track record than the scientific diet that The Elixxir Program is based on.

199 **Permanent Lifelong Weight Loss.** Obesity is now one of the top killers in the U.S. and many other Western or afflu-ent nations which have adopted the U.S. diet. Early effec-tive intervention with the young and overweight is espe-cially important as it otherwise leads to lifelong obesity or morbid obesity with heightened risks for a host of diseases including hypertension, heart disease, cancer, stroke, and di-abetes. These diseases, especially starting in youth or early

middle-age, tax the health care system. And it is in society's interest to invest in and fund weight-loss programs which are effective or have serious promise to prevent or alleviate this epidemic of obesity. It so happens that the scientific anti-aging diet which is the basis of The Elixxir Program is also a proven lifelong weight-loss regimen. So that we would be hitting two goals with one intervention. The ImmorTalist Movement, Party and State strongly support this and any other proven weight-loss program and will use tax credits and state subsidies to encourage the public to get on such programs to prevent obesity and its related ailments, which can overload or even cripple the health care system. This is a serious threat to our national security.

200 The ImmorTalist Movement, Party and State seek to change this unacceptable situation. Overweight and obesity have been culpable in countless needless deaths, chronic ailments, low self-esteem, and lifelong emotional suffering. The ImmorTalist Movement, Party and State will offer preventive programs such as The Elixxir Program to people who want to enhance and preserve their health and at the same time greatly retard their aging and extend their lifespan.

201 **Under the current Mortalist Capitalist system, most people in the world would be unable to afford the coming anti-aging life-extension drugs. We can be sure of this, as most in the world cannot now afford the drugs for AIDS, malaria, tuberculosis, cancer, heart disease etc which can save their lives.**

202 Don't expect the profit-hungry price-gouging pharmaceutical industry to give away the coming anti-aging life-extension drugs that they are working on. That would be the height of wishful thinking. Tens of millions have died in the world from AIDS because they were denied AIDS medicine which could have saved their lives. This is considered "normal" and "acceptable" under the current economic order. The Immor-Talist Party say it is as unacceptable and criminal as denying

an entire population of food and starving it to death. If that be genocide and a crime against humanity, why would denying much of the world (except the rich) a life-saving anti-aging life-extending medication be acceptable? We say it is not, so support us if you agree and don't want to be robbed of your chance to save your Life.

Nothing to Lose but Disease, Old Age & Death

203 We therefore invite all those fighting Heart Disease, Cancer, Stroke, Obesity, Alzheimer's, AIDS, osteoporosis, and all the major killer-diseases to join us. You're the real silent majority. But **silence equals Death**. So support our Total War Against The Real Terrors. Help us fight for new and better treatments, but also cures. If a one-time 3,000 deaths from 9/11 justifies spending trillions, then 2 million American deaths annually from the major diseases require much more funding. With genome mapping, stem cells, and genetic engineering, we have the tools for an all-out drive to find a cure for what threatens to kill you. But the Mortalist parties and the Mortalist State consider that a very low priority. So why continue supporting them? Support The ImmorTalist Movement and Party. It may save your life.

204 We say to the *baby boomers*, join us. Don't go gently into that dark night. You are the front line. You are not done yet. You have the biggest bloc of votes. You ended racial segregation. You broke sexual taboos. You changed music and lifestyles. You stopped a war. Once more, you must shout "Hell, no, we won't go!" You love life, so now fight for it. Stay Young and Save the Planet.

205 We say to *women and gays*, join us. You have been instinctual Immortalists. You have long suffered derision and contempt for your unabashed desire to stay young. You have been

called "bimbos," "queers," "narcissistic," "frivolous," "child-ish," "Peter Pans" by the Mortalist powers that be because of your thirst to stay young.

206 We say to the *young*, join us. Demand the "Impossible," Only the "Impossible" can save us. Refuse to morph into your parents. Choose Life, Save the planet, Make it ImmorTalist. And when you succeed, we would also have saved your parents, your siblings, and your friends.

207 We say to the **Anti-Globalization movement**, join us. Global Warming and Biodiversity Collapse have proven you right. Globalization, by forcing every nation on earth to turn into a market for and a clone of U.S.-style 18th century capitalism, is demolishing not merely our cultures, our livelihoods, our economies, our ways of life, but the very planet itself. Its insatiable lust for profit and its demand for never-ending ever-increasing economic "growth" have proven to be toxic and cancerous, and have led directly to global heating. But you need a viable alternative. Demonstrations are not enough. You need a Party and a new Economy and a new politics. And only Scientific ImmorTalism offers this. It is the alternative to Globalization and U.S. Capitalism.

208 We say to all of you closet Immortalists, join us. To those who feel as we do, but have not found the words, we say join us now. Come out of the closet.

209 Let us organize, march, reason, shout, lobby and vote to make anti-aging research a top funding priority as anti-aging research is the most probable path to a cure for aging-related diseases such as cancer, heart disease, stroke, obesity, Alzheimer's, and osteoporosis.

210 For the sake of our own and the planet's survival, let us accept our **Evolutionary Destiny**. Let us evolve from short-lived to long-lived mortals. Then we shall have a stake in the future and care what happens to the planet.

211 Soon, humanity shall no longer be sentenced to Death. A penalty meted out to everyone from infancy, Einsteins and Hitlers alike, without due process or appeals, without consideration of guilt, innocence, or merit. The Elixxir Society will eliminate this "cruel and unusual punishment" once and for all.

212 "Then shall be brought to pass the saying that is written, Death is swallowed up in victory. O death, where is thy sting? O grave, where is thy victory?" (I Corinthians 15: 54 -55)

213 In our generation, we shall fulfill the promise and vision of all great faiths. This generation shall not pass away until all these things have come to pass. We shall be the first generation to attain the maximum human lifespan and exceed it.

214 Let us be the first generation to make Disease, Old Age and Death optional or obsolete.

215 "We shall not all sleep, but we shall all be changed....in the twinkling of an eye...this mortal shall put on immortality" (I Corinthians 15: 51 -53)

216 Mortals of the world unite! You have nothing to lose but Disease, Old Age and Death!

∞

Women and gays have long suffered derision and contempt for their unabashed desire to stay young.

They have been called "bimbos," "queers," "narcissistic," "frivolous," "childish," "Peter Pans" by the Mortalist powers that be.

∞

∞

In our generation, we shall fulfill the promise and vision of all great faiths.

∞

PART II
The Immortalist Worldview

CHAPTER 1

The Immortalist Interpretation of History

1   History is the story of our quest for immortality.

2   The fear of Death and the desire for Immortality are the primary motivations in human life and history.

3   The goal of human history and civilization is the conquest of Death.

4   The meaning of life is life. The goal of life is more and better life.

5   Human history is a protracted struggle against Death. It is the history of our individual and collective efforts to escape the clutches of mortality — the history of our unflagging desire for immortality.

6   The goal of human history is simple and unchanging: it is to break out from the chains of mortality.

7   What seems to be the problem? Death! What else?

8   Contrary to the propaganda of The Death Ideology, even Jesus was "greatly distressed and troubled" in the face of death. (Mark 14:33)

9   To be afraid of Death is not only *universal*, it is also *natural.* Our Fear of Death arises from our Instinct for Self-Preservation.

10 Therefore, to accept Old Age and Death is nothing less than the perversion of our most basic biological instincts.

11 Mortality is the unique problem of the human species. Homo Sapiens is the only species burdened with full consciousness

of its finiteness. This awareness of our mortality is intolerably complicated by our capacity to dream of an immortal state.

12 The question of the rich young ruler in the gospels has always been the question: what must we do to gain eternal life?

13 Throughout history, many answers have been given. By prophets, magicians, priests, mystics, hermits, alchemists, philosophers, artists, kings, rebels and revolutionaries. Countless creeds and ideologies each purport to show us the way. They have, in the final analysis, fallen short and failed. This is why no one answer has emerged as the answer. This is why the quest continues.

14 We cannot shut off our consciousness of Death completely. We cannot be distracted from its shadow all of the time. Nor can our capacity for denial protect us ultimately. Death is a biological problem. Therefore, it demands a biological solution.

15 This is why the "answers" given by religion, philosophy, art, and politics to the problem of Death are too ineffective, too impractical, too abstract.

16 **Any "answer" or "solution" which cannot cure Old Age and Death is ultimately sophistry, deception, a cruel hoax.**

17 This is not to say that these "answers" or "solutions" have not performed invaluable services for us by providing us with the necessary beliefs, support and distractions to maintain a sane and functional existence in an otherwise untenable situation.

18 All our "answers" are part of the total answer that the human species has fashioned: Civilization. It is from Civilization that humankind expects liberation from the tyranny of the evil trinity — Disease, Old Age and Death. This was most explicit in the Ancient Egyptian Civilization which has been smeared by Mortalism for its supposed "obsession with Death." The only "obsession" the ancient Egyptians had was with Immortality which they saw rightly as the ultimate goal.

∞

**History is the story
of our quest for immortality.**

**The fear of Death and the desire for Immortality are
the primary motivations in human life and history.**

∞

19 Civilization is our collective vehicle for the conquest of Death. It is built by the perspiration, sacrifice, gratification-post-ponement, perseverance, faith, and — yes — martyrdom of countless members of the human race.

20 The struggle against Death is sometimes blatant; most often camouflaged. There would be the flamboyant Ponce de Le-ons, as well as the nerdy scientists who insist their only aim is scientific progress, their only motivation thirst for knowledge.

21 We hide our real target out of prudence. By lowering our ex-pectations, by feigning indifference, skepticism, even cyni-cism, we protect ourselves from disappointment and paraly-sis.

22 Even in primitive societies, the work to subvert our unaccept-able mortal condition proceeded. But it was carried out in se-cret - or subconsciously, for our primitive ancestors were sure the gods would not look kindly on such "hubris."

23 The ability to make fire, the rise of agriculture, the invention of the printing press, the rise of modern science, medicine, and technology, the harnessing of the atom, the discovery of penicillin, the deciphering of the double helix, the creation of Universal Mind through the Internet, the mapping of the hu-man genome, the advent of biotechnology and nanotechnol-ogy - all these are indispensable milestones in our long march to accumulate sufficient firepower for our final showdown with Death.

24 If civilization is our vehicle for immortality, then its institu-tions must be connected in one way or another with our ulti-mate goal and desire — immortality.

∞

**Contrary to the propaganda
of The Death Ideology, even Jesus was
"greatly distressed and troubled" in
the face of death. (Mark 14:33)**

∞

∞

Death is a biological problem.

Therefore, it demands a biological solution.

∞

25 *Modern Medicine* is the institution most directly linked to our quest to banish Disease, Old Age and Death. *Science* provides the new discoveries, knowledge, hypotheses. *Technology* converts them into practical weapons for our liberation from Disease, Aging and Death.

26 The *Social Wellbeing* agencies are supposed to ensure that we not only have quantity but quality of life. *Academia* preserves, propagates, and expands the knowledge humankind needs to triumph over D.O.D. *The Police/Military* is supposed to deter other individuals and nations from inflicting harm or Death on us.

27 *Religion* is our aspirin, our antidepressant, our amphetamine, our opium. It provides us the denial and solace needed to continue to function in the face of Disease, Old Age & Death.

28 *Traditional Marriage and Family* are for procreation, the survival of the species, and **Surrogate Immortality** through children.

29 *Arts and Culture* allows surrogate immortality without children — through art, film, music, books, websites etc.

30 *Government* protects us from homicides, natural disasters, accidents; it legalizes private/public ownership of property (an **immortality substitute**); it protects property, and undertakes projects too big for one or a few, or projects which should not be in the hands of one or a few — whether it be a universal health care system (as in Canada, the U.K. and Europe), or funding basic biomedical research the drug companies are not funding (since they live only for profits and the next quarterly report). (An ImmorTalist Government will be devoted to curing life-threatening diseases like heart disease, cancer, stroke, and to terminating The Aging Syndrome, since heart disease, cancer, stroke are its symptoms.)

31 Death drives us to civilization. Death is our cultural foundation. Death is the mother of genius and invention.

32 *Religion and Philosophy have their foundation in Death*. As Schopenhauer, the German philosopher, pointed out: "All religious and philosophical systems are....primarily the antidote to the certainty of death...."

33 **Fame, power, and fortune**? Why do we rush and run? Why do we hear the clock ticking away? Why is there never enough time? Why are our good deeds never good enough? Why do we always yearn to do better? Why can we never be truly happy? The reason for our insatiable drive? The long shadow of Death.

34 Death makes us run. It is our adrenaline, our pacemaker.

35 *We are driven to productiveness*. We must leave behind traces, footprints on the sand. As the Nobel-Laureate novelist William Faulkner said so eloquently and bluntly, "The aim of every artist is to arrest motion, which is life, by artificial means and hold it fixed so that a hundred years later, when a stranger looks at it, it moves again since it is life. Since man is mortal, the only immortality possible for him is to leave something behind him that is immortal since it will always move. This is the artist's way of scribbling 'Kilroy was here' on the wall of the final and irrevocable oblivion through which he must some day pass."

36 We must influence events, control our children, spouse, colleagues and friends, and even our estate after our death. The more ambitous and enterprising among us build monuments, set up charitable foundations, and give money to have hospitals and schools named after them.

37 Although it can become neurosis, this morbid drive has undeniable value and function in human civilization. It is in fact the engine of human progress and achievement.

∞

Civilization is our collective vehicle
for the conquest of Death.

It is built by the gratification-postponement,
perseverance, faith, and — yes — martyrdom
of countless members of the human race.

∞

CHAPTER 2
The Elixxir Lifestyle™

1 The Elixxir Lifestyle is a nonconformist's lifestyle; it is one of scandalous impropriety.

2 "Propriety" is a Mortalist virtue. It requires submission to a life of toil, repression and unhappiness. And it demands surrender to D.O.D. (Disease, Old Age and Death).

3 We Immortalists refuse to kowtow to a life of mindless toil, of relentless repression, of desperate unhappiness. We do not believe in living for the next generation — or for the "next life."

4 We are neither prim nor proper. We are downright scandalous.

5 **To insist on staying young forever is the biggest scandal in Death Society.**

6 We Immortalists are notorious. Notoriety comes from breaking the rules. We are rule-breakers. The ultimate rule: you must grow old and die. We spit on the ultimate rule.

7 We Immortalists are "irresponsible." We're not as interested in making a living as in making a life. Unlike the Mortalist vulgarians, we refuse to squander our lives hoarding up filthy lucre.

8 *Multiple lives, multiple personas. This is The Elixxir Lifestyle.*

9 We reject Mortalist work — irrational, oppressive, endless, compulsive, and, most of all, joyless. We say No to the Mortalist "work ethic" which is nothing but superstition. The "curse" for the "sin" of Adam and Eve in the Garden.

10 We Immortalists live by "faith" alone. Ours is the true "Christian" spirit. We heed Jesus' words: "But if God so clothe the grass which is alive in the field today and tomorrow is thrown into the oven, how much more will he clothe you, O men of little faith!" (Luke 12:27-28 RSV)

11 We Immortalists don't buy into *the surrogate immortality of children*. We don't give a damn that Mortalist society may try to paint us as "narcissistic" or "immature". ("Narcissism" is an Immortalist virtue.) We have no intention of wasting our lives to prop up The Death Society in its last gasp.

12 Our only responsibility: to do everything in our power to demolish Disease, Old Age and Death, to make sure we live long enough to care about planet Earth's future.

13 It is the Mortalist life that is selfish. Mortalists have children for parental or social approval, to cement their marriage, to make themselves happy, or simply to keep up with the Joneses. But most importantly, kids is their immortality project — to have children to survive them. It is not altruism.

14 There's nothing wrong with having children. But today, a direct approach to immortality is in order. We don't need to rely solely on surrogate immortality through posterity – a consolation prize at best. We say it is time to go for the gold. No substitutes are acceptable.

15 *Hubris, that great Mortalist "sin", is a great Immortalist virtue.* When Mortalists accuse us Immortalists of "hubris," they simply mean that we lack the low self-esteem needed to kowtow to Disease, Old Age and Death. We accept the compliment.

16 *Without "hubris," there would be no war against cancer or heart disease, no effort to treat or cure hypertension, stroke, diabetes, Alzheimer's, Parkinson's. No action to shield us from plagues whether it be Ebola or AIDS.*

17 *Without "hubris," there would be no attempt to protect us from "acts of God" such as earthquakes, tsunamis, floods, hurricanes, typhoons, tornadoes, forest fires, species extinction.*

18 Without "hubris," there would be no airplanes. (It is not natural for wingless humans to fly.) Without "hubris," there would be no ships, swimming faster and further than fish. (If God wanted us to swim, he'd have given us gills and flippers.)

19 Without "hubris," there would be no skyscrapers. (They're towers of Babel.) No human on the moon. (God didn't give us dominion over the heavens.) No Internet. (A devilish attempt to create Universal Intelligence, no doubt.) No nothing!

20 *Humanity needs more "hubris," less "fate."*

21 Even if retarding aging and extending lifespan were a scientific impossibility, it would still be far better to live an Immortalist Life-style than a Mortalist Death-style, to glory in Immortalism than grovel to Mortalism. But **our goal is not only possible, it is not only probable, it is inevitable.**

22 **The only question: how to make it come in time to save us?**

We Eat as We Live

23 *We Immortalists do not compulsively overconsume in life, and we do not compulsively overeat at the table.*

24 We do not grab and hoard in life, so we do not grab and hoard at the table.

25 Since Immortalist self-esteem is by definition high, we do not eat ourselves fat, sick, ugly or old. We take only what we need in life so we will only take what we need at the table.

26 *The way we eat, how much we eat, what we eat, reflect our most fundamental values and beliefs.*

27 "Do not labor for the food which perishes, but for the food which endures to eternal life...." (John 6:27 RSV) We Immortalists believe in this.

28 When the Immortalist heart beats in sync with the most ancient and undying dream of the species, it is closest to Happiness. When it is in tune with humanity's Evolutionary Destiny, it is nearest to Bliss.

29 The Immortalist is always closer to happiness than The Mortalist in the grip of The Death Ideology. An Immortalist life produces more happiness than the "happiest" Mortalist life.

30 Why? Because *given time, ImmorTality is inevitable. Therefore given time, Happiness is inevitable.*

∞

We are downright scandalous. To insist on staying young forever is the biggest scandal in Death Society.

Humanity needs more "hubris,"
less "fate."

∞

CHAPTER 3
The Death Society

1 There is no Elixxir Society yet. We have only The Death Society. Western Europe and Scandinavia are getting closer and closer to becoming Elixxir Societies. Some demographic groups in the United States have fierce Immortalist longings. But the bad news is we all live in Death Society still.

2 What is The Death Society? What are its defining characteristics? First and foremost, in a Death Society, *most deaths are unnecessary or premature.*

3 Since our maximum human lifespan is 120 years, anyone who dies before 120 dies prematurely. It is a scandal that the average lifespan in the U.S. is only 77.9, and its average healthspan (the healthy life expectancy) only 70, behind most of Europe, Scandinavia, Japan, and Australia. For the superpower on the planet, with the most advanced science, medicine, and technology at its command, the average lifespan and healthspan should be much higher.

4 The American Death Society — even in its longest economic boom, even when wallowing in budget surpluses — refused to give its people universal health insurance. It is the nature of The Death Society that, in its "best" years, well over 40 million Americans — including 10 million of its children — are without health insurance. This is incomprehensible except in light of The Death Ideology.

5 The United States, the wealthiest nation in history, ranks 37th in health care, behind Japan, behind Western Europe, behind Scandinavia, behind Canada, and even behind some Middle

Eastern countries. This scandalous state of affairs is confirmed by a new WHO study.

6 The U.S. achieves this dubious distinction despite spending
more on health care per capita ($3,700) than any country in
the world.

7 "Welfare states" like Sweden and France, much-maligned in
the U.S. media, have much more efficient and superior health
care systems than the U.S., the world's evangelist of efficien-
cy and superiority. They spend less of their GNP on health
care and get more "bang for their buck" than the U.S. While
the top 10% of Americans get the best health care, the bottom
10% get health care like sub-Saharan Africa's, and the rest,
the big middle-class, get the most mediocre health care. It is
an unacceptable situation. The notion that the U.S. cannot afford to give its people universal health insurance is a wretched lie which kills Americans every day. Vermont is showing
that even a little state can afford universal health care.

8 And much "poorer" than Vermont, Fidel Castro's **Cuba** has long
proven that even a "poor" Third World nation subject to an
unrelenting U.S. embargo can give its people universal health
care. In Cuba, the result is astounding and should, for objective journalism and historians, eclipse any criticism against
Castro's government: an average life expectancy (ALE) as
high as the U.S.

9 **In Maoist China, average life expectancy went from approximately 35 in 1949 (thanks to the U.S.-supported
dictator Chiang, the darling of Time-Life media tycoon
Henry Luce) to almost 70 when Mao died in 1976.** *In the
life expectancy race, China under Mao almost caught up with
the U.S. and the rich "developed" countries.* A monumental
and unrivalled feat for any state or system. But much more so
for a huge, poor population and country, with an economy totally devastated by war, and its treasury emptied by Chiang's
regime as it fled to Taiwan.

10 <u>When the history of China under Mao is reviewed by real historians, not by Cold War or Neo-Con propagandists, they will weigh the mostly-undocumented, wildly exaggerated claims that Mao and the Communist state were directly to blame for tens of millions of Chinese deaths against two uncontested, irrefutable facts.</u> First, **the Chinese average life expectancy almost doubled in one generation under Mao — an achievement no other government, empire or political system can lay claim to in human history. Second, this Chinese population, stagnant for centuries at 400 million, suddenly and for the first time skyrocketed to 750 million.**

11 *Average Life Expectancy (ALE) matters more than GDP or GNP. Contrary to The Death Society's obsession with GDP and GNP, it is ALE that matters the most to the average mortal, and in The Elixxir Society. Why? Because ALE is without doubt the most rational and accurate yardstick for measuring a society's progress and quality of life.* A virtual doubling of life expectancy in China under Mao literally means hundreds of millions of lives saved. That China's population zoomed from 400 million to 750 million means **roughly 350 million Chinese lives were saved by Mao's People's Republic from the clutches of premature, needless, brutal Systemic Homicide.**

12 Let us take those notoriously-unfootnoted claims of 20 million allegedly killed there, 20 million allegedly killed here in Maoist China. 10 or 20 million. They love nice big round figures. To understand the enormity of Maoist China's accomplishment, let us take those apocryphal 10 or 20 millions bandied about and deduct them from this 350 million increase in China's population under Mao, and Mao's China must still be credited with saving literally hundreds of millions of lives.

13 Mao was not perfect, and the China under Communism no utopia. The Communist Party (and even Mao himself) admitted that major mistakes were committed and that excesses happened under their watch which resulted in significant

lives lost. But then a revolution is no dinner party, as Mao had warned. The choice for China was between Maoist China or Chiang Kai Shek's brutal fascistic regime, which in its 20 year reign of terror, corruption and incompetence gave the Chinese people nothing but grief, poverty, famines, and humiliation. The choice was not between Maoist China and a modern rich European or American system.

14 Just as historians would not condemn Franklin D. Roosevelt solely for throwing all Japanese-Americans into concentration camps in WWII, or damn a Truman solely for dropping atomic bombs on civilians in Hiroshima and Nagasaki when Japan was already on its knees (a war crime and crime against humanity), so neither will history judge a Mao or Communist China only for the unauthorized excesses of the Red Guard during The Cultural Revolution and ignore the unprecedented supreme feat of doubling the average life expectancy of China, a poor and immense Third World country, in a single generation, a historical blink of an eye.

15 When the Post-Cold-War Post-U.S.-Empire History is written, when ImmorTalist history is written, it will recognize and restore the fact that for each of the 27 years under Mao, **while China was industrializing itself at breakneck speed amazingly without foreign investments, expertise or debt, China was also adding more than a year annually to its average life expectancy (ALE) — an increase of 33 years to its ALE in 27 years. This supreme accomplishment is unrivaled by any government, any economic or political system, in all the annals of human history.** The only state which can beat such a record would be an ImmorTalist one. An ImmorTalist state and society dedicated to the extension of youth-span and life-span.

16 What this meant was that at least 350 million lives were given birth to and saved from premature death. As they would be under the U.S.-supported tyrant Chiang, a public admirer of Mussolini, who hanged his political enemies, who had no idea

what "human rights" were, whose family and cronies raped the Chinese Treasury, and yet was portrayed by the U.S. media to the bitter end as a true "Christian" and great "democrat" and leader of "free China."

17 How did China's population grow so fast from 1949 to 1976? It is a historical fact that under the U.S.-supported dictator Chiang and the Emperors, the lives of most Chinese were indeed Hobbesian — "poor, nasty, brutish, and short." The wealth and splendor of the imperial courts and palaces were the birthright of a lucky few. Westerners saw only the lights and glamour of Shanghai (and loved the exclusivity of its No-Chinese-and-Dogs parks in its foreign "concessions"). And after 1949, the Western media can only lament the loss of "freedoms" enjoyed in these cocooned privileged enclaves, created thanks to imperialism, colonialism, racism, and let's not forget "the free market," and yes, "globalization." But that, alas, was not the real China.

18 In Chiang's China, the average Chinese, the overwhelming majority of the Chinese people, did not thrive at all. So the population stagnated at around 400 million which was the same as under the Manchu dynasty for a couple of centuries. So how did it rocket from 400 million under Chiang to 750 at Mao's death? Mao's China inherited one of the highest infant mortality rates in the world (which means millions of babies each year killed) and transformed that almost overnight into one of the world's lowest infant mortality rates. (Now that's really pro-life, unlike the U.S., which has one of the most scandalously high infant mortality rates among affluent countries.) Instead of health care for a miniscule elite under Chiang, the Communist government gave the Chinese people a universal health care system, its most important accomplishment, bar none.

19 Unlike the U.S. health care system, which is high-tech, and exorbitant, and leaves out almost 50 million, the Chinese health care system under Mao was universal and prevention-orient-

ed. It vaccinated everyone, infant, schoolchildren, elderly, for free. Instead of concentrating elite, high-tech, expensive medical care in the cities, Maoist China invented the "bare-foot doctors" during the Cultural Revolution, and redistributed and dispersed health care to rural areas, where most Chinese live. It taught the masses good hygiene. How to use serving utensils. How to wash hands after going to the toilet. 20 Why one should wear a mask, take the day off, or not share bowls when one has the flu or a contagious disease. Why one should not cough without covering one's mouth. Why one should never spit on the ground. Mao's China taught the poor rural masses sanitary waste disposal — and how to turn human waste into fertilizers for farming.

21 Instead of cars, which consumed oil, polluted the cities and contributed to global warming, Mao's China used bicycles as the predominant mode of transport in the cities, which also kept the Chinese lean and fit. In addition, China under Mao built an unprecedented public transport network of trains, buses, roads, bridges, ports and airports which knitted this huge country together, so that one does not need a gas-guzzling car to travel across China.

22 Mao's China took over one of the highest illiteracy rates in the world (80% of Chinese were illiterates) from Chiang and the emperors and turned it into virtually universal literacy, on a par with rich Western countries. How? By grassroots literacy programs and by Free Universal Education. Literate educated Chinese knew how to take care of their health. In the public schools, there was nutritious food for the students, so endemic malnutrition, a perennial curse for China, the "sick man of the East," was wiped out. Excellent pre-natal and post-natal care, subsidies for infants and children, knowing that they would have health care, education, and housing, an "iron bowl" for life, and won't starve — all these made Chinese confident that their babies would have a future, and eager to have them. Except for two or three lean years during The Great Leap For-

ward, starvation and famine (facts of life under the emperors and the Chiang regime), were wiped out. Contrary to Western predictions that a country with a population of this size could never produce enough to feed itself, Maoist China was able to do just that, without any help from the West.

23 In addition, except for the Korean War, which China entered as McArthur threatened to invade and bomb China with nuclear weapons, Maoist China was strong enough to ensure a period of uninterrupted peace, unlike the weak China under Chiang and the dynasties, which were constantly wracked with civil wars and foreign invasions where tens of millions of Chinese perished. And for the first time in Chinese history, most Chinese did not die before old age, but instead could expect to reach old age.

24 And last but not least, homelessness, another "fact of life," was eliminated. Yes, accommodations are not to the new Chinese billionaire's liking, but every Chinese was guaranteed shelter over his head, and that of his or her family. And let's not forget, the "coolie" labor (the serfs that worked endless days for a pittance with no benefits or security, so rampant in pre-1949 "globalization" and "free market" under Chiang) was abolished overnight. Suddenly every Chinese worker was guaranteed "the iron bowl," lifelong work security with benefits and vacations and a decent retirement to look forward to.

25 Historically, there can be no question that the quality of life of the average Chinese in Mao's China from 1949 to 1976 was indeed a Great Leap Forward. In fact, for the first time in Chinese history, life for the overwhelming majority was good, with all basic needs taken care of. That this set of stubborn facts are no longer fashionable to cite, and that most Americans and Europeans have forgotten or never heard of them show the grip of the U.S.-dominated media on our minds, and its ruthlessness in rewriting history to serve its own Mortalist agenda.

26 By all objective historical evaluations, Maoist China must be credited with incredible accomplishments. The pinnacle of which is the unprecedented, unrivalled supreme feat of almost doubling China's life expectancy from 35 to almost 70, and almost doubling its population from 400 to 750 million.

27 Maoist China, historians will point out, was actually a very successful experiment. On top of its monumental overriding track record in extending Chinese life-expectancy, its economic and political system never came close to threatening to destroy the planet — neither through its stockpile of nuclear and biological weapons of mass destruction (as in both the U.S. and the former Soviet Union), nor by an economic system in which 5% of the world's population spews out 27% of the carbon emissions causing Global Warming (as in the U.S.).

28 Even when the U.S.'s own scientists tell the Bush-Cheney regime that Global Warming is real, and will wreak catastrophe in the near future, the U.S., to protect its quarterly GDP growth, refused to sign the Kyoto Accord. Obama, who took over from Bush Junior, has continued Empire's policy not only in Iraq and Afghanistan, but also on the life-or-death issue of Global Warming. Despite the U.S. and Western media's reporting, we now know that Obama went to the Copenhagen Conference to kill it. He went there with demands that he and the U.S. Empire knew would be rejected by China, India and Third World countries. He went there with an "offer" that he knew (and now we know) could not even be passed by his own Congress, even under the Democrats. In other words, it was not a good-faith offer. Obama went to Copenhagen to scapegoat China and India, claiming they are now as big or a bigger problem than the U.S. Actually, that is a Big Lie. China, with 1.3 billion (over four times more than the U.S.) people, has a Per Capita Carbon Emission of 4.91 Tons/Capita . India, with a population over1 billion has a per capita emission of 1.31 Tons/Capita. And the U.S. with a popula-

tion of 300 million, has a per capita carbon emission of 19.18 Tons/Capita (Source: U.S. Dept of Energy, Energy Information Agency). So is it any surprise that China and India were furious and did not see any good faith or any serious intention to negotiate a new treaty?

29 The reason why The Death Society and its propagandists are so vehement in trying to rewrite history? They are terrified that poor Third World countries, after trying U.S.-style Capitalism, "Free Markets" and "Globalization" for decades without much trickle down, might finally wake up and see that the template of China from 1949 to 1976 (sans its excesses and errors ideally) provides a much more plausible, much more promising path to a more planet-friendly industrialization and to freedom from high infant mortality, low life expectancy, grinding poverty, virtual slavery for most, homelessness, lack of health care and rampant illiteracy.

30 We ImmorTalists are not Maoists. We hope U.S. Jungle Capitalism and its orgy of plunder and planet-wrecking do not tempt a return to a Maoist "correction." Having said that, ImmorTalist History will recognize that China under Mao was no doubt greatly preferable, more Life-saving and Life-affirming than China under Chiang Kai Shek or the emperors. To insist otherwise is simply to deny facts, erase history, and engage in a Big Lie. The question is how do we prevent a need to return to something like Maoist Communism? The answer: we must give the world a better alternative. We must convince it that Another Way, Another World, is possible. Unless we do, the world's long-suffering masses will opt for either Religious Extremism or Secular Radicalism.

31 **A collapse in life expectancy in Post-Soviet Russia under U.S. inspired economic "reforms" from 72 to 57 is one of the great crimes of the 20th century.** Unlike Stalin's crimes, this one is invisible, unwritten. The so-called crash course economic" reforms" instigated by the U.S. and imposed by the Yeltsin regime resulted, unsurprisingly, in the systemic

deaths of tens of millions of Russians which continues to this very day. Due to this catastrophic decline in life expectancy, Russia's population is shrinking dramatically. It is Systemic Homicide. And is directly attributable to Capitalist Mortalism.

32 Most deaths from heart disease, cancer, stroke, obesity, diabetes, malaria, AIDS, and pneumonia are preventable, premature, unnecessary.

33 *It is the nature of a Death Society that it has the scientific, health-care and economic resources to minimize or even eliminate most of its top killer diseases but for ideological reasons refuses to.* (The United States is the most egregious example.)

34 Another characteristic of The Death Society: Suicide is rampant and glorified — whether it be "Romeo and Juliet," Marilyn Monroe, Kurt Cobain, Jack Kevorkian or the Euthanasia movement which is now legally enshrined in Oregon. The Elixxir Society will not prosecute someone who wants take his own life, but we condemn the legal enthronement and societal glamorization of suicide. We reject turning doctors into Deputies of Death.

35 The third characteristic of a Death Society: **The Death Society Diet (DSD) rules.** The high-calorie, high-fat, high-cholesterol, high-salt, high-sugar, high-death diet. It's junk-food nation, colonized by MacDonald's and fast-food franchises. And it's designed to make you fat, ugly, sick, and dead before your time. The mantra of every citizen of a Death Society should be "Every day in every way I am getting fatter and fatter, uglier and uglier, older and older."

36 Since everyone knows that this Death Society Diet metes out obesity, heart disease, cancers, diabetes, stroke, not to mention premature aging and Death, subsisting on The Death Society Diet must be considered a form of *slow suicide.*

37 In a Death Society, *there is no time for the great pleasures of life — no time for sex, love, or relationship.* Not even time for food, which has to be eaten on the run, like a coolie.

38 There is no time to sleep. The number of Americans suffering from sleep-deprivation is staggering. America is no longer the land of the free so much as the land of the zombies. New research reveals sleep-deprivation is as hazardous to our health as obesity or smoking. Sleep-deprivation mimics many of the hallmarks of human aging. Thanks to Globalization and supermacho Mortalist Capitalism, the U.S. is exporting sleep-deprivation — just as it has obesity and no-leisure-time – to the rest of the world, especially Western Europe and Asia. Coolies and serfs had more time for eating, sleeping, and shitting.

39 *Mortalist Work is excessive, compulsive, joyless and ultimately punitive.* The template? Serfs from The Dark Ages.

40 Implementing the Genesis Curse hurled by a wrathful Yahweh against humanity after "the fall" ("In the sweat of thy face shalt thou eat bread"), the "work ethic" of The Death Society decrees that punitive toil is our end, not the means to our end.

41 The aim of work in the so-called "global economy" is to deny us any possibility of pleasure, fulfillment, or bliss. This is **Economic Puritanism.** Just as in the sexual realm, it is "the fear that someone somewhere is having fun."

42 In a Death Society, there's always money to burn for the instruments of Death, but little or no money for the instruments of life. A Death Society throws money at its Vietnam, Iraq, Afghanistan misadventures. It writes a blank check for its nuclear overkill to dominate the world. But it has "no money" for retirement pensions, Social Security, Medicare, unemployment benefits, and universal health insurance.

43 A Death Society is run mostly by Nasty Old Men, still fighting the last great war, always blest with a soft spot for deadly

toys which allow them *a la* Dr. Strangelove to take us and the planet with them when they exit this life, which is any day now.

44 Adequate government funding for anti-aging life-extension research? Adequate state funding for research to cure cancer, heart disease, stroke, AIDS, or malaria? Never! In The Death Society, one needs to pass the hat for such "nonessentials." Government has little money for such life-and-death things; one is forced to rely on charity.

45 Deathists squander money on a "national security state" and on "anti-missile missile system" to "defend" Americans from Reds, Islamists, Russia, China, Iraq, Iran, this or that "rogue state" *du jour*.

46 The Soviet Deathists engaged in the same insanity – bankrupting themselves in their arms race with the U.S., trying to match overkill nuclear stockpiles with the world's biggest economy, when a minimal one like the French or the Chinese would have been deterrent enough.

47 **Reality-check: We are a million times more likely to die from heart disease, cancer, stroke, diabetes, AIDS, Alzheimer's, and Old Age than from any "rogue state's" nuclear attack.** Every year, every month, every week, every day, every hour this is proven without fail. And yet The Death Ideology, through its Death Societies spends your hard-earned tax money as if the absolute reverse were absolutely true. (No "rogue state" would even think of a nuclear attack on the U.S. unless the U.S. threatens its very existence. Why? It knows it would be bombed into the Stone Age. Unlike China, the U.S. has always publicly reserved the right to use nuclear weapons in conventional war. Hiroshima and Nagasaki are Exhibits A and B. In criminal law, the use of disproportionate force turns you from defender into aggressor.)

48 The bottom line: money and scientists are diverted from urgent life-saving research which can cure not only heart disease and

cancer but also their primary cause – human biological aging. The grossly-misplaced prioritizing of a Death Society is the equivalent of a shotgun pointing at our heads. It cruelly and maliciously deprives us of the prioritizing and galvanizing of society's resources necessary to triumph against Heart Disease, Cancer, Stroke, Old Age and Death.

49 *In The Death Society, GNP (Gross National Product) or GDP (Gross Domestic Product) is worshipped while ALE (Average Life Expectancy) is ignored, denigrated. Mortalists obsess about "standard of living" and neglect quality of life. They idolize productivity as the absolute end instead of the means to our end.*

50 *The citizens of a Death Society are all languishing on a **Deferred Living Plan**.* They postpone, abstain from, and surrender their prime time, their best years because of their programmed obsession with "retirement."

51 The "golden years" refer not to one's youthful or healthy prime, but rather to the terminal years - where disease, dying, and Death hold sway.

52 In The Death Society, <u>life's focus becomes "financial planning" for old age; life becomes fixation on old age</u>. Success in a Death Society means hoarding up a big "nest egg" for the worst part of life, and stockpiling more than you can possibly spend, so you can pass on a big estate to old "children" who won't even talk to you or visit you while you're alive.

53 The health care system of a Death Society is not only sick, it is perverted. It adamantly refuses to extend our youthful, prime years. Instead it lavishes disproportionate resources on the last few years of an average lifespan – during which most mortals are aged, decrepit, and sick. The result is to extend only the painful, suffering, and dying part of life while willfully refusing to prolong youth, vitality, and health. This is The Death Society's implementation of **The Titonius Curse**. (In Greek mythology, Titonius asked for and received im-

mortality. He forgot to ask for eternal youth, however, so his punishment was that he aged hideously but could not be "released" by Death.)

54 Although The Elixxir Society will never neglect the old, the sick, or the dying, its health care system will singlemindedly concentrate on lengthening youth, vigor, and wellness into an endless summer. So that we shall never become old, ill or dying in the first place. *Just as The Death Society's economic system metes out The Genesis Curse, its so-called health care system executes The Titonius Curse for the "gods."* For daring to desire and request longevity, we are punished with longevity of the chronically-ill and senile kind.

55 In The Death Society, a high level of unemployment, underemployment, financial insecurity, homelessness, downright poverty, just as Disease, Old Age and Death, is *de riguer*. A Death Society is generous to a fault when it comes to building state-of-the-art prisons and Scrooge-like when it comes to even the most no-frills housing for its destitute. *It proclaims itself "pro-life" yet cheers on The Death Penalty.* It is no accident that George W. Bush, Jr. was the Governor of the state of Texas, notorious for its wanton executions of the poor, the "colored," the retarded.

56 *George Bush Junior, Rumsfeld, Cheney are the prototypical leaders for The Death Society.*

57 The American Gulag is the world's largest. **Around 2.3 million people are in U.S. prisons. More than 1 out of every hundred adults in the U.S. are in jail. (Pew Center Report on the States, 2008). Counting those on parole or probation would increase the total "correctional" population to more than 7.3 million. That means a shocking 2.4% of the U.S. population is floating in and out of the U.S. Gulag.** (And that does not count the infamous concentration camp in Guantanamo Bay, the CIA's offshore torture camps, and the outsourcing of torture to American client states.)

58 The U.S. has the largest prison population in the world; it incarcerates a higher proportion of its population than the Soviet Union, Apartheid South Africa, and far, far more than China. By the staggering prison-population facts alone, it is clear that *the U.S. Mortalist Regime tops the Repression Index*. It is clearly the most repressive state on the face of the earth. In this it is peerless. The more crime goes down, the more the prison population goes up.

59 Let's not forget the abolition by the Bush regime of *habeas corpus*, the cornerstone of civil liberties, by the so-called "Patriots Act" (more accurately, The Martial Law Act). One wonders how any credible media could keep telling us with a straight face that the U.S. is a "free" country, and that every country its self-serving State Department "Human Rights Report" points to as "authoritarian" must be.

60 China is not even in the top ten for prison populations. But it must be in the Top Twenty? Top Thirty? No? Top fifty? Impossible. Top 100? Guess what, you're still off. **While the U.S. — "the land of the free" — is number one in rate of incarceration, China, ranks 113!** (Never heard this fact from the U.S. or Western Media? What a surprise.) **China's incarceration rate is a very benign 119 per 100,000, while the U.S. has a staggering 762 prisoners per 100,000. The U.S., the self-proclaimed "leader of the free world," is indisputably number one in the Gulag competition.**

61 At 762 prisoners per 100,000 population, the U.S. is securely ahead of Russia (611 per 100,000), and way ahead of such "authoritarian" regimes as Turkmenistan (489), Kazakhstan (378), Iran (222), and Libya (209). In fact, at 119 per 100,000, China is so laggardly in locking up its own people (a basic definition of a repressive state) that it falls far behind Israel (305), Great Britain (153), Australia (130), Spain (156), and even Luxembourg (160). China is virtually tied with The Netherlands (117), and is just a notch above Monaco (109).

62 The U.S., with only 300 million people, has locked up 2.3
    million. China, with a population of 1.3 billion, has only 1.56
    million prisoners. At the U.S. lockup rate, China should be
    entitled to a jail population of 10 million. But with a popula-
    tion more than four times the U.S., China's prison population
    is much smaller than the U.S. *So which country, pray tell, is
    more repressive, more oppressive, more authoritarian?* The
    U.S. and Western media claim it is China. But on what basis
    is this groundless and bizarre conclusion arrived at? Go fig-
    ure.

63 The U.S. Recidivism rate is 60%. China's recidivism rate is
    6%. The recidivism rate is a dead giveaway as to whether a
    criminal justice system is designed to be punitive, warehous-
    ing, or rehabilitating. In the U.S., it's like The Roach Motel.
    Once you get in, you never really get out. This 60% recidi-
    vism rate reveals the U.S. prison system is not designed for
    rehabilitation, but rather for warehousing and punishment.
    Once you are dragged in, there is a 60% chance you will go
    back. As part of this prison subculture, you are marked like
    Cain. You cannot get a job. Cannot reintegrate into society. In
    China, the recidivism rate of 6% shows that it does rehabili-
    tate its inmates. That people are able to return to society, get
    jobs and be accepted. Otherwise the recidivism rate could not
    possibly be a mere 6%, one of the lowest rates in the world.

64 U.S.-style **Jungle Capitalism** – no universal health insurance,
    little job security, atrocious unemployment rates for young
    African-Americans and Hispanic-Americans, virtual dis-
    mantling of welfare and other safety-net programs, dispro-
    portionate inequality between the rich and the overwhelming
    majority, inordinate stress on material consumption etc. – it
    is U.S. Jungle Capitalism which creates its "criminals" and
    then needs to protect itself (well, its very rich and the sys-
    tem) against "them." This is verified by the fact that Western
    European and Scandinavian states, with their Social-Demo-
    cratic Capitalism, do not need to incarcerate 1 out of 100 of

its adults. But then Western Europé and Scandinavia provide universal health insurance, employment and retirement security, and have lesser economic inequality. In other words, it is not as brutal as U.S. Capitalism, therefore it need not be as repressive.

65 The targets of the American criminal injustice system are the young, the minorities (especially African-Americans and Hispanics), and the poor whites.

66 There is no right to trial for most in The American Gulag since they are coerced into plea bargains by the threat of a more severe sentence. In most criminal cases, there is only the right to incompetent counsel, unless you're rich. Government intentionally refuses to pay enough to attract competent counsel. So most criminal trials in the U.S. are nothing but lynchings in kangaroo courts. Because of this, many inmates should be considered political prisoners.

67 Since it is *The* Death Society, with no universal health insurance, no employment or retirement security, little or no paid vacation, the world's biggest gulag and not just for "terrorists" but for its own people, little wonder that a new study led by a Harvard professor has found *the U.S. to be number one in the world in the incidence of mental illness*. Americans' rates of mental illness are "astoundingly high" – so much higher compared to other rich Western countries, so much higher than China or poor Third World countries.

68 Despite all this, all is not lost in U.S. of A. Immortalist sentiment grows with each passing day alongside Mortalist repression. An overwhelming majority of the American population desire to stay young, slim and healthy. This Immortalist meme is especially strong and widespread among baby boomers, women, and gays. And it is entrenched in its pop culture.

69 As more and more boomers retire without adequate retirement savings or pensions, they must flex their voting muscle to compel the Federal and state governments to expand benefits

for Social Security, Medicare, and the social safety net in general. Their victory will benefit the following generations.

70 In other words, unless Baby Boomers plan to passively accept poverty in their later years, they must force the American government to become increasingly Immortalist. Instead of Germany, France, England and Scandinavia mimicking the United States, the reverse must happen. The United States must become more and more like Germany, France, England, and Scandinavia.

71 It would not be surprising if major anti-aging life-extension breakthroughs continue to come from American laboratories if only to meet the demand of 79 million baby boomers who are not growing any younger.

72 The U.S. can go either way — continue to let The Death Ideology reign, or become a truly great Forever Young Society.

∞

**The citizens of a Death Society
are all languishing on a
Deferred Living Plan.**

**They postpone, abstain from, and surrender their
prime time, their best years because of their
programmed obsession with "retirement."**

∞

∞

**Bush Junior, Rumsfeld, Cheney
are the prototypical leaders of The Death Society.**

∞

CHAPTER 4
The Death Ideology

1   The powers that be have a great attraction to Death. Whether it wields Death as the ultimate threat, glorifies it as martyrdom, exhorts us to submit to it as fate, the powers that be have turned Death into an ideology – The Death Ideology - which permeates our society and dominates our days.

2   What is The Death Ideology? It is the paradigm and worldview which makes Old Age and Death acceptable, even desirable. It is the official but unspoken ideology of The Death Society. Its function is to make Old Age and Death — the ultimate oppression — acceptable, "natural," "God-given". It perverts changeable biology into ontological essence.

3   **It is so crucial to make us swallow Death because once Death is acceptable, all the other lesser deaths — all the other unnecessary social, economic, political evils — become acceptable.**

4   *If The Death Ideology can persuade us that Death is a natural part of life, then we can accept Heart Disease, Cancer, Stroke, low life expectancy, high infant mortality, layoffs, downsizings, lack of health insurance, no retirement security, unemployment, underemployment, deforestation, stagnant or low wages, poverty, injustice, sexism, racism, gross inequality, malnutrition, AIDS, corruption, repression, Global Warming, Biodiversity destruction, as unavoidable parts of life.*

5   Despite the Death Ideology, all through history, philosophers, intellectuals, artists, conquerors, kings and queens, and great civilizations have not hesitated to express their fear of Death and their desire for Immortality.

6 Francis Bacon, the English philosopher said: "I know many wise men who fear to die." Queen Victoria on her deathbed stated: "All my kingdom for a moment of time." Homer, great Greek epic poet, quipped: "Speak not smoothly of death, I beseech you, ... Better by far to remain on earth the thrall of another ... rather than reign sole king in the realm of bodyless phantoms."

7 Martha Graham, the great American modern dance choreographer, whose incredibly productive life was abruptly ended at 98, said: "To me, death is a hateful thing. I am angry at death."

8 Shakespeare stated: "The weariest and most loathed worldly life/That age, ache, penury, and imprisonment/Can lay on nature, is a paradise/ To what we fear of death." Miguel de Unamuno, Spanish philosopher said: "Eternity, eternity! .... that is the supreme desire!" Bronislaw Malinowski, the father of modern anthropology stated: "Personally, to me, nothing matters except the answer to the burning question: 'Am I going to live, or shall I vanish like a bubble?'"

9 Albert Camus, Nobel Prize Laureate '57 stated: "All my horror of dying is contained in my jealous passion for life. I am jealous of those who will continue to live and for whom flowers and the desire for women will give their flesh and blood meaning." Woody Allen, comedian, director, said: "Some people try to achieve immortality through children. I prefer to do so by not dying." David Geffen, Hollywood mogul, explaining our fascination with vampire mythology, said: "Everyone wants to stay young and live forever!"

10 *To the Early Christian Church, Death is "the last enemy" to be vanquished. Early Christians saw the Fear of Death and the Desire for Immortality as "natural." The notion that Death is our "friend" is pagan, not Christian.*

11 After relentless reprogramming by Mortalism over two millennia, too many of today's cognoscenti trample on each other to pledge that they harbor no such fear, no such desire. Many have been herded back into the closet.

12 Through bestselling books and countless sermons in the media, Mortalist evangelists such as the Pope, the Dalai Lama (trendy Tibetan Buddhism teaches acceptance of Death), Jack Kevorkian, Elizabeth Kubler-Ross and the Haters of This Life all preach, prescribe and demand that we die The Good Death, all decree that it is not politically correct to admit any fear of Death, any lust for Immortality.

13 Mortalist propaganda tells us that Asian culture (especially the Chinese and Indians) are not afraid of Death because of Buddhism or Hinduism. The reality: no group of mortals on the planet are more shameless in wanting Longevity and Immortality than the Chinese.

14 China was unified by an Emperor who conquered kingdoms and dispatched expeditions abroad to find the elixir. The Chinese wish their leaders and emperors "Ten Thousand Years." They forbid even the mention of Death with the elderly. This instinctual Immortalism is as strong in the Chinese people today as ever before.

15 Reverencing the Old is different from liking Old Age. Or not being afraid of it. This is an intentional Mortalist confusion. During the Vietnam War, the idea that "they" (Asians) are not afraid of Death became "they" don't value Life the way we (Westerners) do. It was used to justify casualties of over a million Vietnamese. It doesn't really hurt them as much as it hurts us. This is the most lethal "Oriental" stereotype, the ultimate dehumanization.

16 Ancient Egypt was unabashed in its pursuit of Immortality. The Pyramids, the Sphinx, the hieroglyph, the Book of The Dead were all towards this end. The ancient Egyptians understood that the ultimate goal of life is Immortality. Civilization is only the means to this end. It was precisely because the ancient Egyptians loved Life so much that they feared Death and strove for eternity.

17 Where the Life instinct is robust, the civilization is great. Where the Life instinct is decadent, the civilization is dying or dead.

∞

If The Death Ideology can persuade us that Death
is a natural part of life, then we can accept Global
Warming, Heart Disease, Cancer, Stroke, low
life expectancy, high infant mortality, layoffs,
downsizings, lack of health insurance, no retirement
security, unemployment, underemployment,
deforestation, stagnant or low wages, poverty,
injustice, sexism, racism, gross inequality,
malnutrition, AIDS, corruption, repression,
biodiversity destruction, as unavoidable parts of life.

∞

CHAPTER 5
The Death Lobby

1 There is a Death Lobby. You may not know it, but what you don't know *can* kill you. The Death Lobby is the most powerful lobby in the United States. And in much of the Western world. In fact, in all of the world.

2 Dr. Death (aka Jack Kevorkian) has been The Death Lobby's most notorious spokesperson. After some years in jail, he's back. Elizabeth Kubler-Ross, the bestselling author, was an effective Death zealot, until her public ramblings about "the next life" discredited her totally with the scientific community.

3 Even **Betty Friedan**, who ignited the modern feminist movement, unwisely joined The Death Lobby in one of her last books "The Fountain of Age" where she tried her best to give Old Age a mystique, unsuccessfully. (Women are instinctive Immortalist; they've always wanted to stay young!)

4 **Naomi Wolf's** "The Beauty Myth" made her a bona fide lobbyist for the Anorexia Hysteria Cottage Industry, a niche in The Death Lobby. In that book, Wolf made the outrageous claim that the U.S. deaths from anorexia in one year were 150,000! The reality: 54 died from anorexia and none from bulimia in 1991, when her book came out.

5 Obesity is on the verge of overtaking heart disease as the number one killer of Americans, and here she is crying wolf, crusading against anorexia. What Naomi Wolf and the Anorexia Hysteria Cottage Industry don't want to admit: **the only eating disorder Americans suffer from is gluttony**.

6   The Hospice movement has been vastly influential, especially
    institutionally, in getting us to focus on accepting Death and
    Dying, in getting us to die The Good Death. The radical Eu-
    thanasia Movement, which has taken roots in the Netherlands
    and in the U.S. state of Oregon, is gaining ground with each
    passing day. Its mission is to subvert medical doctors, our
    front line, into active assistants for Death.

7   <u>In sheer number of Deaths, nothing is as lethal as The Nico-
    tine Cartel. Cigarettes kill up to 500,000 people every year
    in the U.S. alone. This is roughly nine times the American
    casualties in the Vietnam War — in just one year.</u>

8   *What "rogue" state has caused or is likely to cause this kind
    of carnage every year, without fail, on the American popu-
    lation? It's like Hitler's Holocaust happening every decade
    without any resistance, without any protest, without any me-
    dia coverage.*

9   Cigarettes cause heart disease, stroke, and cancers. Smok-
    ing is more addictive than heroin. And The Nicotine Cartel is
    richer, bigger and more powerful by far than Latin America's
    Drug Cartels. And yet it is perfectly legal. The U.S. Commerce
    Department with able help from the late racist, gay-bashing,
    coldwar-mongering, global-warming-denying Senator **Jesse
    Helms** (whom the Dalai Lama called "my great friend") left
    no stone unturned in their efforts to force American cigarettes
    on poor Third World countries.

10 Just as the British Empire imposed opium on China, so now
    the Death Ideologists in the U.S. government push tobacco
    exports to China and other Third World countries, exporting a
    ticking timebomb of Disease and Death which could collapse
    these countries' fragile health care systems.

11 The Death Lobby also includes the Fast-Food Pushers. Mac-
    Donald's, Burger King, Kentucky Fried Chicken et al spend
    billions every year on advertising and promotion. Galloping
    obesity, heart disease, cancer, diabetes are the harvest we reap

for becoming Fast-Food Nations. The Salt, Sugar, and Fat industries are not too far behind in wreaking damage. It is not that they are inherently harmful, it is that they are inserted into every food in excess.

12 The Death Lobby includes Military-Industrial Complexes, which have priority over health care and retirement security in the U.S. and in many poor, Third World countries. The Military-Industrial Complex is given a blank check to protect us from enemies we won't die from.

13 The Gun Lobby. Deaths from firearms kill anywhere from 30,000 to almost 40,000 people in the U.S. each year. In the past two decades, more than half a million Americans have lost their lives because of firearms.

14 The Fat Extremists are turning obesity, a health hazard which kills hundreds of thousands of Americans each year, into a "civil right." They have successfully pushed for fat "civil rights" law in San Francisco, and have pressured clothing and cosmetics companies to hire fat models who are no role models for children or adults.

15 The Cult of Muscle Queens, brought into the mainstream by Arnold Schwarznegger, is definitely part of The Death Lobby. This insidious cult has speeded the aging of millions and pumped up their bodies into caricatures through steroids and extreme weightlifting.

16 **Mortalist Religions, especially Mortalist Christianity, are still powerful, still dangerous and still the basic text of Western Civilization.**

17 *The unholy cabal of The Death Lobby includes but is not limited to Mortalist Religions (especially Mortalist Christianity), The Nicotine Cartel, The Fat Lobby, The Fast Food and Junk Food lobbies, the Euthanasia-and-Suicide movements, The Gun Lobby, The Bodybuilding Cult, The Anorexia Hysteria Cottage Industry, and of course The Military-Industrial Complex.*

18 Ideas do count. This is why the most influential and insidious elements of The Death Lobby are its most fervent and tireless intellectual evangelists.

19 In March of 2000, a number of its leading lights scurried to a conference convened by the University of Pennsylvania's Center for Bioethics and funded by the wealthy John F. Templeton Foundation. The *New York Times* story about this conference was appropriately titled "In Praise of Death." The summary on page one read: "Ethicists and theologians offered passionate praise of death at a conference on the consequences of advances that extend human life."

20 Passionate praise of Death indeed! From the Lovers of Death of course!

∞

The Death Lobby includes Mortalist Religions (especially Mortalist Christianity), The Nicotine Cartel, The Fat Extremists, The Fast-Food/ Junk-Food Pushers, the Euthanasia-and-Suicide movements, The Gun Lobby, The Bodybuilding Cult, The Anorexia Hysteria Cottage Industry, and of course The Military-Industrial Complex.

∞

∞

The Fat Extremists are turning obesity, a deadly health hazard which kills hundreds of thousands of Americans each year, into a "civil right."

The Cult of Muscle Queens (or Arnold Schwarznegger's cult), is definitely part of The Death Lobby. This insidious cult has speeded the aging of millions and pumped up their bodies into caricatures with steroids and extreme weightlifting.

∞

CHAPTER 6
Mortalism's Arguments for Death Debunked

1   How does The Death Ideology turn Death into an object of desire, the Supreme Good?

2   It has created, perfected, and drummed into us the following arguments for Old Age and Death, all rooted in Mortalist Religion, but all disguised in secular clothing.

3   These arguments for Death are used again and again by the Death lobbyists. You will recognize these arguments and their omnipresence. And the next time you hear someone use them, it will tip you off to the fact that they are a "card-carrying" member of the Death Lobby, or at the very least programmed by it.

4   *Mortalist Argument Number One: Death makes Life meaningful and precious.* "To number our days is the condition for making them count," rhapsodizes Leon R. Kass, Bush Jr.'s "Bioethics" Czar, who teaches at the University of Chicago. "Could life be serious or meaningful without the limit of mortality?" Dr. Kass answers with a vehement no, of course. "Homer's immortals....for all their eternal beauty and youthfulness, live shallow and rather frivolous lives," he argues. This argument is ridiculous even if expounded by a University of Chicago "ethicist." *If immortality must be inherently meaningless, frivolous, and shallow, then Yahweh or God, being very immortal, must live the most meaningless, frivolous, and shallow existence indeed.*

5   Surely Dr. Kass and his fellow Death apologist Richard J.
     Neuhaus (a priest who heads The Institute of Religion and
     Public Life) do not really believe their own argument? All the
     great faiths — Christianity, Islam, Judaism — believe in an
     eternal, immortal God. All great faiths preach that immortal-
     ity is the ultimate state to aspire to, the most precious prize
     awarded to believers. And yet this flimsy argument has been
     trotted out so many times by theologians, "ethicists," Protes-
     tant churches, and most especially the Pope and the Vatican,
     all of whom should know better.

6   It is hard to overestimate The Death Lobby's radical love of
     Death and their fundamental hatred of Life. Dr. Kass assures
     us "The finitude of human life is a blessing for every indi-
     vidual whether he knows it or not." He's a mind-reader too.
     This extra talent must be why the University of Chicago hired
     him? He presumes to speak for you and me, like a god or
     king, though we have not given him our proxy votes.

7   His loathing against Life is so deep that he has serious prob-
     lems even with an increase in your lifespan of only 20 years. The
     shorter a lifespan, the more precious and meaningful it must be,
     he claims.

8   By this reasoning, everyone who lived when lifespan averaged
     less than 50 years must have had a more meaningful and valu-
     able existence that us who are condemned to a lifespan averag-
     ing 75 to 80 years. By this logic, a drifter who died at 26 from
     suicide or drug overdose must have had a more meaningful and
     precious life by far than some overstaying seniors like Picasso
     who lived to be 92.

9   *Mortalist Argument Number Two: Death is a "natural" part of
     life.* It is "natural." But so what? Heart disease, strokes, cancer,
     polio, cholera, smallpox, measles, the bubonic plague, AIDS,
     Ebola, Multiple Sclerosis, Parkinson's, Alzheimer's and obesity
     are all natural too. But that doesn't make them any more accept-
     able.

10 An extension of this argument: one must die in a "natural" way. The reality is that even the most fanatical of the Death lobbyists if afflicted by a painful terminal disease like cancer would beg their doctors for morphine and other pain killers. Dying "naturally" is nasty.

11 *Mortalist Argument Number Three: Death is an "essential" part of life.* Death is that which gives meaning to life, the Death lobbyists tell us. Death is the ultimate aim, the *telos* of life. It is that which opens the door to a superior realm, that which makes human perfection possible. We Immortalists say the Deathists are in this argument confused at best, malicious at worst.

12 The Immortalist answer: *Death is not ontological essence. It is a cruel, dirty, terroristic biological reality. A quick visit to the nearest nursing home or morgue verifies this.*

13 The mischief of this Mortalist Lie is great. If execution of a Jesus or Socrates (or a Gandhi or Kennedy) makes "heaven," "eternity" or life's "ontological essence" possible, then the executioner is cleared of any and all guilt. As he has inflicted no real damage.

14 *If Death is "ontological essence," if it opens wide the door to a better realm, then the Holocaust, other genocides and garden-variety mass murders cannot be that bad.*

15 *Mortalist Argument Number Four: This Life is not the supreme good.* The Blasphemers of This Life are Lovers of The Afterlife. Ah, they tell us, the Afterlife is such a blissful, idyllic state where every wrong will be righted. To divert attention from our daily misery, despair or deprivation, the purveyors of Death still sell us real estate in heaven.

16 We Immortalists care about This Life. We believe that one bird in the hand is better than a hundred in the bushes. *We are tired of buying real estate in heaven from the Vatican or TV evangelists or fundamentalists of any and all stripes.*

17 *Mortalist Argument Number Five: The Good Death follows The Good Life.*

18 A "peaceful," "fearless" and "accepting" dying is claimed to be proof that one has lived The Good or Virtuous Life. If one has led a fulfilling or righteous life, one should not be afraid to meet one's maker, or meet life's end, or so claims Mortalism.

19 **Elizabeth Kubler-Ross**, one of Death's high priestesses, deftly repackaged this old Mortalist superstition into that of The Good Death. Dying, she claimed in her bestselling book, can be broken down into "stages." The Good Death requires you to go through neat stages supposedly ending in — surprise, surprise — acceptance. If you die in acceptance, Death becomes the most fulfilling stage of life, she promised. Kubler-Ross' "science" was not the most rigorous kind, as seen by her claim later on that she also had evidence of the "after life." When facing her own Death, Kubler-Ross insisted "I know beyond a shadow of a doubt that there is no death....The body dies, but not the soul." In other words, Kubler-Ross herself, the preacher of "acceptance" of Death, *never* accepted her own Death. Although she had pontificated tirelessly to us that "acceptance" is the last stage of The Good Death, she died refusing to accept it.

20 We Immortalists say this is voodoo science. The fact that the dying may "accept" Death under great duress does not mean that it equals fulfillment. "Acceptance" of death by the dying is no more evidence of Fulfillment than confession squeezed out by torture is of Truth. The obvious explanation for the so-called "acceptance" of the dying: *the clinical depression of the dying, which is often passed off or confused with "acceptance."*

21 Mortalist Religions always claim their leaders died "peacefully," "without pain," or were surrounded by family, friends, and disciples. This is to impart to us a model of The Good Death. This is to distinguish it from the "terrible" death of infidels.

22 Two recently deceased "princes" of the church, **Cardinal Bernardin** of Chicago and **Cardinal O'Connor** of New York

took great pains to tell Americans and the world that they were not afraid in the face of Death. Chicago's Cardinal Bernardin preached in his dying days that we should see Death "as a friend." But both were eclipsed by the spectacle of the dying Pope John Paul, who was most intent on evangelizing the whole world on the Vatican's notion of The Good Death. *But the Vatican's Good Death is the Greek response to Death, not that of the early Christian Church. It is the response of Socrates, not of Jesus. It is heresy.*

23 **Jesus** saw Death as The Enemy. On the cross, his Death was a horrifying ordeal: "My God, my God, why have you forsaken me!"

24 We Immortalists say if you have had a good life, you should be rewarded with more life, not Death. If you've had a good life, you would want more life, not less.

25 *Mortalist Argument Number Six: Death is The Great Leveler.*

26 It comes to both the rich and the poor, the famous or the obscure, the powerful or the powerless, majority or minority, they tell us. It has no bias towards race, gender, nationality or sexual preference, so it is good, they preach.

27 **We Immortalists point out there is gross inequality and injustice — even in Disease and Death, especially in Disease and Death. Middle-income American adults are 2.3 times more likely to die than their richest counterparts! The poorest American adults are 3.2 times more likely to die than the richest! (1999 New York Times Almanac)**

28 If you are not rich, you may be more than 300% more likely to die. This may be due to the fact that the middle-class or poor are more likely to get sick. Less likely to get excellent or preventive medical care. Less likely to get to a good hospital in an emergency. Less likely to be treated as well in the emergency room as the rich. And often, less likely to get any medical care at all.

29 The rich *are* different; they live longer, they die later.

30 It's easy to see the bankruptcy of The Death Ideology and its *lame* arguments for Death. They are not logical, not rational. They are lightweight and unworthy. This is not because the Death apologists are dumb so much as their cause is indefensible.

31 All they can do is trot out once again those old musty discredited arguments from the dark age of medieval theology. It is Superstition, not Reason, that they offer us.

32 It is why **Father Neuhaus** can only attack the search for immortality as "a pagan and sub-Christian quest." It reeks of Mortalist Religion, not to mention intolerance for non-Christians. *They have no case, period.*

33 What is really lurking behind all these Death Ideology arguments in praise of Death? It is basically Death religionists trying desperately to enforce The Genesis Curse: The Curse of Mortality allegedly imposed on the human race by a wrathful God for "the fall" (that is, Eve's having picked the wrong apple in the Garden to snack on).

34 After Adam and Eve supposedly "disobeyed" God and ate of the Tree of Knowledge of Good and Evil, God "cursed" Adam and Eve: *"...for dust thou art, and unto dust shalt thou return."* (Genesis 3: 17-19 King James Version) And this according to Mortalist Religion is why we die and why we *must* die. We are told that this Curse of Mortality covers not only Eve, the one guilty of this "misdemeanor," but also Adam, you and me, and all of the human species, for all time!

35 If you analyze it, these self-appointed "ethicists" like Dr. Kass and Father Neuhaus (a priest) are nothing but *enforcers* of The Genesis Curse, the supposed curse of Mortality on the human species.

36 What they have done is dress up a medieval superstition in modern secular garb. It's no wonder that so many of these "ethicists" are clergy, ex-clergy, or devotees of Mortalist Religion. They are covering all the bases. While Mortalist Chris-

tianity (with the Vatican leading) roll out the explicitly religious artillery against Immortality, these "ethicists" disguise essentially religious arguments as "philosophy" or "public policy" or "ethics."

37 Rather than say we must remain mortal because we are under The Genesis Curse, they say we must remain mortal because it is "natural," more "meaningful," "ontological essence," etcetera, etcetera. They are the traitors to the species, the Fifth Columnists, the Trojan horses in our midst.

38 Let us deconstruct the Genesis story, as we must every part of the "Old Testament" and "New Testament" (and as we must with every Mortalist basic text of every civilization). This is because Mortalist and Immortalist elements lie side by side, in contradiction and "paradox" and warfare, depending on whether Mortalist dogmas or Immortalist longings get the upper hand on a particular page, in a particular line.

39 Initially, Yahweh (God) did not forbid Adam and Eve from eating of the Fruit of The Tree of Life, which would have given them and the human race Immortality. God told Adam: *"Of every tree of the garden thou mayest freely eat.* But of the tree of knowledge of good and evil, thou shalt not eat of it." (Genesis 2:16) This meant God gave Adam and Eve implicit permission to eat of "the tree of life" which can confer Immortality.

40 This permission to partake of the fruit of Immortality was supposedly rescinded after Eve picked the wrong apple. The rationale? "And the Lord God said, Behold, the man is become as one of us, to know good and evil: and now, lest he put forth his hand, and take also of the tree of life, and eat, and live for ever...So he drove out the man (from the garden)." (Genesis 3:22-24)

41 *Why did God not command Adam and Eve to not eat of the fruit of The Tree of Life? Why indeed if Immortality is bad for "man," if it would lead to a frivolous, meaningless and*

dissipated existence? Why indeed if Mortality is the "nature" and "essence" of "man"?

42 This is something the Vatican and its army of theologicans can never explain. This is something the "ethicists" like Kass and Neuhaus and Callahan can never explain. Even their own basic text — the Bible — tells us that there is nothing inherently wrong, "sinful" or "evil" with the prospect of Immortality for humans.

43 **The sin of Adam and Eve was in *not* having chosen to eat of The Tree of Life and its Fruit of Immortality. The sin was in having said No to Life. This was what the "fall" was really about.**

44 This is *the unpardonable sin* of the Mortalist Religionists, and its theologians, "ethicists" and "philosophers." They have rejected Life Eternal, once again, as in the Garden, when it is being proffered.

45 What are the Mortalist "ethicists" and "philosophers" doing if not guarding the fruit of The Tree of Life and preventing your access to it, and to Immortality?

46 *We Immortalists shall not make the same mistake as "Adam and Eve." We say Yes to The Tree of Life, to its Fruit of Immortality. We say Yes to the Eternal Life that Jesus' Immortalist Christianity offers.*

47 We reject belief in a Mortalist God who would condemn you and me to capital punishment just because "Eve" flunked her little test and chose the wrong fruit to gnosh on. Not even the most unjust, vengeful, and arbitrary hanging judge would dare to impose such an outrageous sentence: Death not only to the "wrongdoer" but also to her mate, to each and every one of her descendants, to her race, her entire species, until the end of time.

No, if we must believe in God, it is an Immortalist God, not this blood-hungry Mortalist skygod!

48 *The Lovers of Death want to force you and me to commit suicide. Yes, to refuse the "elixir" when it is available is to commit suicide.* Just as surely as it is suicide if you have a life-threatening ailment and refuse to take medication which can save you. They want to ban, to pass laws against - if they still have the power. These authoritarians, they have not changed their stripes; they have absolute contempt for your freedom to choose. But then freedom to choose has always been alien to them and their ilk.

49 *We Immortalists will not deny the Death Ideologists their desire to embrace suicide if they so choose.* To not take the "elixir" when it arrives. To exit at the "appointed" time of 75 years, or is it 70, or is it 50? There's a strong case for 35. After all, it is the "natural" lifespan of humans in the jungles or in primitive tribes. And in India under the British and in China under the U.S.-supported dictator Chiang Kai Shek, the average lifespan was around 35. And 35 was the average lifespan in Tibet under the Dalai Lama. So if suicide or a 35 year lifespan makes them blissful and fulfilled and in tune with God and the cosmic plan, so be it. We promise not to stop them. But we draw the line when they demand the power to impose their unnatural craving for suicide on you and me.

50 **We dare and demand that the leaders and apologists of The Death Society and its Death Ideology to sign an enforceable and irrevocable contract that they will reject the anti-aging life-extension medicine or technology in all its forms when it arrives.**

Since he banned stem cells in federal research funding, **Bush Jr. must be the first to sign such an enforceable and irrevocable contract** that he will never use the fruits of stem cell research for the rest of his life. After him, every Republican and Democratic Senator, Representative, office holder or office seeker as well as all the leading lights of the Religious Right plus the Pope must be made to publicly sign such a pledge and contract. **And all hospitals, physicians, nurses, and paramedics in every nation on earth must be made aware of**

this list so as to deny them any and all fruits of stem cell research.

51 We challenge the above to convince their loved ones to sign the same pledge. It must be a legally binding contract. We shall provide a little consideration to make it binding. *If they change their minds, they will have to forfeit their entire earthly estate, which is of no real value anyway to them who are "heaven-bound."*

52 Only when they sign such a pledge and contract can you and I take them seriously. Only then we will not have to worry that they may try to sneak to the front of the line, tin cup in hand, when "the elixir" comes.

∞

What is really lurking behind all these Death Ideology arguments in praise of Death?

It is basically Death religionists trying desperately to enforce The Genesis Curse: The Curse of Mortality allegedly imposed on the human race by a wrathful God for "the fall" (that is, Eve's having picked the wrong apple in the Garden to snack on).

∞

∞

We dare the Death Apologists — especially Bush
Jr. — to sign an enforceable and irrevocable
contract that they will reject the anti-aging life-
extension medicine or technology when it comes.

If they change their minds, they will have to forfeit
to me their entire earthly estate, which is of no real
value anyway to them who are "heaven-bound."

∞

CHAPTER 7

The Crisis of Mortalism

1   The bad news: The Death Ideology is still in power. The good news: it is in crisis. We see signs of this great festering crisis everyday, everywhere.

2   The human genome mapped, genetic medicine, stem-cells growing replacement organs, human cloning, nanotechnology keeping us ever healthy, machine-enhanced humans, breakthrough anti-cancer and anti-stroke drugs. And, last but not least, anti-aging life-extension research giving us the prospect of "eternal" youth - and life. Yes, that most hated word to The Lovers of Death: the "I" word, Immortality.

3   The crisis of Mortalism is also glaringly seen in its paralysis and impotence in the face of the great issues and problems of our day. Exhibit A: *the graying of the rich countries — the biggest threat to their future, bar none.* This dramatic aging of the population and work force threatens to endanger or collapse pension and health care systems, and end affluence and destroy societies.

4   All this because of Mortalist Medicine, which extends dotage instead of youth, metes out The Titonius Curse, decreeing that if we dare to ask the gods for longevity, we must be punished with old age, longer.

5   The solution to the looming catastrophe of an increasingly aged and unproductive population: use anti-aging research and its breakthroughs to give people not only longer life but longer youthful healthy years so they can continue to be productive, and not tax the health care system and social safety net too much.

6   But this goes against **one of Mortalism's core superstitions and dogmas: that the human aging process itself cannot be touched lest the gods rain damnation on us for "hubris."**

7   Mortalist social institutions are ultimately unsustainable. For example, the U.S.'s Social Security and Medicare, or Western Europe's pension plans. These are founded on the obsolete Mortalist assumption that we will be dead soon after we retire.

8   Mortalist Marriage is similarly unsustainable. "Till death do us part" and ironclad monogamy might have made sense when the average lifespan was less than 50, but probably not when it's 75, and definitely not when it's 100.

9   How do we explain the U.S. government's insistence that it must put its quarterly GDP growth ahead of protecting civilization and the planet itself against Global Warming? Only The Death Ideology can explain this self-destructive, planet-killing insanity, this ultimate Crime Against Humanity, which **proves that this regime and economic system are unfit to govern.**

10 Economic growth at the cost of our civilization and the planet's destruction can only be described as insane and *cancerous*. What good is economic growth if we can't breathe or live? What good if the rising sea will drown all our most populated and important cities like New York, Miami, London, Lagos, Amsterdam, and Shanghai. (How about Manila, Pakistani or Indian cities?) What good if drought will turn much of the world into desert?

11 The Post-Mortalist Era has already dawned. The Elixxir Society is coming. And Mortalism can only respond by ranting and raving.

12 Listen to their fulminations. **Dr. Daniel Callahan**, another one of the Death Lobby's "ethicists" at the Hastings Center, threatens to make anti-aging life-extension research "socially despicable." (*New York Times*, 3/7/00 F4) They want to turn anti-aging life-

extension researchers into pariahs. They want to start a new Inquisition. How irrational, desperate and bullying they still are.

13 No wonder we feel a basic disconnect. Mortalism is so desperately behind the times. Its apologist Mortalist Christianity is so unbelievably reactionary. The old men in the Vatican are *still* railing against condoms, still screaming against teaching its use in public schools even in the face of the AIDS epidemic.

14 The Vatican is still against contraception and family planning dooming countries whose exploding populations eat up what little economic gains they eke out. It is still condemning *in vitro* fertilization which has given hundreds of thousands of infertile parents around the world the gift of a child. Despite shrill Vatican condemnations, 75% of Americans support *in vitro* fertilization.

15 The Vatican is the gangleader when it comes to attacking stem-cell research to cure Parkinson's and other terrible neurological diseases. We should not be surprised. After all, the Vatican also condemned Copernicus and Galileo too for the "heresy" that the Earth revolved around the Sun.

16 Death Ideologists, whether Catholic or Fundamentalists, want to ban therapeutic stem-cell research. They're against growing a new heart to replace your failing heart. They're against replacing your liver scarred by cirrhosis with a new one. They don't care about the possibility that it might cure you of Parkinson's. Or save you from vegetation from spinal cord injuries.

17 Some Death Societies have already banned human cloning. Cloning is nothing more than having a twin. Why don't they track down all twins in the land and ban them? It's neo-Luddite!

18 We Immortalists are for perfecting safe, effective human cloning. It is biblical to both Jews and Christians. *God did the first cloning: "God created man in his own image."*

19 This attempt by Mortalism to ban life-saving, disease-fighting, anti-aging or life-extending technology is totally futile and destined to fail. It is like trying to ban the Industrial Revolution and its machines of mass production.

20 If one society banned the new machine, another would have used them. The point is not to ban machines, the point is to make them serve humanity.

21 If the U.S. or U.K. bans stem-cell research or cloning, another country would seize on it, sooner or later, and take advantage of this opening. The same is true for anti-aging life-extension research.

22 There will be money, lots of money, much more lucrative than selling Old Economy cars or planes or sweaters. This Biotech Race will determine which societies flourish and which flounder in the twenty-first century.

23 *The real New Economy of the twenty-first century is not the Internet, it is BioTech with focus on anti-aging and life-extension.*

24 Yes, The Death Ideology is in its death throes. And it will only get worse. The situation in every Death Society is dangerous, complex, even schizophrenic. Because of its crisis, the Death Ideology is losing its grip, but it is not going without a fight.

25 In a big Death Society like the United States, there is now a mixture of Mortalist and Immortalist elements, with the Mortalist having the upper hand, or even barely in control, with Immortalist forces and longings emerging or even dominant in some sectors and demographics. Things are in a state of flux. There is great volatility.

26 The future for Immortalism is not merely bright, it is inevitable.

27 Given that 79 million baby boomers are near to retirement, and the majority have little or no retirement planning, there will be tens of millions of destitute boomers subsisting on Social Security, millions of sick boomers with no money to buy prescription medicine. Since they are the activist generation and have a big-

ger vote than any other demographic group, such a situation will lead to social and political upheaval. It will force an Immortalist restructuring of Social Security, Medicare, Health Care, Retirement, and the entire social system. It will also force government to pour money into Immortalist Medicine and Science — research to not only stop but *reverse* the aging process so boomers can take care of themselves financially and physically.

28 The end result: *American society is going to look more and more like Western Europe.*

29 Even **Paul Krugman**, winner of the Nobel Prize in Economics, MIT economics professor and *New York Times* columnist, glimpses this when he wrote that "the future may belong to the medical welfare state, a state whose slogan might be 'From each according to his ability, to each according to his needs.'"

30 *There is only one way out of the current crisis: a new paradigm.* One not afraid of the Post-Mortalist Era we are now irreversibly in. One not fighting The Elixxir Society that is coming. One which explains the emerging brave new world, and has a perfect fit with it. One which shows us how to save ourselves and the planet by staying young "forever."

∞

**To survive, American society is going to become
more and more like Sweden and the EU.**

∞

∞

79 million baby boomers are near to retirement, and the majority have little or no savings and pensions. There will be tens of millions of destitute boomers subsisting on Social Security. Millions of sick boomers with no money to buy prescription medicine.

Since they are the activist generation and have a bigger vote than any other demographic group, boomers will force an Immortalist restructuring of Social Security, Medicare, Health Care, Retirement, and the entire social system. Benefits will be increased for all Americans. Boomers will also convince government to pour money into research to not only stop but reverse the aging process so all future generations can take care of themselves financially and physically.

∞

∞

Death Ideologists, whether Catholic or
Fundamentalists, want to ban therapeutic stem-
cell research. They're against growing a new heart
to replace your failing heart. They're against
replacing your liver scarred by cirrhosis with a
new one. They don't care about the possibility
that it might cure you of Parkinson's. Or save
you from vegetation from spinal cord injuries.

∞

CHAPTER 8

The Human Condition:
Upgrade by Deleting D.O.D.

1   Life is "solitary, poor, nasty, brutish and short." So wrote the English philosopher Hobbes (1588-1679). For many in the Third World it still is. But for most in the First World, it is no longer as poor or brutish or painful or short as it used to be. And yet people are not truly happy. Something nags at them, haunts them, keeps them on the run, always a distance from that fulfillment they expect would be theirs. Even if we were to eradicate poverty overnight, even if we were to provide everyone the basics — food, shelter, education, employment, security in later years — we would still be far from bliss.

2   Why? Because there will still be the peculiarly human problems of Alienation, Repression, and Oppression. What philosophers have described as, "the human condition."

3   In this new millennium, *Repression, Oppression, and Alienation remain uniquely human problems inextricably linked to our mortality. They will be solved only when the problem of Death is conclusively resolved in our favor.* And this is why humanity cannot be truly happy until it is freed from its mortal shackles.

Repression & Death

4   Civilization is built on renunciation. It is possible only because the human race has learned to postpone immediate for

future gratification — to surrender today for a "newly im-
proved" tomorrow.

5   Since the gratification of the pleasure principle is the prerequisite for human happiness, civilization has — unsurprisingly
— been so far unable to deliver happiness.

6   But what does civilization protect us from? What is it that
we are so afraid of that we would willingly sign away our
chances for bliss and settle instead for a life of chronic, low-
grade depression?

7   Why Death of course! What else can it be? After all, civilization is merely our vehicle in our relentless attempt to obliter-
ate Aging and Death.

8   We are willing to give up happiness today for Immortality
tomorrow. For we know that true Happiness and Fulfillment
are impossible so long as we must grow old and die.

9   The denial or postponement of the pleasure principle is absolutely essential. The human race has decided to forgo pleasure
— and therefore happiness — while it is plotting to vanquish
Aging and Death once and for all.

10 While preparations are continuing, it is important that the
thought, reality and power of Death be deleted or distracted
from the mind. Otherwise, it would be dysfunctional, intolerable and self-defeating.

11 Since Death is so intimately linked with Life, repression of
the thought of Death - of things and situations connected with
it - means deleting a significant part of our reality and experience.

12 This is the human dilemma: to be sane and functional, we need
to shut down, delete or deny a significant part of our reality
and experience. Repression is necessary for our sanity and
functionality because it blocks the part of our reality tainted
by the virus of Death.

13 *So long as Death reigns, there will be repression.*

14 Repression — individually and collectively — shields us from the full brunt of Death. It is self-defense.

15 It is not true that the truth shall make us free. The truth makes us dysfunctional, even mad.

16 *The "neurotic" is choking on reality.* He is tortured by the tenuousness, the lack of justice, the absence of Reason in our mortal condition. She has stared at Truth without the screen of illusions. He has found it unbearable to know that we are all under an arbitrary death sentence which can be meted out anytime for no reason whatsoever. Yes, the "neurotic" is being eaten alive by this unflinching knowledge. *If we are not better at smoke and mirrors, we would be similarly afflicted.*

17 A person who finally gets his act together in life is killed by a car driven by an intoxicated teenager. A doctor who spends his life treating cancer patients dies of cancer. Good people meet an early, tragic, or painful death while evil people enjoy power, fame, wealth and health to a great age. We stubbornly cling to the belief that good will be rewarded, that life has reason, that injustice shall be righted at The Last Judgment or by karma or in the next incarnation. Otherwise, how can we avoid the asylum?

18 Total non-repression will remain a theoretical ideal until Death is annihilated. The life of Truth cannot be lived so long as life ends in Death.

∞

**So long as Death reigns,
there will be repression.**

**The life of Truth cannot be lived so
long as life ends in Death.**

∞

Alienation & Death

19 Alienation exists in human history because of the yawning gap between our needs and our control over nature.

20 This is the alienation resulting from our lack of power over nature. It was the kind suffered by the primitives and by many poor societies even now.

21 But we also suffer from a self-imposed and unnecessary form of alienation — the alienation of labor — which is peculiar to a society with the institution of private property. In primitive society, people are oppressed by nature but not by the products of their labor, or the nature of their labor. But most of us hate work. It is too repetitive, too menial, too manual, too backbreaking, too poorly-paid, or too much of a good thing. This is true in any kind of system.

22 With the great scientific and technological advances of the modern age, it is claimed that the role played by a hostile and untamed nature in our alienation is dwarfed today by economic factors.

23 But this is wrong — dead wrong!

24 While scientific and technological advances have given us more control over nature than ever thought possible, it is still unsatisfactory.

25 We are *still* at the mercy of nature. Although we have sophisticated warning systems against typhoons, storms, tornadoes, earthquakes, and volcanic eruptions, when nature throws its weight against us and brazenly commits "crimes against humanity", all we can do is run, evacuate and hide until its homicidal frenzy subsides.

26 Yes, the rich nations of the world have achieved increasing control over nature. Most people in these countries have the basics of life: food, clothing, health care, and shelter. And yet it is scandalous that so many even in these rich countries,

even in the best of times, still do not have any guarantee of basics in life which should be included in any definition of human rights.

27 But the majority of the human race still has not achieved fundamental control over nature and still suffers from the alienation resulting from lack of such control. For hundreds of millions, food is still at the mercy of unpredictable weather conditions. As in ancient times, a drought means disaster, starvation. Monsoon floods and tornadoes in the Indian subcontinent, Southeast Asia or the Pacific spawn typhoons and rampaging floodwaters which sweep away huts, possessions, and lives.

28 This suffering is unnecessary. It is caused by historical, economic, political and social forces which function to keep such countries in a state of subsistence dependence.

29 To find out if alienation resulting from lack of control over nature is still a major factor in human alienation, we must ask ourselves what is the ultimate goal of our efforts to control nature? It is only when we know our ultimate goal that we can tell how far we are from it. And therefore how important a factor it is in our alienation.

30 We want to control nature to preserve life. *We want to make nature safe for the human race.* And we have made incredible strides. Never in human history have so many been able to live so long.

31 This is obviously truer of the rich nations. But even there the control over natural forces is still not enough. This is because our aim in controlling nature is based on our desire to deprive her of her fangs. We are not satisfied with a control that leaves intact nature's power to impose on us D.O.D. (Disease, Old Age and Death).

32 The "spirit" is willing but the flesh is weak. The "spirit" is eager for continuing health, youth, and vigor. But the body falls into disrepair all too soon, all too easily. This alienation

is even more dramatic in the sick, the elderly, and the handicapped. They know what they desire but their bodies can't function.

33 So long as Death reigns, our control over nature is ultimately as unsatisfactory and inadequate as that of the primitives. So long as Death dominates, human alienation will continue even if we were to eliminate economic and social inequalities.

34 Our lack of control over nature is the more important factor in human alienation. Only when we gain enough control over nature to assure that Death comes only when we wish it to. Only when old age and its wretched infirmities can never molest us. Only then will human alienation be conquered.

Oppression & Death

35 Oppression — the most blatant human problem — is an act, situation or system that seriously diminishes the possibilities for full development of human potential.

36 Slavery is oppressive because it forces people into one arbitrary role. It does not matter if the slaves can be singers, dancers, scientists, or teachers. The institution of slavery allows only one role for people — refusing to see their merit and their potential. Therein lies its evil.

37 In a patriarchal society, women are only allowed three roles: mother, wife and housewife. In a feudal society, there was only lord, vassal, and serf.

38 Today's Mortalist Capitalist society turns people into consumers and producers. I buy, therefore I am. Our responsibility is to toil at jobs we hate so we have enough lucre to consume as much and as irrationally as possible. If you can afford to consume a lot, to gorge on food and things beyond your needs, you are said to be "successful," "happy," even "attractive."

∞

The U.S. spends 16% of its GNP on health care
— more than any other country in the world.
Yet almost 50 million Americans — every one
out of six — are without any health insurance
coverage and its health care system is ranked
34th by the World Health Organization (WHO).

Another 100 million Americans are
dangerously underinsured for a major
health crisis or catastrophic accident.

The irrefutable fact: it is cheaper to
provide universal health care.

∞

39 The oppressed are those who can be everything but are forced to become one thing. The oppressors are those who force people to become less than all they can be.

40 Serfs, slaves, women, and laborers are oppressed because they have been forced to restrict themselves to roles which have already been depreciated by the powers that be.

41 There are two kinds of oppression. One is crude and blatant, such as when the state puts a gun to your head or maims and kills to get its way. The other kind of oppression is systemic and somehow more acceptable. It is the kind that metes out poverty to ten percent of the U.S. population, refuses health care to tens of millions of Americans, and denies financial security in retirement to far too many senior citizens.

42 Countries like India kill and malnourish and cripple more of its people than "authoritarian" ones. It practices systemic infanticide. Just look at its horrendous infant mortality of 55 deaths per 1,000 live births. It kills off more adults prematurely too. Just look at its pathetic average life expectancy of 64.7 years. And it's literacy rate — or is it illiteracy rate? Half the country can't read or write. A "democratic" country like India is more oppressive and *lethal* than even some much-condemned dictatorships. Indians are a great people, but their government stinks. The nation whose people provide a disproportionate amount of the technical talent behind Silicon Valley can surely do better. The great Mahatma Gandhi would be appalled.

43 **Why do African Americans passively accept that their Average Life Expectancy (ALE) is up to 8 years less than whites but get upset when white cops shoot "a brother" forty-one times at point blank? Blacks should be a million times more outraged that they are dropping dead before their time every day.**

44 The gap in life expectancy between blacks and whites is a direct result of the disparity in income between blacks and whites.

45 It is the result of lack of access to adequate medical care, which is more lethal than lack of access to good schools.

46 It is testimony to the effectiveness of The Death Ideology that this criminal situation is accepted without any murmuring. This kind of oppression is silent, invisible, systemic, and relentlessly deadly. And black leaders don't make any noise about it.

47 *Why do Americans agree that the courts should treat everyone, rich or poor, alike, but then accept the notion that health care should be available to only those who can afford it?*

48 Why do almost 50 million Americans without any health insurance put up with this when they have enough votes to get health insurance? Why do they consider it a "natural" state of things when in Europe universal health care is the given, is considered a human right? This is the fatalism which paralyzes us when The Death Ideology holds sway over our minds.

49 Why do Americans accept the ridiculous notion that the U.S. — the world's biggest economy — "cannot afford" to give them universal health care? *The U.S. can afford universal health care even in a depression!* This is the reality. And contrary to the incessant propaganda of The Death Society, the facts are irrefutable: the best way to cut health care costs is to provide universal health care.

50 The United States spends 16% of its GNP on health care - more than any other country in the world. Yet 47 million Americans - about 16% - are without any health insurance coverage and it's health care system is ranked 37th by the World Health Organization (WHO).

51 *Countries which provide health care coverage to its entire population end up spending less of its GDP on health care.*

The Swedish "welfare state" spends only 9.2% of its GDP on health care. Canada 10.1%. France, which spends 11% of its GDP on health care, has the world's best health care system, according to WHO.

52 *The irrefutable conclusion and fact: it is cheaper to provide universal health care.* [Note: Sweden, Canada, and France are all in the top 10 nations for ALE (average life expectancy)]. Applying the more-refined measure of "Healthy Life Expectancy," the U.S. ranks a sickly 24th while Sweden ranks a very healthy third.

53 The Scandinavian countries are all in the top 10 for low infant mortality, while the U.S. ranks 46th! Despite its "pro-children" rhetoric, the U.S. is one of the biggest practitioners of systemic infanticide in the developed world. Lack of universal health care equals more babies dying prematurely, needlessly, outrageously.

54 Human rights include not only political rights but also the right to food, job, housing, and a secure retirement. If "human rights" do not include these, they are worthless — a mere ploy to put one's adversaries on the defensive in the geopolitical struggle. Comprehensive human rights are the kind that The Elixxir Society believes in.

55 Mahatma Gandhi, who led India's epic and inspiring fight for independence from the British Empire, once said, "Even God has to appear to a hungry man in the form of bread." How right he is. What is freedom of speech to a homeless person? What are political rights to someone who cannot feed her children?

56 The powerless have few possibilities. The Christian scriptures say all things are possible for God. Why? Because God is omnipotent.

57 Although oppressors are not omnipotent deities, they have much more power than the oppressed.

58 *Power corrupts — only because we have so little of it.*

59 The abuse of power comes from the need to create the illusion that we are more powerful than we are.

60 Anyone who has dealt with a petty bureaucrat knows how true this is.

61 It is often said that both the rich and the poor have to die. The rich touts this as equality. The poor sees it as consolation. This "wisdom" argues that oppression is relative since we all have to die. But it is misleading and distorts reality.

62 *The rich are different; they live longer.*

63 People differ in the way they relate to Death. Some use Death to oppress others. Others do not. Those who use Death to control others are the oppressors.

64 *Death — being the end of all possibility, all personality, and all individuality — is the most oppressive event in human experience.*

65 No other event in life has the power to end all possibilities. No other event can turn us into an inanimate object. No other event is more arbitrary, permanent and non-participatory.

66 Death is not only the most oppressive human event, it is also the root of human oppression. Death is that which turns every human being into a potential oppressor.

67 **Death is *the* instrument of social control by an oppressive status quo and its most effective justification.**

68 But there is hope. *Oppression, repression, alienation and unhappiness will decrease in proportion to the increase in our mastery over D.O.D. (Disease, Old Age and Death).*

∞

Countries that provide health care coverage
to their entire population end up spending less
of their GDP on health care. The Swedish "welfare
state" spends only 9.2% of its GDP on health care.
Canada 10.1%. France, which spends 11% of its
GDP on health care, has one of the world's best
health care system. Compare the above with the
United States, which spends a whopping 16%
of its GDP on health care and leaves out in the
cold almost 50 million Americans without any
health care coverage. Source: OECD, 2007

The rich are different; they live longer.

∞

'Sin' & Death

69 *Death did not come into the world because of sin. Sin came into the world because of Death.*

70 *Our mortality is not a consequence of sin. Our sinfulness is a consequence of our mortality.*

71 *Sin is simply the negative and destructive manifestation of our struggle against Death.*

72 Our fear of Death has produced not only the creative energy and light called genius. It has also spawned all our destructive orgies of evil. What is human evil but our flight from oblivion?

73 Death gives us a Tolstoy, a Van Gogh, a Dostoyevsky, a Melville and a Tchaikovsky. But it also curses us with our Hitlers, our garden-variety serial murderers, and our killer-kids who want to die in "a blaze of glory."

74 The artistic mode of struggle against Death seeks symbolic immortality by leaving behind footprints in art and literature. The nihilistic mode of struggle against Death attempts to deny human impotence by playing an omnipotent god of destruction who metes out life and death. The killer-kids in Colorado and elsewhere who snatched their fifteen minutes of fame by turning their schools into killing fields were acting out this god-of-destruction role to the hilt.

Death — being the end of all possibility, all personality, and all individuality — is the most oppressive event in human experience.

Death did not come into the world because of sin. Sin came into the world because of Death.

Sin is simply the negative and destructive manifestation of our struggle against Death.

CHAPTER 9
Mortalist Capitalism & Its Discontents

1   What is the root of Mortalist covetousness? Why does it always need more? And why are Mortalists never satisfied no matter how much they hoard?

2   Why do Mortalist billionaires drive themselves to an early grave to grab more? How many foreign sports cars can they drive at one time? How many beds can they sleep in each night? How much food can they pig out on in twenty-four hours? How many corner offices, presidential suites, or mansions can their bloated, expansive, aging bodies occupy at one time?

3   Excessive accumulation of material goods is a Mortalist compulsion, not based on any objective or reasonable needs.

4   You can never have enough of what you don't want. **Immortality substitutes** like Wealth, Power and Fame can never truly satisfy. **Immortality surrogates** like Children ain't the real thing.

5   You see this truth confirmed in Mortalist consumer society every day. The accumulation of money and possessions are no longer rational means to a rational end (pleasure or happiness). They have become ends in themselves.

6   In The Elixxir Society, what's important is *access, not ownership.*

7   We don't need to own a club, we need access to it — i.e. to get in, to use the space, to promote our event. As any club promoter will tell you, it's better not to own the venue, so long as you can access it. We don't need to own software, just be licensed to use it. We don't need to own property, we only

need access — to live on it, to live off it, to walk on it, to drink its beauty.

8   Ownership is exclusionary, access is inclusionary; ownership is for the enjoyment of one, access is for the enjoyment of legion. A glorious Post-Mortalist life can be had based on access.

9   Mortalist Capitalism is never far from psychopathology. The compulsive need to hoard is fixation on the "anal-retention" stage. But it is also understandable. The rich believe they must hoard "filthy lucre" if they are to be considered worthy. They believe that their billions, their mansions, their fleet of sports cars, their garish success will somehow impress God or fate and gain a commutation of their capital sentence.

10 **Capitalism is merely a way of immortality-seeking involving acquisition, expansion and accumulation. The insatiable and compulsive heart of capitalism is a function of our fear of Death and our desire for immortality.**

11 Our compulsion to acquire and accumulate — the cause of so much conflict, inequality and misery in the world — is a result of our half-crazed efforts to escape the clutches of mortality.

12 In their hearts of hearts, capitalist tycoons — and to a lesser extent all faithful consumers — believe that the fruit of life will be awarded to those who grab the most.

13 *There are no more Christians in the United States, only worshippers of the cult of Mammon.* Americans long ago rejected Jesus; they worship the all-powerful, all-pervasive, all-knowing Market. They have rejected Jesus' command to "Take nothing for your journey, neither staves, nor script, neither bread, neither money; neither have two coats apiece." (Luke 9: 3)

14 But money always fails us. Because no matter how much we hoard, no matter how many mansions and cars and office towers we acquire, we still grow old and die. In our sober moments, we know this all too well. This is why there is quiet and not-so-quiet desperation among the rich.

15 Money cannot make us happy until The Immortalist World is
   ushered in. Only then will we not burden it with a function it
   can never achieve — that of procuring for us immortality.

16 Only then will money have a rational basis in our lives — that
   of buying the goods we really need, that of increasing our
   quality of life, not merely our "standard of living." Only then
   will we be freed of the Mortalist compulsion to waste our
   lives hoarding riches which rust.

17 We Immortalists agree with Henry David Thoreau that we are
   not here to make a living, we are here to make a life. We Immortalists agree with John Ruskin that "There is no wealth
   but life."

18 Mortalist Capitalism is a *necessary but transitional state* in
   our efforts to gain enough control over nature to banish Disease, Old Age and Death. Industrial capitalism would not be
   possible without Science and Technology. And Science and
   Technology would not have developed as fast if not for its
   obvious utility for Industrial Capitalism.

19 **Marx**, no friend of capitalism, recognized this fact and gave
   credit where credit was and is due. "The bourgeoisie...has created more massive and more colossal productive forces than
   have all preceding generations together," Marx pointed out in
   "The Communist Manifesto." "*Subjection of Nature's forces
   to man.*...clearing of whole continents for cultivation, canali-
   zation of rivers, whole populations conjured out of the ground
   — what earlier century had even a presentiment that such productive forces slumbered in the lap of social labor?" This is a
   million times truer since Marx wrote these words.

20 The alienation arising from the capitalist economic system is
   ironic since it is a massively successful effort to tame nature.
   After all, it is capitalism that recognized the potential of Science and Technology and has sharpened these weapons for
   humankind in its final drive against Disease, Old Age and
   Death.

21 If capitalism is a colossal effort to eliminate the alienation resulting from our powerlessness over nature, then it has failed. This is because nature still kills.

22 Mortalist Capitalism as a mode of immortality-seeking has given humanity more power than ever before. But it has concentrated this power in a tiny elite in its winner-takes-all system.

23 Its apologists claim that the outrageous, ever-growing disparity between the rich and the rest of the population is a necessary evil, and that without the possibility of becoming as rich as a Rockefeller or a Bill Gates, people won't become enterpreneurs, won't work hard, won't produce more and more and even more.

24 And yet *every great enterpreneur from John D. Rockefeller to Bill Gates insists that it's not the money that drives them!* After a point, it's not the money, it's the game.

25 Otherwise, there would be no enterpreneurs in Western European societies where the gap between rich and poor is not allowed to be so wide. Otherwise, the French, the Germans, and the Swedes would have stopped going to work every morning a long time ago, and their economies would have collapsed into utter ruins.

26 The Elixxir Society (which might employ Immortalist Capitalism, of which Western European nations have been inching ever closer to) will neither allow nor need outrageous inequality as an incentive to fuel the economy.

27 Rest assured, The Elixxir Society will allow for more than adequate remuneration, more than enough to make people want to go to work, to want to be enterpreneurs. *But surely, no one really believes that economic doomsday will descend on us if we allow for mere millionaires, and not billionaires!*

$$\infty$$

Mortalist Capitalism is merely a way of immortality-seeking involving acquisition, expansion and accumulation. The insatiable and compulsive heart of capitalism is a function of our fear of Death and our yearning for Immortality.

$$\infty$$

28 But unlike Mortalist Capitalism, which has come to believe its own press releases, Immortalist Capitalism understands that money is not everything, that the greatest mortals like Albert Einstein and The Wright Brothers pushed themselves not in hope of gaining lucre, that all the dollars in the greatest economy in human history are not enough to bribe even one sane mortal to give up his life for something he does not believe in.

29 *Mortalist Capitalism exhorts us to its "work ethic," to live for posterity, to abhor pleasure, to accept little or no leisure time, to deny our bodies, to neglect our health, to surrender our dreams for "security" in old age, to turn work into bondage, to worship productivity as The Supreme Good. In other words, to abandon all hope for happiness in this life. Mortalist Capitalism is also known as "The New World Order," or "Market Globalism."*

30 *Implementing The Genesis Curse hurled by Yahweh against humanity after "the fall" ("In the sweat of thy face shalt thou eat bread"), the "work ethic" of The Death Society decrees that punitive toil is our end, not the means to our end. The aim of work in the Mortalist Capitalism of the "global economy" is to deny us any possibility of pleasure, fulfillment, or bliss. This is Economic Puritanism which, as in the sexual realm, is 'the fear that someone somewhere is having fun'.*"

31 <u>The stability of the Mortalist social order depends on our saying no to Life, on our dying little "deaths" along the byways and highways of Life. The Mortalist social order demands toil, resignation and sacrifice of our lives at its altar</u>. It persuades us this is only "normal," "mature," "responsible."

32 **Soviet Communism failed.** It became a repressive, puritanical regime engaged in a nuclear arms race and empire-building which bankrupted it. Instead of a champion of life, it became an instrument of Death, as demanding of self-denial and sacrifice as its Capitalist foe. But for all its fatal flaws, Soviet Communism can claim credit for bearing the brunt of defeat-

ing Hitler and Fascism much more than the U.S. or U.K. Soviet Communism industrialized a huge feudal country in record time. Most importantly, it increased life expectancy from 32 in 1896 under the last Tsar to 70 in 1987, which more than neutralized the deaths ascribed to its policies or to Stalin. Unlike U.S.-style Capitalism, it is a fact that Soviet Communism was a minor and Johnny-Come-Lately contributor to Global Warming.

33 Communism did put economic equality on the agenda. And in this sense, it had a reason for being. But economic equality is a universal ideal — to be found in the Bible and practiced by the early Christian church, as well as in the French and American Revolutions. We will appreciate the absence of gross economic inequality when the anti-aging life-extending drugs and technologies arrive.

34 We need **a real third way**, and **The Immortalist Worldview is the real Third Way — looking at the world beyond right and left, beyond black and white, beyond male and female, beyond straight and gay.**

35 *Immortalism is based on our primal and undying desire to stay young and live forever. This desire is our natural instinct for self-preservation speaking. This instinct for Life is universal, much more than capitalist greed, much more than socialist solidarity. It is true for every race, every nation, every culture, every age, every gender, every class and every epoch.*

36 A historical struggle between the Mortalist and the Immortalist worldviews is raging. The climactic battle is joined between an Immortalist world that's being born and a Mortalist world that's dying.

∞

**Mortalist Capitalism is Economic Puritanism.
As in the sexual realm, it is the fear that
someone somewhere is having fun.**

**Mortalist Capitalism exhorts us to its "work ethic," to
live for posterity, to abhor pleasure, to accept little
or no leisure time, to deny our bodies, to neglect
our health, to surrender our dreams for "security"
in old age, to turn work into bondage, to worship
productivity as the supreme good. In other words,
to abandon all hope for happiness in this life.**

**Mortalist Capitalism is also known as "The
New World Order," or "Market Globalism."**

∞

CHAPTER 10
The Genesis Curse: The Origin of the 'Work Ethic'

1 What is the origin of the Mortalist "work ethic"?

2 Why do mortals feel so guilty about not working? Why are we so resentful and punitive about the apocryphal "idleness" of "welfare queens"? When they can't hold a K-Mart candle to the actual idleness of The Filthy Rich, their spouses, and their trust-fund brat kids.

3 Why is there such inability to enjoy leisure time? What happened to the abundant leisure time that the powers that be promised in the 1960's?

4 What is the root of our compulsion to be incessantly "productive"? Why are we working so much overtime? Slaving at two jobs? Why are we on call seven days a week by cell phones and emails? Why do we submit to being cogs in this relentless, insatiable, life-sapping wheel of U.S.-Style Extreme Capitalism (i.e. Mortalist Capitalism)? Why do so many toil so much more than they need to? Is it only because of greed? No, there's something more to it.

5 The Mortalist "work ethic" is contained in The Genesis Curse. After Adam and Eve supposedly disobeyed God and ate from the Tree of Knowledge of Good and Evil, God told Adam: *"cursed is the ground for thy sake; in sorrow shalt thou eat of it all the days of thy life...In the sweat of thy face shalt thou eat bread, till thou return unto the ground; ...for dust thou art, and unto dust shalt thou return."* (Genesis 3: 17-19 King James Version) [The other half of this "curse" is the curse of Mortality. Another core Mortalist belief and superstition.]

6 In addition to having to return to dust in Death, the "punishment" for our "fall" is a life of sweat and toil: this is a core Mortalist belief and superstition.

7 We are allowed to live, to eat, only if we submit to a life of *punitive* toil.

8 Therefore too much leisure is a violation — an offense to this angry, vindictive Mortalist God.

9 The "work ethic" is Mortalist penance, self-flaggelation, masochism.

10 We must work, and this work must be unending, exhausting, and lifelong. No other kind of toil will appease the Mortalist god.

11 We Immortalists unconditionally reject this Mortalist "work ethic." It makes work irrational — way beyond our needs — and condemns humankind to a treadmill of joyless and unfulfilling labor. It reeks of the worst of Calvinism, Lutheranism and Judaeo-Christianity. It is a primary crime of Mortalist superstition.

12 The Jesus of the Gospels was radically different from the Yahweh of Genesis. This Jesus tells us to "Consider the lilies, how they grow, they neither toil nor spin; yet I tell you, even Solomon in all his glory was not arrayed like one of these."

13. We Immortalists invoke *Jesus the Bum.*

14. The Jesus who spurned bondage to work and the work ethic. The Jesus who was "idle," who talked instead of toiling as a carpenter. The Jesus who drifted instead of settling down to the immortality substitutes of family and children.

15. The Jesus who had no home to call his own, who lived in other people's homes, who ate and drank what they offered him. The Jesus who hoarded up no nest egg, and died dead broke. The Jesus who rejected Mortalism's Deferred Life plan, and preached and lived "The Abundant Life"! This is the Jesus who says No to the Mortalist Work Ethic which destroys all possibility of The Abundant Life. We celebrate this Jesus!

∞

The roots of the Mortalist "work ethic" is in The Genesis Curse. After Adam and Eve supposedly disobeyed God and ate from the Tree of Knowledge of Good and Evil, God told Adam: "cursed is the ground for thy sake; in sorrow shalt thou eat of it all the days of thy life...In the sweat of thy face shalt thou eat bread, till thou return unto the ground; ...for dust thou art, and unto dust shalt thou return." (Genesis 3: 17-19)

∞

CHAPTER 11
Why Mortalist Love Fails

1 Love can make us immortal — but only for a fleeting moment.

2 "Love can do all but raise the Dead," the American poet Emily Dickinson tells us. Alas, raising the dead is exactly what we demand of it.

3 Lovers are a different species. They inhabit a glorious distant planet. They don't walk, they float. They don't talk, they swoon. They don't need gods to worship, they have each other.

4 *Falling in love is a common mode of immortality-seeking.* Falling in love is resurrection and rebirth. We are cradled in the womb once again. We are given a new start on life. Everything is possible. We feel all-powerful. We are, for one shining moment, beyond time.

5 The Spanish philosopher Miguel de Unamuno sees clearly when he writes that "The thirst of eternity is what is called love among men, and whosoever loves another wishes to eternalize himself in him." Or, as Sigmund Freud puts it "Love cannot be anything but egotistical."

6 When lovers make love, their bodies seem made for each other. They intertwine perfectly. It's destiny.

7 Love is all about merging. Two become one. One consolidates with the lover, becomes perfect, attains eternity.

8 Great love is, by definition, foolish and childish. When in love, we demand the impossible: relentless bliss, absolute loyalty, undying fervor.

9   Love gives us a foretaste of divinity. So we keep coming back to its well. To drink of its elixir. To partake of its mysteries. Just one more time. Oh, we implore the gods to be kind, and grant us one last fling.

10 Love competes with religion for our time and zeal. This is why the old religions look with suspicion and hatred at love.

11 There's a reason why lovers describe their experience as "rapture". It is a form of religious ecstacy.

12 The "wise" do not make great lovers. Love requires passion — and by definition, foolishness.

13 The "wise" and the "mature" surrender romance for stability. They forgo adrenaline for security. They give up "eternal love" for "growing old together." The "foolish" and the "childish" find this unacceptable. They insist on nothing less than passion. If the flame has turned into dying embers, they abandon ship and frantically attempt to duplicate their experience of divinity one more time.

14 Always one more time. Perhaps this time it will last. Perhaps this time it will work. And though we hope against hope, **so long as Death reigns, love always disappoints**.

15 We marry or live together for security. We need to know that in this world, someone is ours. But the price of security is familiarity, and familiarity breeds contempt.

16 For passion to flourish and continue, we need illusion. But illusion is impossible to maintain when two live together in close proximity. We are appalled to find that our lover farts, belches, even shits. We did not know he or she suffers from body odor or "morning breath." These are understandable for other mortals. But we didn't know they also apply to our beloved. Our illusion of perfection, of divinity, is thus punctured.

17 So long as we die, illusions are as essential as the air we breathe. The question is not should we have illusions, the question is what are the most beneficial illusions?

18 Passion is the necessary ingredient for great love. But it soon becomes poison - and in the end it suffocates love. And yet we yearn and crave again and again for its taste — for passion suspends time while it lasts.

19 Mortals can never fully love because mortals can never fully trust.

20 Obsession comes from the need to possess. We want to hold the lover in our hands and be assured that he or she is ours to keep. Not just for now, but forever.

21 Love always fails — because our lover is ravaged by Time. She gains weight. He wrinkles. She gets cellulite. He grows a beer-belly. She acquires stretch marks. He goes bald. She becomes double-chinned. He becomes stooped. She shrinks.

22 Yes, love gives us a glimpse of the divine state, of bliss beyond time. But therein lies its cruelty. We cannot linger. Instead, we are soon confronted with a lover who reminds us of the inexorable passage of time, who cruelly mirrors and mocks our own aging — our impending slide into the abyss.

23 Time always turns our lover into a stranger - physically. Love always becomes tragedy — worse, a farce. We grieve. We surrender. The loss is enormous — and unacceptable.

24 No wonder middle-aged men trade in their loyal wives for young bimbos. Beauty may be skin-deep, but it's deep enough.

25 We fall in love with beauty, with youth, with energy — with Life. We did not bargain for ugliness, obesity, decline, and loss. But that is what we end up with.

26 Love and Death are inseparable. Even Christianity glimpses this truth as it intertwined Love and Death on the cross.

27 For those who die, love must always be passionate - the last train out of a doomed city.

28 Until now, love has always failed. Why? Because lovers invest in each other as if they will last.

29 "I lived in misery," Augustine screamed upon the death of his beloved friend, "like every man whose soul is tethered by the love of things that cannot last and then is agonized to lose them." "What madness," he concluded, "to love a man as something more than human." Many centuries later, his insight still rings true.

30 Love fails. It never lasts. Love fails. It's always subverted by Death.

31 Before we attain the dream, while Age, Disease and Death share our bed, while a gun is aimed at our head, let us love the best we can. But let us save enough passion for the dream — so that glorious day foretold by our ancestors may come to pass in time for us.

32 In The Elixxir Era, love will be freed of the chains of Disease, Old Age and Death (D.O.D.). Passion will be stripped of its self-destructiveness. Love in this coming age will be a perfectly new dance. An unimaginable feast. An eternal flame. Even so come, True Love!

∞

**Falling in love is a common mode
of immortality-seeking.**

∞

∞

Falling in love is resurrection and rebirth.

∞

CHAPTER 12
The End of Loneliness

1 The loneliest people in the world are in rich Western societies. The denizens of the great western metropolis are atomized, stranded, abandoned, friendless — in a sea of humanity.

2 In the New Economic Order, we are expected to prey on each other, to never let down our defenses. We are afraid to be Good Samaritans, lest we be sued. We dare not look each other in the eye or smile, lest we become obligated.

3 Children are taught from day one to be suspicious: don't talk to old men and strangers with candies. Many parents no longer dare to show physical affection to their kids, much less be alone with them; they are afraid of being accused by their own children of "inappropriate" behavior. Our medicine and food have to be sealed because of the fear of tampering. There is a complete breakdown of trust.

4 In our "free market," we think nothing of moving thousands of miles from home to get a job. We move when our company moves. We leave behind parents, friends, spouses and lovers. We commit our parents to nursing homes when they become inconvenient. And when our children grow up, why they incarcerate us in nursing homes too and hope we understand.

5 Countless millions live with nobody caring, and die with no one remembering. Having spent their lives toiling for the system, they are left to rot unceremoniously. No 21-gun salute for them.

6 In the fully-realized Elixxir Society, loneliness will not exist. This is because human loneliness is existentially based. Its foundation is the consciousness of our own mortality.

7   *When we banish Death, loneliness will disappear like the morning fog.*

8   In our mortal state, we know that one day we will be cut off eternally from our family and friends and everything we care about in life. This is an awesome, terrifying, and dysfunctional knowledge. And it explains why, till we vanquish Death, there is a core of loneliness in each mortal that cannot be dispelled.

9   Mortals are by definition a lonely species. They are born alone, and die alone.

10 Money cannot banish this foreboding. Neither can fame. Nor power. For even the rich, the famous, and the powerful know they will not be spared.

11 Marilyn Monroe was beautiful, rich, famous, adored by millions. Yet she was devoured by a loneliness which drove her to take her own life. There are more rich, famous or beautiful people like her than we imagine.

12 Power and wealth isolates. The more power and wealth, the more isolation.

13 Power and riches breed suspicion. The powerful and wealthy believe everyone is out to get them, or get something from them. So they hire people to "protect" them, to screen out the undesirables, the riff-raff. To safeguard their precious time and ensure their sacred privacy. The result? They cut themselves off from anyone who can make them happy, and end up only with maids and secretaries.

14 Once in a while, we hear of a maid, secretary, or stripper marrying a wealthy, famous or powerful person. We wonder how this could be? After all, the great man or rich heiress can have anyone he or she wants. But that's only the façade. The maid or secretary saw through it — and filled the void.

15 It's like the most popular girl in class. All the guys assume they haven't got a prayer. So they don't even bother to ask

her out. So every Friday and Saturday night, she stays home — alone.

16 But don't feel too sorry for the rich, the famous and the beautiful. They do have more ways of distracting themselves than the rest of us.

17 The human species is obviously not the only species cursed by Death. Other species die too. But they are lucky not to be stricken by Death-consciousness.

18 In the West, single people spend so much of their money to have their own apartment. And then they spend even more to try to find someone who will relieve them of the loneliness of living alone in their own apartment.

19 We claim we treasure privacy. But in old age, this "privacy" degenerates into solitary confinement. Our grown-up children move out of the "nest" to attend college or to get married. Following their jobs, they move away, often far away. Their visits and phone calls dwindle. This is the privacy we claim we want. But when we grow older, in our hearts, we know what we really want is more "intrusions" into our privacy.

20 Unlike the Western societies, The Elixxir Society will be the most close-knit community in history. Why? Because we Immortalists understand *it is only as a community that we can overcome Death.*

21 In this struggle to achieve the goal of all human history, it gives us great joy and honor to be part of this irresistible evolutionary tide sweeping towards Life.

22 In our final push for Life, there will be challenges daily. But one thing is certain — there will be no room for loneliness! As we are in the company of comrades and friends. There is *direction, meaning, and purpose* in *our* lives. And <u>what can be more exciting and fulfilling than being part of this grand immortal fellowship and movement spanning the ages, aiming for the goal of all human history</u>.

23 *To be out of sync with our Evolutionary Destiny, with the dream of all human history, that is the path to loneliness, unhappiness.*

24 **To be in sync with our Evolutionary Destiny, with the next step in evolution, with the dream of the human species, this is the *only* path to true happiness.**

∞

**When we banish Death,
loneliness will disappear like the morning fog.**

∞

CHAPTER 13

Mortalist Religion v. Immortalist Religion

1 Just like sexuality, procreation and family, the Church is an institution with obvious links to our fear of Death — and our quest for immortality.

2 The Religions which address our fear of Death and our demand for immortality prosper. Those which do not don't.

3 Death — and our desire for immortality — is the fountainhead of all religion.

4 Most Mortalist Religions, though now instruments of The Death Ideology, started by grasping the truth of our mortal condition and its unacceptability. They discerned that there is no greater terror than that of Death, no greater craving than for immortality.

5 Even "Saint Paul" was inspired in his visions about our leap from mortality to immortality. We find Immortalist prophecies sprinkled throughout the books of Isaiah, Daniel, Revelation, and in the Gospels. We need a bit of sifting through the garbage of Mortalism to find the nugget of Immortalist gold. We can similarly find Immortalism in the basic texts of other major faiths. (Even in the writings of secular, atheistic writers.) Rising above the din of Mortalism, the voice of our Evolutionary Destiny cannot be suppressed.

6 *Without Death, there is no Religion. With Death, there will always be Religion.*

7 Early Christianity triumphed because it offered *physical* "eternal life" to believers. For those who are old, dying, or dead,

it promised the *physical* resurrection of the dead. Although this resurrection of the dead was considered crass and scandalous to the learned and the sophisticated, it was precisely the reason why Christianity triumphed over Greek Paganism. Christianity's reign over the past two millennia is testament to the power of our fear of Death, our thirst for immortality.

8 **Buddhism started with the fear of Disease, Old Age and Death.** When the young Buddha asked his father to assure him that his life would not end in Death, that sickness would not follow health, that age would not follow youth, his father was forced to admit he could not. Because of this, the young prince left and began the quest which eventually made him founder of a world faith.

9 We hope religion shields us from the brute force of nature. We hope our prayers, penance, and groveling to the gods will spare us the fate which has so far befallen all mortals. We hope to find the fire-escape to the next life.

10 Christianity and Islam offer an afterlife in the crudest and most blatant way. This is why they have become the world's foremost religions.

11 In Christianity, Jesus is both human and god. This is our way of saying that humans should be gods, that mortals should become immortals.

12 Buddhism, Taoism and Shintoism have all been modified by popular piety.

13 Scholastic Indian Buddhism taught that the point of life is to overcome the cycles of rebirths by attaining Nirvana — originally a state of nonbeing. But it misses the point. We do not desire Nirvana — a state of nonbeing.

14 **If salvation is release from life, then we want to be damned.**

15 When Indian Buddhism reached China, it was modified by popular piety to address the faithful's real desire: Immortality. Nowhere is this more evident than in the popular tale of

the "Monkey King," who stormed the heavens to snatch the Pear of Immortality from right under the gods' noses. In the Chinese Classic "Journey to the West," the Monkey King upstaged the monk who traveled to India to bring a basic Buddhist text back to China..

16 The Pure Land School of Buddhism emerged in China and quickly became widespread with the T'ang dynasty. Instead of Nirvana and its tortured path, the Pure Land School taught that the Great Buddha Amitabha has prepared a paradise called the Pure Land to the West. And anyone who calls upon the name of the Buddha in faith will enter that paradise upon death.

17 There is no qualitative difference between this and the Christian doctrine of "salvation by faith alone" — or between this and the "born again" Christian insistence that we must accept Jesus into our hearts to gain eternal life.

18 The same fate befell Taoism. What was originally a mysticophilosophical system became a religion of magic, alchemy, esoteric exercises, and the quest for the elixir of life.

19 Shintoism is no exception. Initially, it was not concerned with the afterlife. After some time, it developed a populist doctrine of paradise and taught that it would be the reward for those who faithfully serve the emperor.

20 The popular versions of Buddhism and Hinduism offer an afterlife in basically the same way as Christianity and Islam. They have been popular because they give their followers what they really want.

∞

Without Death, there is no Religion.

With Death, there will always be Religion.

Christianity and Islam offer an afterlife in the crudest and most blatant way. This is why they have become the world's foremost religions.

∞

Elixxir...The Only Anti-Aging Guru who has Actually Stayed Young

(Investor's Business Daily, Marilyn Much)

Reveals

How To Look 20-Something At Past 50!

1. Slash your Risk for Cancer, Heart Disease, Stroke, Diabetes, Osteoporosis, Alzheimer's

2. Lose Weight by Staying Young

3. Reverse 70% of your Age-Related Changes in Gene Expression in a Few Weeks

4. Look Years Younger in 72 Hours

Plus — a $500 gift

Imagine living to 120...with youthful vigor, free of disease... Elixxir is living proof — **Life Extension Magazine**

Elixxir is Most Amazingly Youthful...He is his own best argument — **Dr. David Weeks, BBC** Broadcaster, Bestselling Author, Expert on the SuperYoung & **Jamie James,** former **New Yorker** magazine art critic

Seeing is Believing! — **Marilyn Much, Investor's Business Daily**

Dear Friend,

My classmates and childhood friends have all grown old, fat, and ugly. I can still **pass for 20-something at past 50.**

I'm still getting carded. Still chased by suitors half my age. I've stayed as slim as in senior high. I make love with the potency and stamina of a young man. No Viagra.

And I just love family and class reunions!

My name is Elixxir. I've been on the only scientific anti-aging program for a third of a century.

Want to learn how I've stayed young and how you can too?

You can in my executive report

How to Look 20-Something at Past 50!
The Elixxir Program Executive Report

Science knows of <u>only one way</u> to dramatically retard your aging and greatly extend your maximum lifespan potential of 120 years by up to 50%.

The **New York Times, Wall Street Journal, AP** etc. have all reported this scientific fact. Proven repeatedly in prestigious laboratories around the world.

Life Extension Foundation calls it "the only method proven to slow aging and extend lifespan in mammals."

The Elixxir Program is *based on* the landmark anti-aging disease-preventing life-extending discovery by **Dr. Clive McCay, M.D.**at **Cornell Medical School**.

Still our *only scientific* anti-aging breakthrough!

So powerful it can *reverse* up to 70% — yes, 70%! — of **age-related changes in your gene expression** *in a few weeks.* (Proc Natl Acad Sciences, Sept. 4, 2002, Stephen Spindler, Ph.D.)

Even in old rats. Great News for those of us who weren't born yesterday.

Dr. Stephen R. Spindler, Ph.D., who led this University of California research team said "**Older people may be able to benefit rapidly from switching (to such a program).**

You want to put the brakes on your aging and extend your lifespan? The **New York Times** concludes the scientific foundation of The Elixxir Program is "**the best—in fact the only bet.**"

TO ORDER with our 60-Day Money-Back Guarantee, just go to http://www.Elixxir.com

Even **Dr. Atkins** admitted it is "**the best researched and most generously documented** (of all anti-aging programs)."

Barry Sears, Ph.D. calls it "**the Holy Grail of anti-aging.**"

But amazingly most people still don't know about it. Or if they do, they've been told it's "too difficult."

Well, what if they're wrong? Dead wrong?

For three decades, I've tackled this challenge and transformed this scientific anti-aging regimen into *la dolce vita* (**The Sweet Life**). I call this eating program The Elixxir Program™.

The result? After seeing Elixxir in person, the senior reporter of *Investor's Business Daily* crowned Elixxir as.........

"The <u>only</u> anti-aging guru who has <u>actually</u> stayed young."

Yes, probably like you, this veteran reporter has had enough of so-called "anti-aging gurus" who look *older* than their age.

Why model yourself after failure?

Dr. David Weeks, BBC Broadcaster, known for his long-running study of those who look at least 10 years younger than their age, raves...

**"Elixxir is Most Amazingly Youthful ...
He is his own best argument"**

Seeing is Believing

- My face is **wrinkle-free**. My skin **glows**. It's **baby smooth**.

- My body is virtually **fat-free**.

- A 26 inch waist. My BMI (body mass index) is that of a **teenager**.

- **Cellulite-free tight**, **smooth buns**, **Fat-free abs** Without Gym Torture.

- **A full head of hair, still black. No liver spots, no turtle neck**.

- **Watch your Excess Weight & Ugly Fat Melt Away on The Elixxir Program**

- And *Keep them Away for Life—Without Gym Slavery.*

Too good to be true?

Just look at my most recent pictures. Elixxir is Baby Boomer but could pass for Generation X.

This is why Investor's Business Daily's Marilyn Much exclaims after meeting Elixxir, *"Seeing is believing!"*

Your Best Insurance against Heart Attack, Cancer, Stroke & Major Killer Diseases

Staying young is the best disease-prevention. The Elixxir Program not only dramatically slows down your aging, it also **slashes your risk for** Heart Disease, Cancer, Stroke, Diabetes, Hypertension, Osteoporosis & Alzheimer's.

At the same time you're staying young, slim, and beautiful. Only the Elixxir Program can achieve both for you.

Order with Mastercard, Visa, PayPal. It's easy!
Just click or go to http://www.Elixxir.com

See your Blood Pressure, Bad Cholesterol, and Blood Sugar Plunge...and Your Immune System Supercharge....Within a few weeks to a few months on The Elixxir Program.

The Sweet Life *(la dolce vita)*

On The Elixxir Program. Here's why...

Eat Anything

No ban on carbs or meat. Don't have to give up pasta or rice like on Atkins. You don't have to become almost vegetarian like on Pritikin or Ornish.

Champagne Is Fine

So is fine wine, Cognac and Calvados. A toast to the Forever Young Life!

No Hunger

Never feel hungry or deprived—ever again!

Safeguard Your #1 Asset

Legendary financier Sir Nathan Meyer Rothschild declared "I've got to keep breathing. It'll be my worst business mistake if I don't."

What is your most valuable asset? Your health and life. Without that, you have nothing.

Can You *Afford* to Grow Old & Die?

On her deathbed, **Queen Victoria** desperately offered *"My kingdom for a moment of time."* Don't wait until a heart attack, stroke or cancer strikes to 'get it.' You don't have time to reinvent the wheel. Can't afford to nickel and dime yourself. Or do trial and error.

As *"the anti-aging guru to the pampered set" (Investor's Business Daily),* retaining Elixxir as your coach will cost you. Perhaps a million dollars.

Limited-Time Offer

But for a short time only, Elixxir's Executive Report **How to Look 20-Something at Past 50!: The Elixxir Program is yours for only $99 + $15 shipping & handling* (total US $114).**

Learn about Elixxir's Million-Dollar Anti-Aging Program for only $99 (plus S&H). You don't get value like this every day.

Risk-Free 60-Day
Money-Back Guarantee

If *for any reason* you are not fully satisfied,
just return Elixxir's Executive Report in
60 days (2 months), you will get your $99 back.

No Questions Asked. Hassle-Free Refunds.

(Shipping & Handling not refundable)

So what do you have to lose?
Disease, Old Age & Death?

Order with Mastercard, Visa, American Express, Discover

or PayPal. It's easy! Just go to http://www.Elixxir.com

Gift #1 if you order now

$500 Value Credit Voucher towards personal coaching by Elixxir & Associates and a personal invitation to join Elixxir and his beauties in one of their international playgrounds. (Credit Voucher not exchangeable for cash)

Gift #2 if you order now

Elixxir reveals, in a short personal memo, the easy way to

"Look Years Younger in 72 Hours!"

Your spouse, loved ones, friends will <u>notice at once</u>. And wonder what you did. The value of an excellent facelift.

Order Now Risk-Free
with Mastercard, Visa, American Express, Discover or PayPal.

It's easy! Takes just a Minute!

You have Nothing to lose...
Everything to Gain.

TO ORDER with our 60-Day RISK-FREE Money-Back Guarantee, just go to **http://www.Elixxir.com**

Note: Our Bonus Gifts of 1) $500 value Credit Voucher towards personal coaching by Elixxir & Associates, and 2) Elixxir's memo on "Look Years Younger in 72 Hours!" may be revoked at any time. So order now to make sure you claim your bonus gifts.

12 ImmorTalist Warriors
Elixxir Wants You

"Before this century is over, billions of us will die, and the few breeding pairs of people that survive will be in *the arctic region*, where the climate remains tolerable." — *Dr. James Lovelock, Eminent Climate Scientist*

We have only a few years left to prevent the apocalyptic scenarios of Global Warming from destroying civilization. The U.N. Panel on Climate Change. NASA scientists. Al Gore. The U.N. Secretary-General. Climate Change Scientists Worldwide. They all agree on this.

Elixxir is searching the four corners of the earth to find The 12 ImmorTalist Warriors.

Where have you been? Elixxir's been waiting for you.

If you've read this book, and agree with even just 50% of it, what are you doing there? Running The Rat Race? Playing their rigged game where you end up loser?

What happened to all your dreams of great deeds? Your talents? Your idealism?

If you've had your wake-up call from Cancer, a Heart Attack, a Mini-Stroke, why haven't you awakened yet?

Doing more of the same will only get you more of the same.

Step Forward and Offer Yourself. There is no time to lose.

Conquer Cancer, Heart Disease, Stroke. And all the other major killers. Including the master disease — The Aging Syndrome.

The Twelve will join Elixxir's mission. Are you one of the Twelve?

Then you are one of the chosen. To help humanity conquer Disease, Old Age & Death. To save the Planet. And you will learn from Elixxir how to stay young on The Elixxir Program.

The Death Society wants you to be all alone. Demoralized. Exhausted. Afraid.

They want us to do politics with no community, with no support system. Like a Don Quixote tilting at windmills.

Alone you are impotent and easily discouraged. As part of The Elixxir Society, you are powerful and you will persevere till victory.

If fishermen can create a new faith with a carpenter's son, if they can make the Roman Empire fall to its knees, why can't you?

When Disease, Old Age and Death are looming, when Global Warming's apocalypse is descending on us, saving yourself and the planet is **the only sane and rational thing to devote your life to.**

To apply and get more details, write an e mail — 500 words maximum — to Elixxir on why you believe you are one of the twelve, what you can bring to the table, and why you would like to stay young on The Elixxir Progran and save the planet.

Send e mail to **12immortalists@gmail.com**
or go to **http://www.immortalism.com** or
http://www.ElixxirSociety.com and follow instructions.

CHAPTER 14
Mortalist Christianity v. Immortalist Christianity

1   Early Christianity triumphed over the pagan cults because of its outrageous and incredible doctrine of The Resurrection of The Dead.

2   What can be more appealing to immortality-seeking mortals than the teaching that corpses will rise at the Second Coming of Christ. The doctrine says the resurrection body will be transformed (that is, it can no longer fall prey to Disease, Old age, or Death).We are promised a basic continuity from our carbon-based mortal body to this eternal, resurrected body. What is paramount is the promise that our consciousness will continue in this resurrection body. This is the genius of Christianity.

3   The Greek philosophers derided Paul and the early Christians for this "vulgar" and "offensive" doctrine. They were worldly intellectuals. They offered the vague concept of the immortality of the soul. But there were many more takers for Christianity's "crude" offer.

4   Since early Christianity blatantly sought physical and bodily immortality, in terms of our drive for immortality it was a great advance over Greek Paganism which only offered a vague and effete spiritual immortality.

5   Early Christianity divined that "eternal life" (longevity) is somehow linked to "bread" — to diet, to eating. This was why the most important sacrament was the Eucharist, the Holy Communion, or the Lord's Supper. This was why the

last act of Jesus with his disciples was the breaking of bread, the drinking of wine.

6   Jesus offered himself as the "bread of life" which gives eternal life. "I am the bread of life, he who comes to me shall not hunger, and he who believes in me shall never thirst." (John 6:35 RSV) *I am the bread of life. Your fathers ate the manna in the wilderness and they died. This is the bread which comes down from heaven; if any one eats of this bread, he will live for ever*; and the bread which I shall give for the life of the world is my flesh." (John 6:48-51 RSV) "This is the bread which came down from heaven, not such as the father ate and died; *he who eats this bread will live forever.*" (John 6:58)

7   The "miracle" of the Loaves and Fishes, the one that fed "five thousand" with a few loaves and fishes, was possible because the crowd all ate less. No such miracle is possible in the land of double portions.

8   The Eucharist, the Holy Communion, the Lord's Supper is the secret rite of Immortalist Christianity, of original Christianity. So much so that when some in the early church fell ill and dead, the culprit was believed to be a violation of this life-giving sacrament.

9   The centrality of the Lord's Supper in the life of the Early Christian Church was recognized by its enemies. In their attempt to scandalize this practice, they spread rumors about how believers ate human flesh, drank human blood.

10   To the early Christians, the eating of bread and wine in the right way was sacred. Sharing food and drink ritualistically as a community meant smaller portions. The bread and wine were rationed. There were no second helpings. No gluttony, which was seen as a sin.

11   <u>Food is the bridge to eternal life, the key which unlocks the secret door to immortality: this was the belief of Early Christianity, Immortalist Christianity.</u>

12 Today Immortalists can avail themselves of the only scientific anti-aging program which can prevent the top killer-diseases, slow aging dramatically, and give us a real shot at exceeding the maximum human lifespan of 120. Elixxir has transformed this 100% scientific eating program into *la dolce vita*, and he calls it The Elixxir Program.™ It is the only thing known to 21st century science which extends your youth and buys you time so that you will be around for the breakthroughs, for Virtual Immortality, for Actual Immortality. You can update the vision and spirit of the Lord's Supper today through The Elixxir Program.

13 **Immortalist Christianity is true Christianity.**

14 **Mortalist Christianity is heresy.** It is a subversion of Jesus' message by The Death Ideology. Jesus taught that his mission was to conquer Death (his healings were all previews and rehearsals for this main event). The core early Christian Church's beliefs and teachings were the Rapture (believers need not pass through Death to gain eternal life) and the Resurrection of The Dead. They are Radical Immortalist. It was only when Christianity became the state religion (and Jesus tarried) that it became allied with The Death Ideology, that it degenerated into the image of the AntiChrist, that it launched inquisitions and wars, that it became Death-breeding instead of Life-producing.

15 **The subversion of Immortalist Christianity into Mortalist Christianity is without question Mortalism's greatest coup. It laid the foundation for Western Civilization's subservience to the "Beast," to his cult of Death.**

16 *All great faiths have been perverted by Mortalism from their original Immortalist foundation* — the fear of Death, the desire for Immortality. They have made 180 degrees turns from their original mission — the destruction of Death — and have degenerated into Death's apologists.

17 We expose The Death Ideology (Mortalism) for hijacking the "good news" of Jesus of Nazareth. It was a hostile takeover. It forced Christianity to betray its Immortalist roots.

18 *Today's "Christian" theology is nothing but Mortalist Revisionism. It blinds us to the radical Immortalism of the early Christian church.* We forget that the early Christians believed "eternal life" is possible without having to pass through the Valley of Death, that even the deadest of the dead shall be raised. The early Christians refused to settle for the immortality of the "soul" and demanded the immortality of the body.

19 The takeover of Immortalist Religion and its perversion into Mortalist Religion affects every life today. **Mortalist Religion is repackaged in secular form and arguments for easier consumption and digestion. It pervades even the most secular societies, and manipulates even the most secular of mortals in subtle, sophisticated, invisible ways.**

20 Despite the Scopes Trial, despite the TV evangelists' scandals of Jim and Tammy Bakker, Jimmy Swaggart and Oral Roberts, despite the great disappointment of millions of "born again" Christians that Jesus was a no-show in 2000, Fundamentalist Christianity has managed to not only survive but thrive. Why? Because it promises what we really want — physical immortality. And if desperate mortals know of no other way, they will continue to buy real estate in heaven.

21 Why has the liberal "mainstream" wing of Protestant Christianity declined so precipitously since the 1950's? Why have the liberal state churches in Western Europe withered into irrelevance? The answer is obvious. Even in this day and age, churches which promise "eternal life" will prevail any day over the ones which offer only reason, good works, and demythologizing.

22 One third of the American people — living in the most scientifically and technologically advanced society in human history — believes in an afterlife in heaven rather than accept the

more "rational" message of liberal Christianity or religions which offer no immortality, no resurrection of the corpse.

23 We Immortalists understand that Mortalist Religion must be defeated. And that **the only way to defeat Mortalist Religion is by Immortalist Religion.**

24 The "New Age" movement, the descendant of the ancient pagan cults of "special knowledge" and "fertility rites," is the hope of some to replace Christianity. But just as the pagan cults were no match for early Christianity, so the New Age movement is currently no match for a fundamentalism that is so tightly organized and militantly fanatical.

25 We want and need to believe that Death is not the end, that there is meaning in our short, painful, brutish existence. A religion must satisfy these basic needs or be rejected.

26 *Aside from propping up the status quo, religion preserves our sanity and functionality in the face of Death.*

27 Religion shields us from premature and intolerable exposure to the truth — the whole truth — of human reality.

28 But Religion is not only a shield, it is also a sedative — calming us down when we have every reason to be hysterical.

29 *The harsher life is, the more religious Mortals are.*

30 Americans are the most religious people in the "developed" world. Americans are so much more religious than Western Europeans and Scandinavians. This is because life under U.S. market capitalism is so much harsher, economically and psychologically, than life in Western Europe. This is also why black Americans are much more religious than white Americans. Life has been much harsher for blacks than for whites.

31 The illusions of the old Mortalist Religions kept us sane — when we were not strong enough to do anything about Death. But now that we are ready for the final assault on this evil fortress, they have become a major obstruction — a traitorous

fifth column — which must be swept away so the Kingdom can be ushered in.

32 The great leap forward in our "spiritual" evolution will occur when we realize that *there is no salvation outside the human race. The kingdom of God is within us.*

∞

Today's "Christian" theology is nothing but Mortalist Revisionism. It blinds us to the radical Immortalism of the early Christian church.

We forget that the early Christians believed "eternal life" is possible without having to pass through the Valley of Death, that even the deadest of the dead shall be raised. The early Christians refused to settle for the immortality of the "soul" and demanded the immortality of the body.

∞

CHAPTER 15
Mortalist Medicine v. Immortalist Medicine

1   *The National Institute on Aging (NIA) is spending over half — yes, over 50% — of its budget on Alzheimer's research. This is as crazy and idiotic as dumping half of the funding for AIDS research into one single symptom or complication of AIDS.*

2   Why? Alzheimer's is a terrible disease. A mind is indeed a terrible thing to lose, just ask Ronald Reagan. Alzheimer's should get adequate research money. But it is irrational and imprudent to plunk down half of the NIA's limited budget on one symptom of aging which afflicts at most 1.6% of the U.S. population. (An ImmorTalist government will *not* cut Alzheimer's funding. It will grow the NIA budget so that the bulk of its funding focus on curing The Aging Syndrome. Alzheimer's funding will become proportional to its 1.6% affliction rate. Focusing on The Aging Syndrome is the best bet to find a cure for Alzheimer's.)

3   Alzheimer's is not a disease which can spread sexually like AIDS. It is not contagious like Ebola. So there's no justification for this irrational extravagance on the part of the NIA. It is bad stewardship and totally out of proportion to dump over half of the NIA's limited budget on an ailment which afflicts such a small percentage of the U.S. population.

4   Even the man responsible for pushing Alzheimer's research has said enough already. He is no other than the late Dr. Robert Butler, one of the forces behind the creation of The National Institute on Aging (NIA), its first director, and one of

the most influential American gerontologists. In an interview in the March 9, 1997 issue of *The New York Times Magazine*, Dr. Butler admitted that the overriding emphasis on Alzheimer's research is "out of balance."

5   We give Dr. Butler credit for his candor, and much credit for helping forge the NIA. But we must ask why the NIA's bureaucracy insists, despite Dr. Butler's reassessment, on continuing on its merry, deluded way. Why it insists on wasting your hard-earned tax money on its disproportionate funding of Alzheimer's to the detriment of everything else? Especially the all-important basic research into the biology of your aging, the *only* thing which will save you, your loved ones, and every member of the human race. Why?

6   The ultimate reason: just like the U.S. government and every government out there, the NIA has been working from a Mortalist paradigm.

7   *This Mortalist paradigm breeds Mortalist Medicine which restricts itself to trying to treat only the* symptoms *of aging —heart disease, cancer, stroke, obesity, diabetes, Alzheimer's etc. — which it wrongly diagnoses as "diseases" of aging.*

8   Why did Dr. Butler push for this "out of balance" stress on Alzheimer's at the NIA? He told the New York Times, "*my perception was that we shouldn't just focus on aging, because aging was not considered a disease and was obviously not something that was immediately eradicable.*"

9   Butler's core assumption which led him astray was that Aging is not a disease. This Mortalist assumption directly resulted in the NIA's fixation on Alzheimer's and its unwillingness to make basic research into why you age its priority *numero uno*.

10   If Butler was worried that declaring Aging a disease might increase Ageism, should we then say AIDS is not a disease to prevent homophobia? Of course not. Because if AIDS is not a disease, then the government is not compelled to fund

AIDS research or treatment. Note: Immortalism is anti-Old-Age, *not* anti-Old-People.

11 As to Butler's claim that aging "was obviously not something that was immediately eradicable," if we were to accept this argument, we would not have put any money into cancer research. When the U.S. government started its War Against Cancer in the 1970's, cancer was definitely not something that was "immediately eradicable." This did not deter the U.S. government from pouring billions into cancer research and rightly so.

12 The same can be said for AIDS research. Why have we put any money into AIDS research? Most scientists, even with the AIDS cocktails, do not see the disease as "immediately eradicable."

13 In fact, why bother to do research on *any* disease? When we begin looking at any disease — whether it be polio, measles, smallpox or Alzheimer's — it is usually not "immediately eradicable."

Beyond Mortalist Medicine

14 So what lurks behind this uncharacteristic lapse in reasoning from someone as intelligent as Dr. Butler? It is the unspoken dogma of Mortalist medicine that though doctors and researchers are allowed to tinker here and there with the *symptoms* of Aging, *it is verboten to touch the biology of human aging itself.*

15 Why this failure of nerve when for the first time in history, we have the tools to decrypt the secret code of our biological aging? Why when we may soon deploy stem cells to regenerate our bodies and restore our youth - to be 'born again'? It's Mortalist superstition, pure and simple: the belief that we can tackle Alzheimer's but not Aging itself.

16 To solve the riddle of human aging is like eating the forbidden fruit in the garden; it is "hubris," it will offend the skygods and rain down damnation and destruction.

17 The Elixxir Paradigm, on the other hand, breeds Immortalist Medicine. *Immortalist Medicine's strategy is to focus funding, research and treatment on the aging process, The Aging Syndrome,* to understand why we grow old, to figure out how to retard this process, stop it, and finally reverse it, no matter how old we are. *It is from research into the aging process that humanity will get its big payday, and Immortalist Medicine gets this.*

18 It is all very logical, very elegant. By preventing or greatly retarding Aging, Immortalist Medicine "kills" many "birds" with one stone. **By preventing The Aging Syndrome, we prevent all its symptoms — whether it be depression, obesity, cancer, heart disease, stroke, diabetes, pneumonia, weakened immunity, or Alzheimer's.**

19 Aiming at the human aging process, The Aging Syndrome, instead of its symptoms, is the cheapest and fastest way to conquer our major killer-diseases like heart disease, cancer, stroke, obesity and Alzheimer's. It's also *the most cost-efficient way to protect our health care systems from possible collapse.*

20 But why the reluctance to see Aging as a disease, a syndrome just like AIDS? Why when The Aging Syndrome puts you at extremely higher risk for obesity, for clinical depression, for heart failure, heart attacks, stroke, for lung, breast, or prostate cancer, for diabetes and dementia?

21 The fact that an increasing number of people who are not chronologically old are afflicted by the above diseases is no argument against The Aging Syndrome. Firstly, due to The Death Society Diet which is high-calorie and high-fat, and the pervasive lack of exercise, many teenagers today are already suffering from aging-related diseases like diabetes and hyper-

tension, not to mention obesity. So many of the young are already victims of one of the byproducts and side-effects of The Death Society: *Premature Aging*. The ever-earlier onset of puberty (caused by excessive feeding) and the epidemic of teenage obesity are two dead giveaways of **the Premature Aging Syndrome.**

22 Secondly, people without HIV or AIDS may come down with pneumonia or lymphoma or weakened immune systems too. But this does not alter the fact that someone with AIDS is at extremely higher risk for a host of afflictions such as pneumonia and lymphoma.

23 It is beyond the shadow of a doubt that older people are at much higher risk for heart failure, cancer, stroke, diabetes, hypertension, Parkinson's, Alzheimer's, and obesity. **Conclusion: There is every scientific reason and medical precedent to officially recognize human biological aging as a master disease and a master syndrome: The Aging Syndrome.**

24 *This is not mere semantics. Acceptance of this new paradigm on Aging is a life-and-death matter worth lobbying and fighting for.* **Why? Because it will finally result in every government giving us the funding for research on human biological aging *in direct proportion* to it being The Master Disease and the Number One Killer, the Foremost National Security Threat, the one disease and threat that will sooner or later kill every one of us alive on this planet today, unless we decrypt and defuse its lethal terror code. (An ImmorTalist Government, by definition, will accept and fund this new paradigm and research strategy. Not merely that, an immortalist government will declare War on D.O.D. (Disease, Old Age and Death), and make it the highest national priority, bar none. And this means number one in the budget.)**

25 We are on the verge of unraveling the secrets of aging. There can be no doubt about it. It is five minutes to D-Day. We must concentrate our funding resources and pile it on.

26 Instead of lavishing 50% of the NIA's budget on Alzheimer's and the rest on things like "the psychology of aging," we should spend much more than 50% of the NIA's budget on unraveling the secrets of our biological aging.

27 The best way to fight Alzheimer's is by getting to the *cause* of our biological aging. If we stop Aging, we stop Alzheimer's. We cannot win the war against Aging by squandering half of our resources on one battle against one of its symptoms. The way to conquer Alzheimer's is to conquer Aging. We need to get our priorities and paradigm right.

28 **We Immortalists demand that the National Institute on Aging's budget be dramatically increased.** How dramatically? Even a token increase of 20% at this hour of imminent anti-aging breakthroughs is simply not enough. In fact, it's an insult and outrage.

29 How much of an increase do we need and how much is justified? We must look squarely at the undeniable fact that The Aging Syndrome and its symptoms (heart disease, cancer, stroke, diabetes, obesity, pneumonia) slaughter more than two million Americans each and every year. So if the Pentagon gets trillions to prevent a repeat of 9/11 and its 3,000 deaths, then to prevent two million deaths year-in and year-out, we demand a budget of $888 billion. **To start with, we will accept a preliminary increase in the National Institute on Aging's budget to that of the Pentagon budget for its Iraq-Afghanistan debacle.**

30 **If The Death Society won't give you this, The Elixxir Society will.**

31 Because The Elixxir Society recognizes that **it is a million times more likely for mortals to die of The Aging Syn-**

drome and its symptoms than of pesky missiles from some "rogue" state.

32 Where do we find the money? For starters, we find the money in the approximately 25% of the Pentagon's budget that then U.S. 'Defense' Secretary Rumsfeld admitted could not be accounted for.

33 No, that crumb thrown at aging research by the Mortalist regimes is no longer acceptable. Not when we are on the verge of major breakthroughs. Not when time is running out for hundreds of millions of people of a certain age, or who are facing life-threatening ailments.

34 We refuse to be suckered into fighting each other over a grossly-inadequate funding pie. Divide and conquer won't work with us. *There should be more than enough money for Alzheimer's, cancers, heart disease and other top killers and still be more than enough money for an all-out, no-holds-barred War against Aging. And in The Elixxir Society, there will be.*

35 The U.S. Congress throws hundreds of billions each year on military bases that even the Pentagon admits it doesn't need after the Cold War. And Congress and the White House have the nerve to tell the American people that the biggest economy in the world can only afford $83 million on basic anti-aging life-extension research —less than the average cost of a Hollywood movie! — research which will save up to 2.2 million Americans from the grave in one year alone. And this same outrageous situation prevails in most countries around the world.

36 We demand that the NIA (National Institute on Aging) budget for basic research into why we age and what can be done to retard, stop or even reverse it, be equal at least to the military budget for the occupation of Iraq and Afghanistan, which like Vietnam will cease to be any threat to Americans as soon as the U.S. withdraws.

37 **We demand that the U.S. Mortalist regime shuts down its empire, the world's largest empire, with more than 700 military bases around the globe. This is why there's no money for universal health insurance, for schools, for bridges, for airports, for parks, for children, and last but not least, for anti-aging disease-curing lifespan-extending research.**

38 General Charles de Gaulle had the courage and good sense to withdraw French troops from Algeria and shut down the French Empire which was bleeding the economy and depriving its citizens. As a result, the French have enjoyed the good life since. Germany and Japan were forced to shut down their empires after the Second World War. And it was the greatest boon for the Germans and Japanese. Without the need to feed a rapacious warmongering military, Japan and Germany can focus on developing their economies distributing its fruits to the people. The result? Japanese and Germans (and the French) have been enjoying a sweeter higher quality of life than when their countries were in the empire racket. And as we can see, since they no longer go around invading countries and killing innocents from "drones", there is practically no threat to Germany or Japan's national security. It is time the American people get smart.

39 We must leave no stone unturned. We must explore all avenues of research into why we age. We cannot afford to have credible researchers complain they don't have sufficient funding or any funding.

40 We must compel the government to give us the benefit of every doubt. It is more prudent by far to err on the side of spending more than too little on research into The Aging Syndrome which will lead to prevention, treatments or downright cures for heart disease, cancer, stroke, Alzheimer's, obesity, etc.

41 *To guarantee that the anti-aging life-extension drugs or technologies are affordable to you and as many people as quickly*

as possible, the government should get into the business of researching and manufacturing such drugs.

42 This will avoid a repeat of a situation like the AIDS cocktails which cost up to $15,000 a year and which has meant unnecessary death for millions of have-nots in Africa and elsewhere. It will prevent a situation like the new cancer drug which costs up to $2,400 a month or $28,800 a year.

43 The problem? Drug companies claim such astronomical prices are necessary. They argue that research is very costly and risky and the patent gives only "a few years" to exploit and make a profit.

44 The solution? *Do the research in government labs with government monies. And do it as fast and well as The Manhattan Project or The Apollo Space Program. Then there's no need to recoup on "investment" and no need to gouge us blind or leave us to die, in the name of dirty profits. Either this or the government must pay for those anti-aging life-extension drugs and the resulting cures for diseases when they arrive.*

45 If nothing else, the government jumping into this race for the anti-aging life-extension drugs will spur the drug companies. They will want to outrun the government, just as in the genome mapping project. This means the life-saving breakthroughs will come sooner, in time for you and me.

46 **There is nothing more important that the U.S. government or any government is doing right now than funding and conducting anti-aging disease-curing life-extension research. Nothing, period. It will save countless millions facing life-threatening diseases from imminent death. It will also solve the problem of our graying populations. And since a society retooled to conquer Disease, Old Age and Death will be clean and green, and since most voters will accept staying youthful, healthy and living longer as a great bargain for giving up a way of life which aggravates**

global warming, it will be our best hope for responding effectively to the Global Warming crisis.

47 Tax breaks — small or big — are scams. They aren't going to save you from decline and debilitation, from the cold embrace of The Grim Reaper. Don't be conned by the Deathist politicians. Don't trade your personal survival for a bowl of pottage!

48 Your chances of dying at the hands of the Russians or Chinese or North Koreans or Serbians or Iraquis or Afghans or Iranians or Timbuktuans are nil. So it's unconscionable that one stealth bomber shot down over Serbia, or one lousy spy plane, costs almost as much as the entire National Institute on Aging's budget for biological aging research, which is your only hope. But this is why we all live in The Death Society. And why it has to go.

49 You deserve better, much, much better. But <u>unless you do the right thing, and do it now, the chances are excellent that, just like all your ancestors, you'll rot in old age and end up as food for worms</u>.

50 The Immortalist Paradigm rejects the ancient superstition, taboo, and injunction against tampering with Aging and Death.

51 In the pursuit of Life, we Immortalists say nothing is off-limits. *The goal of Immortalist Medicine and Science is the cure of Aging, the extinction of Death.*

52 Therefore it is a life-and-death matter that we compel Medicine and Science to shift from the Mortalist to the Immortalist paradigm at this critical hour.

∞

We demand that the National Institute on Aging budget be dramatically increased and focused on human biological aging: The Aging Syndrome. This is the way to cure all The Aging Syndrome's symptoms — including heart disease, cancer, stroke, diabetes, and Alzheimer's.

If the U.S. government can find $3 trillion (so far) to invade and occupy Iraq, then we demand as much for anti-aging research which holds the best promise of preventing, treating and curing heart disease, cancer and stroke, obesity, diabetes, Alzheimer's and all other major killer-diseases.

∞

∞

To guarantee the anti-aging life-extension drugs or technologies are affordable to you as quickly as possible, the government should get into the business of researching and manufacturing such drugs.

We must avoid a repeat of a situation like the AIDS cocktails which cost up to $15,000 a year and which has meant unnecessary death for millions of have-nots in Africa and elsewhere. It will prevent a situation like the new cancer drug, which costs up to $2,400 a month or $28,800 a year.

∞

CHAPTER 16

Mortals of the World, Unite!

1 Why have all human attempts to eliminate Oppression, Alienation, and Repression been unsuccessful? It is because we have the wrong diagnosis of the human condition.

2 Without the correct diagnosis, the right cure is not possible.

3 Religion (especially Christianity) teaches that "sin" is the cause of evil, oppression, and Death. So it has tried to conquer evil, oppression, and Death through the elimination of sin.

4 The symptom of Death — sin — has been confused with its cause. The symptom of mortality mistaken for its cause.

5 "Sin" is the superstitious' feeble attempt to explain why we grow old and die. We must have done something terribly wrong; we must have committed a great evil — "the unpardonable sin." This is why we are under the curse of decay and Death.

6 Psychoanalysis — which studies human desires - has also failed to pinpoint the root cause of evil and oppression. Towards the end of his life, Freud - the father of psychoanalysis — became convinced that the blame for human evil could be laid at the door of "the death instinct."

7 But the "death instinct" is nothing more but the Freudian analogue for the Christian concept of "original sin." Freud turned the real cause of evil — Death — into a part of human nature — the "death instinct."

8 Suicide does not "prove" the "death instinct." There is no "problem of suicide." There is only the problem of depression.

9 Mortals kill themselves only when clinically depressed. Clinical depression short-circuits their normal instinct for self-

preservation. When the "suicidal" are given anti-depressants, their darkness lifts, they no longer wish to die.

10 Suicide is not an argument against our fear of Death, our desire for Immortality. Rather, it is an argument for effective antidepressants.

11 The question is not why suicides, but why so few?

12 Humans overwhelmingly choose Life even when it is grinding poverty, life imprisonment, death row, chronic ill health or agonizing pain. Humans choose Life even when they are completely paralyzed by a stroke or a spinal injury. Just ask Christopher "Superman" Reeves.

13 If Thanatos ("the death instinct") is a reality and more powerful than Eros (the life instinct), then there is no hope. Instead of our healer, psychoanalysis becomes our prophet of doom.

14 Like suicidal persons who internalize hatred and hostility against themselves, Freud led us astray by internalizing the problem of Death in this phantom called "the death instinct."

15 Existentialism has seen that it is our situation of finiteness, in which life is inevitably and arbitrarily ended by Death, which is the cause of human anxiety.

16 But it has done humanity a great disservice by claiming that the solution lies in our acceptance, our affirmation of Death.

17 It is no surprise that out of the Death-friendly soil of Hegel grew the cult and orgy of Death that was The Third Reich.

18 We reject "The Good Death" — the Mortalist dogma that everyone goes through the same "stages" in dying, that an "authentic" and "fulfilling" Death ends in "acceptance." This "acceptance" of Death, it is the most unnatural, for it is the pathetic spectacle of the decadence of our most natural instinct of self-preservation. Mortals resign themselves to Death only when their instinct for survival has rotted beyond repair. So this Good Death peddled so fervently by the likes of Elizabeth

Kubler-Ross, one of Death Ideology's propagandists, is both ridiculous and insidious.

19 It is bad enough to be dying. One does not need to feel guilt-ridden about not enjoying it.

20 If one has made a good accounting of one's life, one should be rewarded with more life, not Death.

21 A person who has lived a good life will naturally face Dying and Death with trembling and trepidation. He will not go gently into the dark night. He will go screaming and kicking. He will have to be evicted like an unwanted tenant. This is not evidence that he has led a "sinful" life. But rather evidence for the exact opposite. That he has led a good life, and naturally, logically, and unsurprisingly, desires more of it.

22 If your life is worth anything, Death will not be welcomed. A life that ends in Death is not acceptable. Not now. Not ever.

23 **Death is more than an ideology, it is a fact of life. Therefore, to eliminate Oppression, Repression, and Alienation, we must destroy not only The Death Ideology, but also its foundation, Death.**

24 Humanity will be freed at long last from the curse of mortality. Humans will no longer be meted an arbitrary Death sentence from birth.

25 The Elixxir Society will do away with this "cruel and unusual punishment" — often meted out without even allowing time to say goodbye. A fate worse than that suffered by our worst criminals. Humanity will be liberated from this arbitrary and unprincipled condemnation.

26 Then we can declare in unison "O grave, where is thy victory? O death, where is thy sting?"

27 Let The Death Society tremble at The Immortalist Revolution.

28 Mortals of the world unite! You have nothing to lose but Disease, Old Age and Death!

PART III

ROADMAP & GAMEPLAN for THE ELIXXIR SOCIETY™

CHAPTER 1
110 Year YouthSpan™ :
The Elixxir Society's Goal

1   This is the Goal of The Elixxir Society: a 110 year average lifespan in youthful and healthy vigor. That's why we call it 110 Year YouthSpan.

2   In The Death Society, the increase in lifespan (which has plateaued at around 80) is mostly an increase in the years of old age, disease and senility. This is the Titonius Curse of Greek mythology where eternal life is really being old and decrepit forever.

3   The kind of longer ALE (average life expectancy) you want is the kind that keeps you young and healthy and vigorous. It is the kind of healthy ALE increase that protects our health care system while allowing you to continue being productive and to continue contributing into the system.

4   The Death Society will not allow this. Their regimes are warning about how you are living too long and how it will ruin everything. Especially Social Security or Pensions. The most The Death Society will allow is an average life expectancy of around **80 years**. But this is **only two-thirds of your maximum human lifespan potential of 120.** In other words, **The Death Society is robbing you of one third (33%) of your lifespan.**

5   **ALE (Average Life Expectancy), NOT GDP, is the KEY STATISTIC for The Elixxir Society. ALE is the measure by which ImmorTalism and ImmorTalist History will judge a society, economy or state.**

6   Why? Because ALE is about LIFE. An increase in life expectancy means lives saved. Literally. It means dying or not dying from cancer, heart disease, or stroke. It means having or not having health care when you get sick with cancer, stroke, heart disease, diabetes, etc. Getting or not getting good medical care when you fall ill. It means babies not born dead or dying within the first year. It means babies born healthy and easily surviving childhood. But this does not mean much in The Death Society. Its media, its political chatter give hardly any notice to the ALE while it obsesses over the GDP.

7   **The goal of a 110 Year YouthSpan can already be achieved without any further breakthroughs** by using The Elixxir Program. Entire populations can partake of its anti-aging life-extending anti-cancer, anti-heart-disease, anti-stroke benefits. *Now.* While we wait for more breakthroughs to come from science labs.

8   **Is it a pipe dream to have a goal of 110 in 20 years? Absolutely not. In fact, an increase of 33 years in 27 years has been done before.** And not just by a small rich country, but by a poor, underdeveloped, war-torn and infrastructure-destroyed country that had a population one quarter of humanity.

9   And that country was **China. From 1949 to 1976. During the Maoist era.**

10 In most of the developed countries, like Sweden, Scandinavia, France, Germany, U.K., U.S., the ALE is already close to 80 years or past it.

11 Why is ALE of primary importance? Because **ALE affects every major indicator of relevance and interest to the average person. ALE is correlated with health care access, education, income or quality of life and so on down the line.**

China's Great Leap Foward in ALE (Average Life Expectancy)

12. In 1949, when the Communists took over, China's population had been stagnant for centuries at around 400 million.

13 From 1949 to 1976, a most amazing thing happened. The Chinese population under the Maoist People's Republic shot up from 400 million to 750 million.

14 In other words, **the Maoist state added or saved 350 million Chinese lives. An awesome, unprecedented and irrefutable historical accomplishment which is well-documented. And which is unrivalled by any state or system in all the annals of human history.**

15 In contrast, under the brutal, corrupt and incompetent dictator Chiang Kai Shek (whom the U.S. lauded as a great "Christian" and leader of "Free China" and gave billions of dollars in arms aid), China's life expectancy was at a rock-bottom 35 years, the same as in Tibet when the Dalai Lama temporarily held sway.

16 **To put China's feat under Mao in perspective: The U.S. Average Life Expectancy (ALE) in 1900 was 40. And in 1976 (when Mao died), it was about 73.**

17 **It took the Rich Capitalist U.S. 76 years to add 33 years to Americans' average life expectancy while it took poor Maoist China only 26 years to add as many years to the Chinese average life expectancy.**

18 *In the ALE race, China under Mao almost caught up with the U.S. which was then the wealthiest country in the world.*

19 We ImmorTalists give ALE credit where ALE credit is due.

China 1949-1976 Without Cold War Lenses

20 We are not oblivious to the Cold-War U.S./Western claims of mass murders being committed under the Maoist regime. We take them into serious consideration and evaluate them. Thousands were killed during the Cultural Revolution but this must be compared to the over 600,000 butchered in the American Civil War which the U.S. media and movies still glorify. (In hindsight Mao could claim he was absolutely justified in launching The Cultural Revolution as his avowed goal was to prevent a restoration of Capitalism). Yes, there were serious food shortages in the late fifties in China which resulted in malnutrition and premature deaths no doubt. But there was severe drought in India too at the same time which resulted in less food and deaths too. So to blame whatever deaths resulted in the late 1950s all on the Maoist state and not on the Indian state shows definite Cold-War bias. No Mortalist state is free of the taint of blood. Perhaps this is not possible for any kind of state.

21 **We ImmorTalists certainly have no problems accepting the Holocaust in which there is much factual evidence to support the claims that Hitler's Third Reich killed millions of Jews. Nor is it hard to accept that Stalin went after his political enemies and killed them by the thousands. Nor is it hard to accept that Cambodia's Pol Pot regime's killed hundreds of thousands; there are far too many mass graves attesting to its killing fields.**

22 But the claims of mass murder and genocide of up to a hundred million against the Maoist Chinese State just do not bear up under the slightest scrutiny. It relies on no primary sources. It relies on secondary or tertiary sources which are at best hearsay, apocrypha or unsubstantiated allegations by sources with too obvious an ax to grind. The books and articles cite each other in circles and none have any primary sources to back up their monumental claims.

23 Against this lack of evidence stands The Fact, documented and irrefutable, China's population leaped from 400 million to 750 million under Mao. History, freed from Cold War propaganda, will no doubt take due note of this feat and give credit where it is due.

Nobel Laureate in Economics Praises Maoist China's ALE Feat

24 Despite the U.S. and Western media totally blacking out this historic achievement of Maoist China in ALE, the facts are indisputable. It is recognized by everyone. Even Deng Hsiao Ping and his heirs, no fans of Mao, did not dispute these facts. Even the CIA recognized them.

25 Amartya Sen, the Nobel Prize Winner in Economics, for example, has repeatedly given Maoist China the credit it deserves on ALE as any scholar who is not a propagandist would. Sen confirmed in amazement that under the Maoist era, "the Chinese life expectancy was already 68 years; the Indian life expectancy was 54 years, 14 years behind it."

What Adding 33 Years Would Mean in Different Nations

26 **If the U.S. becomes an ImmorTalist State and increases Average Life Expectancy (ALE) by 33 years in 26 years (as Maoist China did), by 2036 it would have increased American life expectancy from 78 to 111. Within range of the maximum human lifespan of 122.**

27 **If an ImmorTalist Party were to win in Japan and increase Japanese ALE by 33 years, Japanese life expectancy would jump from 82.6 (current world champion) to 115.6 years.**

28 If the United Kingdom were to turn ImmorTalist and boost its current ALE by 33 years, British life expectancy would zoom from 79.4 to 109.4 years.

29 If Germany were to turn ImmorTalist and add 33 years to its ALE, the German ALE would jump from its current 79.4 to 112.4 years.

30 If France became an ImmorTalist state which increases its life expectancy by 33 years, then French ALE would jump from 80.7 to 113.7.

31 If Sweden were to become an ImmorTalist State and increase its ALE by 33 years, the Swedish ALE would leap from 80.9 to 113.9. Almost 114 years.

32 If the Chinese government were to decide to repeat China's historic feat on life expectancy, the Chinese ALE (average life expectancy) would take another great leap forward — from its current 73 to 106 years.

33 If Spain were to become an ImmorTalist state, increasing its ALE (average life expectancy) by 33 years, the Spanish ALE will go from 80.9 to 113.9. Approximately 114 years.

34 If Greece were to become an ImmorTalist state under which its ALE rises by 33 years, its ALE would leap from 79.5 to 112.5 years.

35 *If Cuba's Socialist State were to now extend its ALE by 33 years, Cubans' life expectancy would rise from its current 78.3 years to 111.3.*

35A   Remember, an ImmorTalist state is dedicated to adding not merely 33 years, but 33 years of good health and youthful vigor. *La dolce vita.*

Even Poor Third World Nations Can Do It

36 What Maoist China did in extending life expectancy 33 years was especially awesome since in 1949 China was not merely poor, it was destitute. Wracked by a long brutal resistance against Japanese occupation which killed up to 20 million Chinese, bankrupted the country's economy, and devastated its infrastructure.

37 Upon this wretched foundation, Mao had to build his new People's Republic. And it *managed right from the start to give the Chinese people universal health care, universal education and literacy, mass vaccinations, low infant mortality, great improvements in hygiene and sanitation, job and retirement security.*

38 The Mortalist regime in the U.S., whether under Democrats or Republicans, has told the American people with long grim faces that the government simply cannot afford to give the people universal health care, even in the Clinton boom years. China and Cuba have proven that it is entirely possible for even a "poor" Third World nation to do what one of the world's richest countries claimed it can't afford to.

Cuban Socialism Beats U.S. Capitalism

39 Castro's Cuba has overtaken the U.S. in the race for ALE (Average Life Expectancy), the only race that matters to The Elixxir Society.

40 Why isn't this a raging issue in U.S. political campaigns? Why aren't resignations demanded and given? Why aren't heads rolling? Why isn't this lagging behind Fidel's Cuba a political scandal of the first magnitude covered relentlessly by investigative journalists? Why aren't the so-called "patriots" boiling? An ImmorTalist Party must and will make an issue of this.

41 Cuba's ALE is unrivalled in the Third World. Cuba's ALE outshines every Latin American country except for Chile (78.6) and Costa Rica (78.8), which are a notch higher but were far ahead of Cuba in 1959.

42 **Despite Maoist China's Great Leap, Castro's Cuba's ALE now outshines China in ALE. As Nobel Prize in Economics Amartya Sen has pointed out, China has increased ALE by only a few years since Mao died in 1976.**

43 This startling ALE achievement by Cuba is of course not news worth trumpeting in the U.S. or Western Mortalist media at all. Apparently it is more important to report about how old U.S. cars from the 1950s and 1960s are still being used in Havana. (Thanks to the economic embargo.) Yep, and cars like those are being driven with great pride every summer by Swedish hobbyists in Stockholm too.

44 Just think how many millions of people the Communist government in Cuba has saved when it increased life expectancy from 58 under the U.S.-supported dictator Batista to the current 78.3. An increase of over 20 years. Just as the great leap forward in China's ALE (average life expectancy) was reflected in her population jumping from 400 million to 750 million, so too this happened in Cuba. In 1959, the Cuban population was 7 million. Today it is 11.2 million people.

The Elixxir Program

45 **What if there's a new drug that can give you permanent weight loss and prevent obesity, lower your blood pressure by 30%, prevent and reverse heart disease and arteriosclerosis, prevent or greatly delay all types of cancer, slash risk for breast cancer to virtually zero, slash your risk for stroke, avoid mental decline and Alzheimer's, prevent diabetes or reverse its symptoms, prevent osteoporosis, rejuvenate your immune system, slash your body**

fat, **postpone menopause and prolong fertility, increase testosterone naturally, give you a chance of attaining or even exceeding the maximum human lifespan of 122, and last but not least, reverse up to 70% of your genetic/cellular aging in two to four weeks?**

46 You would assume that this wonder drug would be headline news around the world, and everyone would be buzzing about it, and lining up for it. And every government would be forced to pay for it due to popular demand. Right?

47 **There is no such wonder drug but there _is_ a proven eating program which can give you all or most of the above life-saving benefits with no serious side effects. The Elixxir Program™ is its most doable adaptation. But it's ignored in The Death Society by its media and by its governments.**

48 For over sixty years The Death Society has known about this anti-aging health-preserving life-extending dietary intervention. And for over sixty years, it has done nothing. Nothing. This is another reason why we call it The Death Society. What government which is in favor of Life could have ignored such a life-saving intervention?

49 The Mortalist Regime's excuse for this? It claims that it is not 100% proven that its anti-aging effects will work in humans as in mice and every species so far put on this regimen. And it would take far too long an experiment to find out if it truly can extend maximum lifespan in humans by as much as in rats.

50 But this diet is not only about retarding aging and extending lifespan, it is also able to prevent or reverse arteriosclerosis, prevent heart attacks, prevent strokes, prevent all kinds of cancers. So even if despite its working in every single species so far, its anti-aging life-extending benefits don't somehow work in humans, it is still proven (and can easily be proven) that it is the best prevention we have against heart disease, cancer, stroke, diabetes, overweight, obesity, just to name a

few. And that should be enough to get any half-awake government's attention.

51   The Elixxir Program, the eating program of ImmorTalists and ImmorTalism, happens to be based on and adapted from this the only proven scientific anti-aging disease-preventing life-extending program. This is why we call it The Elixxir Program. Not just because it is named after its creator, but more so because it is truly the closest thing science has come to a "silver bullet" against disease, and to the mythical "elixxir" of "immortality."

52   Instead of the junk food and fast food dispensed by Death Society, we choose to eat well, live well, and stay young and live long on The Elixxir Program.

53   **The Elixxir Program will be the cornerstone of Public Health and Disease Prevention Policy in the coming Elixxir Societies.** In the long run, it would mean that it would cost The Elixxir Society less of its GDP to care for a population whose ALE is 110 than for the current Mortalist population whose ALE is at best a miserly 80 or thereabouts.

54   It will be the best thing for our health care systems to have drastic cuts in obesity, heart disease, cancer, stroke, diabetes, Alzheimer's, osteoporosis etc Aging-Related diseases. It will mean great savings which we can then spend on anti-aging research and other worthy endeavors.

55   The Elixxir Society will invest in and become partner with a program such as The Elixxir Program and help make it possible for it to be rolled out to teach, train and maintain an entire population on it.

56   Our ImmorTalist Government will invest in different versions of this eating program if need be. And the government stake in such ventures will prove to be very wise as it will reap not merely a good return money-wise (so that the Elixxir Society will have more revenues for its anti-aging research etc) but also health wise because it is the best guarantee of a healthy

and productive population over the long run, the best insurance for the continued viability of any health care system and for any economy.

57 An Elixxir Society will pay its willing citizens and residents to live on a program such as The Elixxir Program as a mass scientific study and a mass demonstration project. As a mass scientfic study, it will prove beyond a shadow of a doubt that this anti-aging life-extending disease-preventing intervention works also in humans. As a mass demonstration project, it will showcase the dramatic desirable anti-aging disease-preventing life-saving benefits for all of humanity to see.

58 This demonstration project can be done not only in the scientifically advanced nations of the E.U., Japan, U.S., Singapore, or China, but it can also be done in Cuba, Venezuela, Vietnam, Brazil, or Ecuador. This is the kind of life-saving scientific competition that countries should engage in. The country that wins and is the first to demonstrate that The Elixxir Program works on a signficiant human Population will land in the history books and win humanity's eternal gratitude.

59 **The Elixxir Program will buy Time, not to mention Youthful Health and Vigor, while we are waiting for further anti-aging life-extension breakthroughs.**

60 **It is less expensive to put the entire population of the United States, China, the E.U. or Russia on a program like The Elixxir Program than it would be to put ten percent of such a population on the HIV drug cocktails or on Viagra.**

61 Of course The Elixxir Society will not force anyone who does not want to get on The Elixxir Program. No Mortalist mortal longing for Death will be prevented by our ImmorTalist society from living one extra day beyond what he or she believes to be the "natural" human lifespan. (Of course the "natural" human lifespan is seen when mortals are put in the jungles — it is around 30 to 35.)

62 Anyone can opt in or out of The Elixxir Program. Every citizen and resident of The Elixxir Society has the freedom to decide if he or she wants to be fat, get sick, grow old, get ugly, and die on cue, *or not.*

63 *We are willing to give the voters and public a real choice. They can choose between The Death Society's ALE of at most 80 years or so, filled with Disease, Aging, Decline, and Suffering. Or they can vote for The Elixxir Society's 110 year Youth-Span, filled with youthful vitality and lifelong health, productivity and happiness. We are confident most people, if allowed such a choice, will choose our 110 Year YouthSpan and The Elixxir Program.*

64 Unlike the HIV drug cocktails, heart transplants, brain surgery, or even Viagra, The Elixxir Program (and its anti-aging disease-preventing lifespan-increasing benefits) is something that any "poor" Third World nation can afford. Yes, Cuba can easily afford to put its entire population on The Elixxir Program and be the first society to give its people 110 years of glowing youthful life. (That would go down in the annals of history indeed.) A North Korea can do The Elixxir Program too. So can any of those Sub-Saharan nations.

65 In summary, a 110 Year YouthSpan is the Goal and Promise of The ImmorTalist Party and The Elixxir Society. It is absolutely doable. China's experience in extending the Chinese ALE (Average Life Expectancy) by 33 years in a short time is our guide and assurance that our 110 year goal is realistic and achievable. Adding 33 years to the roughly 80 year ALE will actually exceed 110. And this feat does not require any new drug or breakthrough. It can already be accomplished with the help of a dietary intervention such as that which The Elixxir Program is based on.

∞

A wonder drug which can give you dramatic permanent weight loss and prevent obesity, lower your blood pressure by 30%, prevent and reverse heart disease and arteriosclerosis, prevent or greatly delay all types of cancer, slash risk for breast cancer to virtually zero, slash your risk for stroke, avoid mental decline and Alzheimer's, prevent diabetes or reverse its symptoms, prevent osteoporosis, rejuvenate your immune system, slash body fat, postpone menopause and prolong fertility, give you a chance at attaining or even exceeding the maximum human lifespan of 122, and last but not least, reverse up to 70% of your genetic/cellular aging in two to four weeks?

There is no such drug. But there is an eating program (The Elixxir Program is its most doable adaptation) which can give you all or most of the above life-saving benefits with no serious side effects. But it's ignored in The Death Society.

This anti-aging eating program will be the cornerstone of Public Health and Disease Prevention in The Elixxir Society.

∞

CHAPTER 2

No Money for a War Against D.O.D.?

1   <u>Where do we find the money</u> for an all-out War Against The Real Terrors? Disease, Old Age & Death™ (D.O.D.™)? Where do we find the money to prepare our societies and civlization against the coming onslaught of Global Warming?

2   Where do we find the money for a quantum leap in the budget of the NIH (National Institutes on Health) and NIA (National Institute on Aging)?

3   If we are to believe the rulers in Washington and Wall Street, and their blue-ribbon panels, there is simply no money left since the U.S. government has a huge budget deficit (racked up by them of course) and we have no choice, they claim in unison, but to cut "entitlement" programs like Social Security, Medicare and Medicaid.

4   Not true! We do have a choice!

5   We've followed the money trail, and we've found the money and the solutions.

6   Below are *where* the money for a Total War Against Disease, Old Age & Death (D.O.D.) can be found. And on top of it, we can still *increase* Social Security and Pension benefits, *lengthen and increase* unemployment benefits, have paid *maternal and paternal leaves* as in Sweden and other E.U. states, and finally give universal health care (a primary human right) to the long-suffering American people. This is what The ImmorTalist Party stands for. And what The ImmorTalist State will do.

I   Big Business in U.S. Pays No Taxes. Make Big Business Pay.

7   "Some of the world's biggest, most profitable corporations enjoy a far lower tax rate than you do — that is, if they pay taxes at all," *Forbes* magazine pointed out recently. This is the same *Forbes* magazine which prides itself on being a "Capitalist Tool." But even it ran an exposé publishing a list of what top corporations pay (or rather, don't pay) in taxes.

8   Exhibit A: General Electric — "The most egregious example is General Electric. Last year the conglomerate generated $10.3 billion in pretax income, but ended up owing nothing to Uncle Sam. In fact, it recorded a tax benefit of $1.1 billion." (Forbes)

9   "Two out of every three United States corporations paid no federal income taxes from 1998 through 2005, according to a report released Tuesday by the Government Accountability Office, the investigative arm of Congress," the *New York Times*, hardly a radical rag, reported.

10   72% of all big foreign corporations and 57% of U.S. big corporations doing business in the United States did not pay any federal income taxes at all for at least one year between 1998 and 2005.

11   In that same period, over 50% of foreign corporations and 42% of U.S. corporations paid no U.S. income taxes at all for two or more years. (Reuters, Aug 12, 2008)

12   During this period from 1998 to 2005, corporate sales in the U.S. racked up a total of $2.5 trillion.

13   These scandalous damning facts were revealed by the U.S. Congress' own GAO (Government Accountability Office) in a 2008 study commissioned by no less than Senators Carl Levin of Michigan and Byron Dorgan of North Dakota.

14   Senator Dorgan called the report "a shocking indictment of the current tax system." The report made clear, according to Sen-

ator Levin, that "too many corporations are using tax trickery to send their profits overseas and avoid paying their fair share in the United States."

15 Yes, the two Senators are right. But who made it possible for Big Business in the form of giant corporations to evade taxes with tax-loopholes which turn the U.S. into a de facto corporate tax haven? Why the U.S. Congress itself of course.

16 Exhibit B: Exxon Mobil, the octopus oil giant, reported in 2009 a record $45.2 billion profit. But not one cent of its taxes went to the IRS. Why? Because Exxon has 20 wholly-owned subsidiaries domiciled in the Bahamas, Bermuda and the Cayman Islands that (legally) shelter the cash flow from its operations in Angola, Azerbaijan or Abu Dhabi. "No wonder that of $15 billion in income taxes last year, Exxon paid none of it to Uncle Sam, and has tens of billions in earnings permanently reinvested overseas," Forbes revealed.

17 It's time to make Big Business and Multinational Corporations pay taxes. Then the U.S. government won't be broke. And the "little people" (the average American) won't have to pay the taxes that G.E. and Exxon are evading or deferring forever.

18 If the big corporations pay taxes, there'll be more than enough to fund a real war against cancer, heart disease, and stroke, as well to fund anti-aging research to save 79 million baby boomers.

II **The Pentagon cannot account for $2.3 Trillion (Yes, Trillion! That's 2,300 billion dollars!). This is 25% of the the U.S. Military budget that the Pentagon cannot seem to locate. An ImmorTalist Party and State will make (or help) the Pentagon find this missing loot and use it for a Real War Against The Real Terrors: Cancer, Heart Disease, Stroke.**

19 This incredible statistic came from no less than **Donald Rumsfeld**, the day before 9-11, when he was at the height of his power as the "Defense" Secretary under Bush Junior.

20 Rumsfeld for once was right on target. He told reporters **"The adversary's closer to home. It's the Pentagon bureaucracy."** He said **the $2.3 trillion wasted by the U.S. military posed a serious threat to U.S. national security. "In fact, it could be said it's a matter of life and death."**

21 It *is* a matter of life and death. **As *CBS News* pointed out, the $2.3 trillion amounts to $8,000 for every man, woman, and child in the United States.** So you see there is more than enough money for a War Against Heart Disease, Cancer, Stroke and all the big killers. **We could have had such a war funded to the tune of $8,000 per man, woman, and child in the U.S.!**

22 So this unconscionable Pentagon waste (most of it no doubt swallowed up by corruption) means a stagnating budget for the NIA (National Institute on Aging) and its aging research which could be our best new route to a cure for cancer, heart disease, stroke, diabetes, and Alzheimer's. It *is* a matter of life and death to lose 2.3 trillion dollars. It means a death sentence for you and your loved ones.

23 With part of this $2.3 trillion, we could also financially bailout every American going broke because of cancer, heart disease, stroke, or Alzheimer's which require intensive hospitalization or long term nursing care.

24 The ImmorTalist State will invest $3 Trillion in a Real War Against the Real Terrors.

25 Let's make the Pentagon find this missing cash. We may even put Rumsfeld in charge of this Easter Egg hunt.

Note: The fact that the Pentagon cannot account for 25% of its budget means it can do without a quarter of its budget.

26 Can you imagine the Social Security Administration not being able to account for 25% of its monies? The powers that be would have no qualms turning its entire piggy bank over to Wall Street's kleptomaniacs to "privatize." If it were Medicaid or Medicare or any of the social service programs that

the rich don't need and so demand to do away with, such a program or agency would not survive.

27 There would be no end to the fire-and-brimstone from the Republican Party led by morbidly-obese Rush Limbaugh, Glenn Beck and their ilk. And there would be no end to the stories from the U.S. Pravda....erh, Rupert Murdoch's *Fox "News" Network* and Murdoch's new rag *The Wall Street Journal.*

27A But 2.3 trillion disappeared from the Pentagon budget is not a talking point for U.S. media. It reveals the Sacred Cow in the U.S. Mortalist Regime and Society. And tips off anyone who is not blind to what kind of state the U.S. really is.

27B **Fact: U.S. military spending is bigger than China, Russia, France, Germany and the rest of the world's military spending combined.** The better for "full spectrum dominance" — the official U.S. policy and goal.

III The Iraq War costs at least $3 trillion and counting. Stop this lost war based on a big lie and spend a good part of this $3 trillion over 8 years for a total War Against Heart Disease, Cancer, Stroke,and other terrors. Increase U.S. Average Life Expectancy (ALE) by 30 years. Part of this $3 trillion should go to an ironclad guarantee of Job and Retirement Security. Not just for 79 Million Boomers but also for the younger generations.

28 Since 2 million Americans die each year from cancer, stroke, heart disease, etc killers compared to the one-time 3,000 deaths from 9/11, <u>we demand Washington at least match the $3 Trillion for a Real War Against The Real Terrors (Heart Disease, Cancer, Stroke etc.).</u>

IV <u>Shut down the Iraq and Afghanistan wars which cost at least $16 billion a month.</u> That will save us $16 billion every month. Those two wars are unwinnable and already lost. Spend that $16 billion a month on anti-aging research since cancer, heart disease, stroke, Alzheimer's, and osteoporosis are Aging-Related diseases.

29 In one month alone, the U.S. occupations of Iraq and Afghanistan cost 16 times as much as the entire National Institute on Aging (NIA) budget for biological aging research, the most important thing the U.S. government is doing right now, bar none! So <u>We The People will take that $16 billion a month and put it in our War Against Cancer, Heart Disease, Stroke.</u>

V   The U.S. Embassy in Baghdad — the largest in the world, the size of Vatican City, rivaling Saddam Hussein's palaces — cost at least $736 million to build. As if this isn't outrageous enough, it is projected to cost an extra $1.2 billion a year to run it. (Shut down the embassy and sell it while there are suckers who might still buy it.)

30 $1.2 billion annually to run the Baghdad embassy is 20% more than the 2009 budget for the National Institute on Aging. $736 million is what the NIA budget was not too long ago.

31 Prediction: This "Mega-Bunker" in Baghdad, as *Vanity Fair* christened it, will be abandoned when the U.S. forces flee Iraq in the same way it did Vietnam. As even *Vanity Fair* saw and pointed out, *the war in Iraq had already been lost*. So this is simply throwing good money after bad. It's not only Iraq that is lost, but also Afghanistan. So as any wise general, like Eisenhower or de Gaulle, would know it's time to cut one's losses.

The Military's Real Share of U.S. Spending

32 The refrain we hear ad nauseam in the media is that to cut the budget deficit, we have no choice but to cut Social Security, Medicare, Medicaid. Not to mention slash lifesaving research at the NIH's institutes which is the best hope for the 2 million Americans dying each year from predators like Heart Disease, Cancer, Stroke, Diabetes, Alzheimer's, Osteoporosis, Pneumonia, Spinal Paralysis, AIDS, and Obesity.

33 There is no mention of the fact that much of our budget deficit is the result of Empire's wars (e.g., Vietnam, Iraq and Afghanistan). There is absolutely no talk at all of the grotesquely bloated Pentagon budget (which is as if the Second World War is still raging). Nor is there any talk of the ruinous and disastrous wars in Iraq and Afghanistan which eat up $16 billion each month.

34 <u>Two months of Iraq and Afghanistan is enough to pay for a long extension of unemployment benefits.</u>

35 It is amazing that even in *The New York Times* and *Washington Post's* stories on budget deficits, this party line is swallowed hook, line, and sinker. There's nary a mention of a military budget which would be appropriate if the U.S. were still fighting Herr Hitler and his Third Reich. No mention of the two wars in Iraq and Afghanistan which are a bottomless pit.

36 Just Iraq has cost the U.S. $3 trillion so far, according to the best estimate by 2001 Nobel Prize winner in Economics Joseph Stiglitz.

- **An ImmorTalist State believes in military defense, and is not pacifist, but it does not churn up reckless, needless, ruinous wars. And it does not have Empire's lust for "full spectrum dominance." If a crazed rogue state were to really attack an Immortalist State, the rogue state would find that the ImmorTalist State would put up one hell of a fight. That it knows how to protect itself. That it has the will to victory because it has the Will to Life.**

37 How does the U.S. Mortalist Regime hide the cost of the Empire from all the investigative reporters of *The New York Times, Washington Post* and the financial reporters of the *Wall Street Journal*, all of whom should be able to understand basic accounting?

38 Amazingly simple, it turns out. All you have to do is use Washington's Funny Accounting 101. Which by the way was in-

vented only as recently as the Vietnam War. And this funny accounting is one of the few things in Washington that Republicans and Democrats agree on.

39 The problem? How to shrink or hide the disproportionate bite of the Pentagon and its wars (e.g. Iraq and Afghanistan) in the U.S. federal budget? So that Americans voters won't get uppity.

40 The solution? **Sneak in Social Security contributions into Washington's annual budget and pretend they are regular tax revenues. (Note: Social Security is supposed to be a trust fund, and payroll contributions to it are not supposed to be included with run-of-the-mill income tax revenues and raided for every little invasion from Vietnam to Bosnia to Iraq to Afghanistan.)**

41 Let's you and I learn this U.S. Accounting Trick and see how it works like a charm in the 2009 Budget.

42 The Tricks: 1) Ignore that Social Security is supposed to be a Trust Fund. Mix payroll contributions to this trust fund (which is supposed to be set aside for Americans' retirement) into the federal revenues. 2) Don't distinguish Past Military Expenditures (veterans benefits and *interest on debt for past wars*) from nonmilitary spending. 3) Don't include Iraq and Afghanistan spendings of $16 billion a month in the Pentagon's budget. Nope, call them emergency appropriations. Even after seven years.

43 If you count Social Security contributions as tax revenues and you do not distinguish Past Military spendings from Nonmilitary spending, then you get the *official* pie chart of the Congressional Budget Office for Fiscal Year 2008. Voila! You see on this magic chart that "Defense" spending is only 20% while "Medicare, Medicaid & Other Mandatory" constitutes 33%. And Social Security is 21% of budget spending.

44 If you take out Social Security contributions (which belong to our Trust Fund and should not be in the general budget), and

tease out expenditures for Past Military Adventures (e.g. life-long benefits for limbless or traumatized veterans and interest on debts funding past military adventures) and not hide them in Non-military expenditures, then you see the real picture.

45 In 2009, if we set aside and not count Social Security Trust Fund contributions, the total U.S. tax revenues was 1.15 trillion. The grand total for the U.S. military was $874 billion. This means that **the U.S. Military eats up at least 76% of the U.S. government's total receipts. (Gore Vidal, one of the few truth-tellers, in 1988 counted over 90%.)**

Why We Can Increase Social Security and Other Benefits

46 If the above facts were known to every American, he or she would have no problem understanding where Washington's amazing ever-growing budget deficit comes from. And why Washington and its "wise guys" are trying to con retiring Americans into believing that there is no choice but to slash Social Security, Medicare, Medicaid.

47 **The facts above also explain why E.U. countries like Sweden and Norway can afford to have world-class universal health care, "generous" unemployment and retirement benefits, 4 to 6 weeks of paid vacation annually, up to 6 months each of paid maternal and paternal leaves, and still have a balanced government budget, no deficits, in fact surpluses! And no, Swedes and Norweigians are not being taxed to death. In fact they have more disposable income and a higher quality of life than the average American.**

48 Obama's blue-ribbon committee on how to solve the Federal budget deficit was handpicked and stacked to tell him and the U.S. Congress what they wanted to hear: that the budget deficit gives them no choice but to slash Social Security, Medicare, Medicaid.

49 That is simply a bald-faced lie. We reject their fraudulent conclusions based on fraudulent accounting.

- **Social Security is actually a very solvent fund.** In
2009, for example, it took in $949 billion in payroll
contributions and paid out $944 billion. A net surplus
of 5 billion dollars for 2009. The only problem with
Social Security is that Washington's kleptomaniacs violates this Trust Fund by treating it like an all-purpose
piggy bank. To be raided with bipartian abandon. For
everything from Bill Clinton's Bosnian Adventure to
Bush Junior's Iraq and Afghanistan Debacles.

50 *If the manager of a trust fund does what the White House and
U.S. Congress do routinely to Social Security (the trust fund
for 79 million retiring baby boomers), that trust fund manager would be in jail with the keys thrown away for life.*

51 **The Budget Deficit is most certainly not because of Social
Security or Medicaid or Medicare spendings. Scandinavian
countries have some of the most comprehensive social safety-net programs in the world. Yet a country like Sweden
can boast of balanced budgets, little or no deficits, and is in
impeccable financial shape compared to the U.S.** *And this
happened mostly under "leftist" governments. And what's
more, Sweden now tops the U.S. in global competitiveness.*

Bankruptcy or Life?

52 Obama was asked soon after his inauguration when the U.S.
government would run out of money. And he blurted out
"We're out of money now." And this was on *CNBC*.

53 It is a miracle of *faith* that there are still buyers of U.S. Treasury bills. That there are still those who cling to the *belief* that
the dollar and U.S. government bonds are "safe haven." The
true believers include countries whose governments should

know better. Governments which should know how to read balance sheets. They should see that the U.S. Empire is broke.

54 As Nobel Laureate in Economics **Joseph Stiglitz** wrote: "Until recently, many marvelled at the way the United States could spend hundreds of billions of dollars on oil and blow through hundreds of billions more in Iraq with what seemed to be strikingly little short-run impact on the economy. But there's no great mystery here. *The economy's weaknesses were concealed by the Federal Reserve, which pumped in liquidity...*" (Joseph E. Stiglitz & Linda J. Bilmes, "The Iraq War Will Cost Us $3 Trillion, and Much More," *Washington Post* Op-Ed piece, March 9, 2008)

55 Translation: the Federal Reserve has been frantically printing money. The endgame is near.

56 If the U.S. Federal Reserve (Central Bank) is going to print dollar bills like a Banana Republic, then we must make the U.S. government lavish all the dollars it sees fit to print on anti-aging research. On research to cure cancer, heart disease, stroke. On a bailout of the tens of millions of Americans afflicted with life-threatening diseases. Two million of whom are going to die this year, next year, every year. Just in the United States alone. Yes, we'd better make the U.S. government spend on our life agenda while there are still takers for dollar bills and Treasury bills.

57 The choice is crystal clear. The U.S. can spend on a War Against Disease, Old Age & Death (D.O.D.), or the U.S. can go bankrupt with Empire and "war on terror."

58 It's time for Americans — especially boomers — to wake up, march and fight again. Or they shall soon be facing a very cold, very ugly, and very poor future.

CHAPTER 3

Paradigms & The War Against Cancer

"There is no such thing as research in the absence of any paradigm."
— Thomas Kuhn, "The Structure of Scientific Revolutions"

The Mortalist Paradigm

• Disease, Aging, Old Age, and Death are "natural" and "inevitable" parts of life or "acts of God" and therefore must be submitted to;

• God made us mortals and therefore we cannot extend the human lifespan

• Wealth, Fame, Power, Success are the highest good;

• Mortalist Medicine is palliative — it should not seek to cure the underlying master disease: The Aging Syndrome;

• This is because as per The Genesis Curse, mortal life must be Blood, Sweat and Tears, and must end in Death.

The ImmorTalist Paradigm

• **Disease, Old Age & Death are no longer necessary or acceptable;**

• **Human biological Aging — The Aging Syndrome — is the master disease, and cancer, heart disease, stroke, Alzheimer's, diabetes, Parkinson's, osteoporosis, obesity, etc. aging-related ailments are its symptoms;**

- **Wealth, Fame, Power, Children are immortality surrogates and substitutes and therefore cannot make us happy;**

- **The Fear of Death and the Desire for Immortality are the engine of human creativity and productivity;**

- **The conquest of Death is the fulfillment of the promise of all great religions; if Methuselah lived to 969 years, and Enoch supposedly never died and Jesus cured Disease and "conquered" Death, then Judaeo-Christianity is not against vanquishing Death.**

Do Paradigms really matter?

1 Does it matter if society operates under The Mortalist Paradigm or The ImmorTalist Paradigm? Does the wrong paradigm, The Mortalist Paradigm, really kill? Or is that merely overheated rhetoric or polemics?

AIDS RESEARCH PARADIGM POINTS THE WAY

2 What would have happened if scientists did not accept the paradigm of AIDS? As a master disease syndrome, of which a cluster of serious ailments such as Kaposi Sarcoma (a skin cancer), Lymphoma, or Pneumonia are its symptoms?

3 They would not have recognized Kaposi Sarcoma, Lymphoma and Pneumonia as its symptoms or "complications".

4 How would such a paradigm have impacted research strategy, research funding and research results?

5 Research strategy would have gone after Kaposi Sarcoma, Lymphoma, Pneumonia etc. — the symptoms or "complications" of AIDS — as if they were unrelated ailments. Under this paradigm, funding strategy would have poured money into all the different ailments like Kaposi's sarcoma, Lymphoma or Pneumonia instead of on the AIDS virus.

6   Funding would probably have ended up more expensive with less results. Instead of going after one master disease syndrome, the NIH would have had to fund more research into something like half a dozen to a dozen different serious diseases.

7   The result of such a research and funding strategy? Probably not very productive. It may have come up with some treatments for Lymphoma, Pneumonia, Kaposi Sarcoma, etc. ailments but we would still have been unable to prevent their incidence or occurrence in more and more people.

8   We would probably not have the AIDS drug "cocktail" which has proven very effective in preventing those infected with HIV from advancing to full-blown AIDS, and in cutting the death rate from AIDS, and in allowing many HIV positive people to live a "normal" span.

9   Paradigms matter. Choosing the right paradigm is a matter of life and death in the AIDS issue. And it is also a matter of life and death in the struggle against cancer, heart disease, stroke, and other killer diseases.

Lack of Results in Cancer War says New Paradigm Needed

10 It has been forty years since U.S. President Nixon's 1970 declaration of a War on Cancer. Nixon had long disappeared, disgraced by Watergate, but Cancer in all its forms is still here and in fact has overtaken heart disease in the U.S. as number one killer.

11 Unlike wars which Presidents and Prime Ministers are terrified of losing under their watch, there are no political repercussions whatsoever for the War on Cancer's lack of victory. There should be.

12 Despite the so-called War on Cancer, there is still no cure for any kind of cancer. Nor is there any drug or vaccine which can prevent any or all kinds of cancer. And though there has been a decline in the cancer death rate from 1950 to 2005, after adjustment for size and age of population, it is only 5%.

13 Although the National Cancer Institute's 4,000 employees and the $105 billion it spent over fifty-five years on this "war on cancer " pale in comparison to the U.S. budgets for just the Iraq and Afghanistan wars, a five percent lower cancer death rate is still a meager return.

14 What do generals and heads of states do when their strategy for a war proves fruitless or victory-less? If they are wise, they conclude it is the wrong strategy and change it.

15 The lack of results we have to show after a war against cancer over four decades is a telltale sign and wakeup call that we are laboring under the wrong paradigm.

16 The lack of significant results also means millions continue to die each year from cancers in the U.S. and around the world.

17 It is high time to explore and fund an alternative paradigm which is very likely to bear more fruit.

Anti-Aging Research to Cure Cancer, Heart Disease, Stroke, Diabetes, Alzheimer's, Osteoporosis, Obesity, etc.?

18 How can we prevent, in one sweep, with one silver bullet, all the top killer diseases like Heart Disease, Cancer, Stroke, Obesity, Diabetes, Osteoporosis, Alzheimer's, Parkinson's?

19 The key to the answer lies in the fact that they are all "Aging-Related" diseases, or are "highly correlated" with growing older. In other words, the older you get, the more likely you

are to get cancer, a heart attack, heart failure, a stroke, Alzheimer's, or osteoporosis.

20 Mortalist Science and Medicine are in universal agreement that all the above major diseases are *aging-related* or highly correlated with our biological aging. This makes it all the more amazing, puzzling, and revealing why Mortalist Science and Medicine cannot or will not take this all the way to its logical conclusion.

21 *What exactly would be the logical conclusion? It would be that Cancer, Heart Disease, Stroke, Diabetes, Obesity, Alzheimer's, osteoporosis, and hypertension are <u>symptoms</u> of our biological aging. Therefore, just as AIDS is the syndrome for its cluster of ailments, <u>our biological aging must be The Master Disease Syndrome.</u>*

22 New Paradigm for Research: Aging is Master Disease; Symptoms include Cancer, Heart Disease, Stroke, Alzheimer's, Hypertension, Diabetes, Osteoporosis, Obesity. (Note: We advocate that this new paradigm be explored and funded *in addition* to the traditional paradigm and strategy of research.)

23 There must be something that prevents highly intelligent scientists, physicians and researchers well versed in logic from taking this very logical, and rather small step. Why when they are halfway there in their agreement that diseases like cancer, heart disease, stroke, Alzheimer's are "aging-related" or "highly" or "heavily-correlated" with growing older?

24 What is that mysterious something holding the scientists and administrators at the NIA and NIH back?

25 That something is what we call **The Mortalist Paradigm which declares Aging to be "natural" — an "act of God." Therefore, since Aging is not a disease, it is not to be cured.**

NIA Bows to Mortalist Paradigm

26 NIA is Exhibit A for how real and how potent The Mortalist Paradigm is in its impact on scientific research and on the very direction of the NIA as an institution.

27 The original NIA charter from Congress came as close as possible in The Death Society to saying Human Biological Aging is a Disease. But instead of recognizing it as a disease, the U.S. Congress, in passing this rather incredible piece of legislation creating the NIA, compromised, describing Aging as "the condition common to us all." The Congressional mandate to the NIA was explicit: it was ordered to do basic research on the human biology of aging.

28 What happened? The NIA's mission to go after human aging was subverted, with the complicity of its own founding director Dr. Robert Butler, M.D., an eminent gerontologist, who had lobbied hard for its creation.

29 Being a pragmatic fundraiser, and grasping the Mortalist Paradgim that Aging is no disease, Dr. Butler decided that he was not going to get as much funding for the NIA going after Aging as a disease , but that he would raise much more from the Mortalist Congress if he would go after one of Aging's symptoms — Alzheimer's.

Symptoms-Chasing, Not Source-Seeking

- Under Dr. Butler and ever since, Alzheimer's has eaten up a dementedly disproportionate chunk of the budget for the National Institute for Aging. In the NIA's Fiscal Year 2006 budget, Alzheimer's research grabbed 62% of its entire budget! ($643 million for Alzheimer's out of an NIA budget of $1,045 million.) In Fiscal Year 2009, the NIH spent a total of $534 billion on Alzheimer's research. This is still 51%

of the FY 2009 budget for the National Institute on Aging.

- This is like spending all the AIDS research budget on Kaposi's sarcoma, a "complication" of AIDS, instead of going after HIV, the cause of AIDS.

30 Dr. Butler confessed to serious misgivings many years later when confronted by a *New York Times* reporter as to why Alzheimer's research routinely gets over half of the NIA's budget. But despite Butler's public misgivings, this mindless Alzheimer's juggernaut at the NIA rolls on.

31 Butler was director from 1975 to 1982. By the time he left, he had made Alzheimer's research such a disproportionate priority at the NIA that it completely eclipsed what was supposed to be the NIA's main chartered priority – that of basic research into human biological aging.

32 The result of all this Alzheimer's funding at the expense of aging research funding? Little or nothing to write home about, as *The New York Times* pointed out recently.

33 This bears witness to the wrongness of the Mortalist paradigm which allows only feeble attempts to tinker with the symptoms of The Aging Syndrome but bars us from a frontal assault on the root cause of Alzheimer's: human biological aging.

34 Alzheimer's is a dreadful disease and must be conquered. But it must be put in perspective. Currently, 5.3 million Americans are estimated to have Alzheimer's. That is terrible. But at the same time, out of a total U.S. population of over 300 million, the incidence of Alzheimer's is 1.8 %.

35 Since Alzheimer's is a disease of aging, the best route is, in addition to Alzheimer's research, to focus research on The Aging Syndrome (human biological aging) and discover how Alzheimer's could be prevented, short-circuited, slowed down, or cured by stopping or retarding The Aging Syndrome.

Progeria & Werner Syndrome

36 Aside from all the Aging-Related Diseases, there is also the disease known as **Progeria** or Werner Syndrome (adult progeria) in which a chronologically young person is afflicted with many Age-Related diseases like cancer, heart disease, or even stroke.

37 *There can be no more compelling evidence that Aging is a disease than the dramatic premature aging we see in Progeria or Werner Syndrome.* And maybe this is why they are neglected in research and funding in The Death Society on the flimsy excuse that they are a "rare disease."

38 Progeria proves in the most unmistakable way that there is such a thing as Premature Accelerated Aging and that it is a disease. There is no dispute on this. The National Institutes of Health calls it a "disease" – albeit a "rare disease" - and so does every scientist, physician, and researcher who has studied it or encountered it.

39 Does it take an Einstein to grasp that this rare disease Progeria may help us unravel the mystery of human biological aging?

40 A new study has found that progerin, the abnormal protein which causes Progeria, is present in the vasculature of the non-Progeria general population and increases with age. So our hunch is correct. There are parallels between "normal" aging and progeria aging. Progeria is probably "normal" aging speeded up. (*Arteriosclerosis, Thrombosis, and Vascular Biology* August 26, 2010)

41 So why is The Death Society neglecting this "rare disease" when it could give us leads in our fight against cardiovascular disease, cancer, hypertension, diabetes, and stroke?

42 What's even more tantalizing is the fact that all this speeded-up aging resulting in heart disease, cancer, stroke, hypertension, wrinkled skin,and diabetes, seems to be caused by only one tiny mutation in one single gene.

43 <u>But for Mortalist reason, Progeria research is subject to not-so-benign neglect in The Death Society.</u>

Premature Aging in The Death Society

44 But if diseases like diabetes, cancer, obesity, hypertension are Aging-Related ailments, are symptoms of Aging, then how come a small percentage of those who are afflicted with diabetes, cancer, hypertension are teenagers or twenty-somethings? And why is the incidence of diabetes among the young on the rise? Why, indeed if diabetes is a symptom of aging?

45 Answer: Because an increasing number of the young are suffering from Premature Accelerated Aging.

46 It is not as extreme as that seen in Progeria, but it is quite noticeable not merely physically and visually, but also in statistics about diseases afflicting the young.

46A 70,000 Americans from 15 to 40 get diagnosed with cancer annually. There is a 50% rise in strokes in the 15-35 age group.

47 **Earlier Puberty** — American and Western girls are undergoing puberty earlier and earlier. Increasingly, eleven or twelve year old girls and boys look and behave and weigh like fifteen or sixteen year olds.

48 The young in Death Societies like the U.S., the U.K. and even in Scandinavian countries like Sweden are coming down early with ailments like diabetes because **they are aging faster and prematurely.**

49 **Rising Incidence of Diabetes** — Diabetes is the tell-tale disease of premature accelerated aging. Why? Because diabetics exhibit many of the biomarkers of aging.

50 Diabetics suffer an earlier decline in immune function. Their collagen shows changes characteristic of old people. The gamma-crystallin from their eye-lens protein are lost at a

speeded-up rate. Their connective tissue cannot divide as many times as in the young. Another characteristic of older people. High blood cholesterol, decrease in the good HDL, increased risk for arteriosclerosis, earlier incidence of cataracts, heart disease, nerve disorders, kidney damage. These complications of diabetes are caused by diabetics' elevated blood sugar which causes great injury to the cells. Therefore, diabetes is the canary in the coal mine revealing that speeded-up aging is happening.

51 So the fact that the young are increasingly afflicted with Aging-Related diseases like Diabetes does not contradict our new Paradigm in which Diabetes et al are seen as diseases of aging. This phenomenon is clear evidence of premature and accelerated aging among an increasing percentage of the young resulting from their eating of The Death Society Diet and their bondage to its Death Styles.

52 *Cause of Premature Aging?* The most probable cause is the excessive feedings of The Death Society Diet, with its high sugar, high fat, high sodium, and, most of all, high calories. This undoubtedly is speeding up the biological aging process of the young, not to mention the chronologically advanced.

NIA — The Premier Institute

53 NIA should and would get the most funding of all NIH institutes under The Elixxir Society. Why? Because as the U.S. Congress admitted when it created the NIA, aging is the conditon common to all. So it should get the highest priority and the most funding. In the U.S. alone it is about to doom 79 million baby boomers.

54 The Death Society is not willing to recognize Aging as a Disease even when it is chartering the NIA to be an institute at the NIH. Even though other NIH institutes are devoted to curing "diseases," not mere "conditions."

55 The ImmorTalist Paradigm (and Movement) supports an overall dramatic increase in the funding for the NIH and similar
government institutions around the world. People suffering
from cancer, heart disease, stroke, Alzheimer's, and AIDS
should not have to fight for crumbs from the funding table,
and should not have to fight among themselves as to who gets
the biggest crumb.

56 But how do we split up the NIH pie in a fair and rational way,
and not its current status quo where you need big, rich, organized lobbies to get more money for your pet disease?

57 *Under an ImmorTalist government, funding for a disease will
be directly proportional to the percentage of the population
afflicted by it.*

58 This is the only fair allotment of the NIH's funding to its various institutes and to specific diseases. Under this guideline,
**the NIA will and should rightly get the most funding of the
NIH institutes as it is chartered by the U.S. Congress to
research and cure "the condition" most common to us all.**

59 Not only that, it is Aging Research — the NIA's domain —
which is most likely to lead to more effective treatments and
faster cures for cancer, heart disease, stroke, Alzheimer's,
obesity, diabetes, osteoporosis and all the other top killers.
Since they are all Aging-Related diseases.

"Normal" and "Healthy" Aging?

60 In The Death Society, all scientific and medical research is
done under the rubric and prism of The Mortalist Paradigm.
The NIA and its founding director Dr. Robert Butler. M.D.
are Exhibit A.

Basic Dogma of The Mortalist Paradigm: Aging is "Normal" — not a Disease.

61 So we hear, even at the National Institute on Aging (NIA), the constant refrain of "normal aging" — a Death Society core belief — as one of its goals. This is an ideologically-limited goal to which even the NIA's founding director Robert Butler and his successors must genuflect to in each and every budget request to Congress.

62 *But "Normal Aging" and "Healthy Aging" are oxymora. It is no more possible to have "normal aging" or "healthy aging" than it is to have "normal cancer" or "healthy cancer."*

63 The only thing that makes human biological aging "normal" and acceptable is that everyone is eventually afflicted by it, and dies of it. But if that's what makes for "normal" and acceptable, then heart disease, cancer, and stroke which 70% of the population dies of year in and year out must be very "normal" and should be very acceptable indeed.

64 But the NIA — and the NIH's Cancer and Heart Institutes — rightly sees this unholy trinity of heart disease, cancer, stroke to be just what they are — diseases to be hunted down by scientists and treated and cured if at all possible.

Prevention-Cure: The Best & Cheapest

65 The best and cheapest "cure" for Cancer, Heart Disease, Stroke, Obesity, Diabetes, Alzheimer's, osteoporosis, Parkinson's is to *prevent* them. This is part of the ImmorTalist Strategy for the conquest of cancer, heart disease, stroke, Alzheimer's, osteoporosis, AIDS, and obesity.

66 An ounce of prevention is definitely worth a pound of cure, especially since we don't have the cures yet. So research under this new ImmorTalist Paradigm would also include an

aggressive all-out effort to develop vaccines which can prevent these killers.

67 The most promising, potent and efficient route to prevention of cancers, heart attacks, strokes, hypertension, diabetes, Alzheimer's and osteoporosis is through the eating program discovered by Dr. Clive McCay at Cornell University in the 1930s.

68 The Elixxir Program is based on this. But while retaining its "active ingredients," The Elixxir Program has evolved this impeccably scientific but daunting regimen into a popular adaptation which does not require the semi-starvation, the obsessive calorie-counting, the life-sucking online chattering, the *de facto* vegetarianism with bans on alcohol advocated by The Caloric Restriction Society or its late guru Roy Walford.

69 Instead, The Elixxir Program is very doable for a successful person living a modern, hectic, demanding lifestyle who does not have the time to reinvent the wheel. To figure out how to work it. And who wants to make sure it works. As the stakes are too high to do it wrong.

70 This anti-aging eating program points to *a most elegant and cost-effective path* to conquering cancer, heart disease, stroke. By preventing them. Through a natural diet based on foods you can easily find at any supermarket in any country. And yet the U.S. and all other Death Societies have basically completely neglected the funding of any significant research on this diet and on how to apply it to its populations.

71 The best prevention-cure is already here. It has been here and known to Science and Medicine since the 1930s. For over six decades. And The Death Society with its Mortalist Paradigm steadfastly dismisses the McCay-Cornell Breakthrough which can slash our risks for all the major diseases. The Death Society acts as if this anti-aging breakthrough does not exist. Even though it can prevent all the killers the NIH is commissioned to find cures for.

72 Why is this? Could it be that the McCay-Cornell Breakthrough, on which The Elixxir Program is based, is of no interest to The Death Society not because there is no evidence that it can prevent cancer, heart disease, stroke, diabetes, obesity, but because there is too much evidence it could *also* greatly retard aging, and greatly extend even maximum lifespan?

73 The U.S. and most other Death Societies spend little money on prevention. But it costs so much more to treat cancer, heart disease, stroke than to prevent them. The Elixxir Society will spend more money on prevention, as prevention is the best "cure." And the cheapest and least painful one too.

The Diet Cure

74 Dr. Clive McCay discovered at his Cornell Lab in 1935 that mice fed on optimal calories with optimal nutrition extended their maximum lifespan by up to 50% and also stayed youthful, healthy and vital.

75 You would think that such a diet which also dramatically reduced the incidence of tumors in the lab mice would be thrown money at by Washington and other governments. Absolutely not.

76 The lack of interest, it was claimed, was because of the belief that this diet would not work in humans. But was this belief reasonable?

77 If this were a discovery with potential for military use, Washington would have lavished funding on research to find out how to overcccome any and all obstacle.

78 But no, apparently not for something which has the potential to retard aging and extend maximum lifespan by 50 %.

79 So seven decades were lost without any serious government follow-up research of Dr. McCay's landmark discovery.

80 It was not until the 1990s, over half a century after McCay's discovery that, with ominously aging demographics looming, the U.S. finally funded two significant studies of monkeys on this diet.

81 When the McCay breakthrough occurred, it caused no ripple of interest at all in Washington, London, Paris, Tokyo, Rome or Berlin. No, the Mortalist schoolyard bullies were all too busy with their feverish preparations for war. The McCay milestone was dismissed by these Death Societies. All through the 1930s and 1940s, Death Societies were only interested in creating new and more lethal weapons of mass destruction.

82 It is a "cop out" to say it takes too long to prove the diet can extend life or retard aging in humans. *It could have been easily and quickly proven that the diet can lower hypertension, blood sugar, control diabetes, cure obesity, prevent stroke and heart attack and slash risk for cancer in humans.*

83 <u>These experiments should and could have been done on humans over half a century ago. If they were, they would have resulted in dramatic results which could have encouraged tens of millions to get on this diet, resulting in millions of lives saved.</u>

84 This is no aberration. No isolated case. When we examine the history of The Death Society, we see that this is its nature.

85 At every turn, faced with a choice between Life and Death, The Death Society chooses Death. This is why we call it The Death Society, It's not polemics: it's the best description.

CHAPTER 4
Systemic Homicide

1   *Systemic Homicides* are *preventable, needless, premature* deaths caused by an economic, political or social system through its institutions, laws, regulations, or lack thereof. The preventability, needlessness, or prematurity of such deaths can be seen by comparison to other countries or systems.

2   Systemic Homicide is on a scale unimaginable to the garden-variety serial killer. Committed by the Mortalist economic-political system, it goes on right under our noses. But we are oblivious to it. It is invisible to us as our brains and eyes have been taught to see it as "natural," "unavoidable," "an act of God." The sytemic murders go on day in and day out, with no mercy or letup. But there are never any murder trials, no indictments, no prosecutions, no convictions. It is the best testimonial to how well we have been programmed by Mortalism and how lethal its consequences are.

3   Not surprisingly, since Death is ultimately acceptable in The Death Society, deaths from Systemic Homicide receive little or no attention from its government, media, or politics.

4   In the 1960s, and to a lesser extent now, India was touted in the U.S. media as the Asian showcase of "democracy" and capitalism. But the yawning gap in ALE between China and India makes us wonder what kind of showcase India was, is.

5   **ALE is not an academic statistic of no significance in our lives. It is *the* Life-and-Death statistic. This is why it is the least publicized and most ignored in The Death Society.** A shocking ALE gap of 14 years means that hundreds of mil-

lions of Indians are dying prematurely and needlessly under Indian "capitalism" and "democracy."

6   The U.S. ALE is shorter than Cuba, shorter than Sweden, shorter than Japan. The U.S. ranks a shameful 38 in ALE in the world. This is the result of the intentional and premeditated policies of the American Death Society. It is outrageous and unacceptable Systemic Homicide. And it means the premature, needless, tragic deaths of millions of Americans.

7   This does not count for news in The Death Society. But it will be the greatest of scandal enough to bring down any government in The Elixxir Society.

Case Studies of Systemic Homicide
Case Study I. U.S. Health Care Lack Kills 45,000 Americans Each Year

8   A Harvard Medical School study published in September 2010 found that nearly 45,000 people die every year in the United States because of lack of health insurance.

9   Who are among the 45,000 Americans who died last year and the 45,000 Americans who will die this year? Americans fighting cancer, heart disease, stroke, diabetes and obesity and all the other killers. The working middle-class. The poor.

   •   45,000 deaths from lack of health care. This is 15 times 9/11 in one year. Every year. 45,000 is almost as much as all the combat deaths suffered by U.S. during the entire the Vietnam War. What's worse, this 45,000 deaths is not a one year aberration, it is an annual atrocity.

3 Million Americans Killed by U.S. Since 1945

10 45,000 deaths each year means 450,000 deaths every ten years. That's almost half a million needless, premature, preventable deaths for each decade.

11 To see how egregious this lack of universal health care in the U.S. is, we must note that the notion of universal health care is nothing new. Germany has the world's oldest universal health care system. It harks back to Bismarck's social reform legislation in the 1880s. In Great Britain, universal health care took its first steps in the National Insurance Act 1911. It culminated in the National Health Service in 1948 which extended health care security to all legal residents. Britain was financially spent after the Second World War and could have pleaded no money.

12 Universal health care systems in the rest of the E.U. were implemented soon after the Second World War as reforms designed to make health care available to all, to fulfill the requirement of **Article 25 of the Universal Declaration of Human Rights of 1948**, signed by every country.

13 **Except the U.S. The self-styled champion of human rights has refused since 1948 to ratify the social and economic rights sections, which includes Article 25's right to health care.**

Health Care is Basic Human Right

14 Article 25 of the Universal Declaration of Human Rights states:

- (1) Everyone has the right to a standard of living adequate for the health and well-being of himself and of his family, including food, clothing, housing and medical care and necessary social services, and the right to security in the event of unemployment, sickness, disability, widowhood, old age or other lack of livelihood in circumstances beyond his control.

- (2) Motherhood and childhood are entitled to special care and assistance. All children, whether born in or out of wedlock, shall enjoy the same social protection.

15 **Every day the United States is in violation of the basic human right guaranteed in Article 25. A fundamental human right recognized in all of the European Union. And in Castro's Cuba and Maoist China.**

16 Where is the loud and incessant demand by the human-rights organizations in the U.S. and Europe about this outrageous U.S. refusal to ratify? This scandalous denial by the U.S. of the most basic human right? Where are *The New York Times* and *Washington Post* articles and editorials? How come the vociferous champions of human rights in both parties are totally mute on such a life-and-death human right?

17 *So how many decades of Systemic Homicides due to denial of universal health care is the U.S. Mortalist Regime guilty of?*

18 Let's be extremely charitable. Instead of saying it should have started as early as Germany in the 1880s, or as early as 1911 in Great Britain, we shall limit the period for which it must be held culpable to only right after The Second World War, when the U.S. Empire was at its height, and when it was indisputably the richest country in the world, able to afford universal health care better than any other nation on earth.

19 From 1945 to now is 65 years. We must make the U.S. Mortalist Regime at least responsible for the deaths incurred in these 65 years as a result of lack of health care. This means 450,000 a decade multiplied by 6.5 decades. This comes out to about 2.9 million American deaths.

20 **Almost three million needless, premature, outrageous American deaths.** Directly and intentionally caused by a System which denies health care, a basic human right recognized in Article 25 of the Universal Declaration of Human Rights of 1948, a human right which Mao's China and Castro's Cuba fullfilled its obligations to with flying colors. (See Chapter on 110 Year YouthSpan)

21 **This roughly 3 million deaths meted out by the U.S. Mortalist System does not include the "excess" deaths resulting from the U.S. ALE (Average Life Expentancy) which is behind Japan by 4.4 years, and behind Sweden and Spain by 2.7 years, and is even lagging behind Castro's Cuba now.**

22 **In ALE, the U.S. now ranks a dismal and shameful #38.**

23 So this almost 3 million U.S. deaths is only a small part of the Systemic Homicide perpetrated by the U.S. Death Society. And this is merely one Death Society.

Seriously Under-Insured Body Count Adds Another 45,000 Dead?

24 These 45,000 deaths every year from lack of health care, and the almost 3 million deaths from lack of health care since 1945, do not count the big number and high percentage of Americans who have **seriously inadequate health insurance. The seriously under-insured.** Many of whom are working middle class. Most with only token health insurance.

25 A 1995 study found at least **19% of the non-elderly U.S. population are under-insured when confronted with a catastrophic illness. Another study found the seriously under-insured to be as high as 32%.**

26 Seriously inadequate health insurance deters people from seeking medical help, putting it off until they have a life-threatening situation. A cancer that is discovered not in its early stage, but in its late stage. The net effect of serious under-insurance is basically the same as total lack of health insurance: it deprives people of access to health care.

27 This 19% seriously under-insured statistic is shocking as it was for the much-vaunted Clinton boom years. The figure must be higher than 19% today. What with the most serious economic crisis since the Great Depression still roiling. Its high

unemployment, underemployment, slashed income, and high bankruptcies. We are waiting for Harvard Medical School to do another study on how many more deaths result each year from seriously inadequate health insurance coverage.

28 If 15.5% of the U.S. population (Americans without health insurance)results in 45,000 deaths a year, then what would another 19% of Americans (57 million Americans) or another 32% of Americans (96 million Americans) who are seriously under-insured add to this already obscene body count?

29 Surely it is reasonable, even conservative, to estimate another 45,000 dead can be added to this confirmed 45,000 U.S. death toll. This would mean at least 90,000 American deaths each and every year just from the U.S. denying its people universal health care. The guilt for every one of these 45,000 to 90,000 should be laid directly on the U.S. Death Society.

U.S. Refuses Universal Health Care Even Though It's Cheaper

30 Amazing but true. In these days when the U.S. government bellyaches about how its budget deficits (which it created) forces it to slash what little remains of Americans' social services, health care, and employment/retirement security. The Republican Party and a substantial slice of the Democratic Party reject outright the giving of real universal health care to the American people. Even though this would result in the U.S. spending less of its GDP on health care. And benefitting at least 50 million more Americans who are without any health care coverage whatsoever.

31 A Universal Health Care System is cheaper by far than the monstrosity that the U.S. imposes on its longsuffering people. This has been proven by all the E.U. countries with universal health care system like the U.K., France, Germany, Sweden, Norway all of which spend much less of their GDP on health

care than the U.S. And all of which manage to cover their entire population with world-class health care.

32 Per capita heath care spending in many E.U. countries with universal health care is *as low as half of what the U.S. spends per capita.* And yet the U.S. insists on leaving around 50 million Americans out of health care totally, and tens of millions more who can only afford token health insurance.

33 The facts leave us no choice but to conclude that **the U.S. government would rather deny its people universal health care than spend much less of its GDP on health care.**

34 *It is intentional and premeditated.* It has insisted on doing so, against all facts, reason, logic or fiscal responsibility, for well over half a century while the E.U. states have given their citizens universal health care as a basic human right, and have leapfrogged over the U.S. in ALE (Average Life Expectancy).

35 Without any compunction, the American Death Society is still meting out The Genesis Curse of Blood, Sweat & Tears. By, among other things, denying its people universal health care coverage. 15.5% of Americans (almost 50 million) have no health care coverage whatsoever, and probably at least the same percentage and number are inadequately insured. **Young Americans are disproportionately under-insured.**

36 This is why we call the U.S. a Death Society. In fact, it is arguably the most unabashed and extreme of all Death Societies.

Case Study II. **U.S. Kills 8,000 Babies Each Year**

37 U.S. – 6.8 deaths per 1,000 live births

Cuba – 4.4 deaths per 1,000

Sweden – 2.3 deaths per 1,000 live births

Source: The World Bank, WDI and GDF 2010

What do these figures mean?

38 Let the U.S. National Center for Health Statistics tell us. It calculated in a 2009 report and analysis that "If the United States had Sweden's distribution of births by gestational age, nearly *8,000 infant deaths would be averted each year* and the U.S. infant mortality rate would be one-third lower." (Mac-Dorman MF, Mathews TJ. Behind international rankings of infant mortality: How the United States compares with Europe. NCHS data brief, no 23. Hyattsville, MD: National Center for Health Statistics. 2009)

39 But since 2004, the U.S. infant mortality rate has gotten worse and Sweden has gotten better. Sweden now has an infant mortality rate of only 2.3 and the U.S. has a shocking 6.8 infant deaths per 1,000 live births. This means that the U.S. Death Society, with its intentional lack of universal health care, is systemically killing more than 8,000 American babies each year.

40 Where are all the so-called "pro-family" "pro-child" people? Why are they not screaming and damning on this?

41 The infant mortality rate belies the U.S. claim that it is "pro-family" or "pro-children." The only conclusion that could be drawn from 8,000 excess deaths at birth every year is that the U.S. is not really "pro-family" or "pro-children" and in fact is anti-family, anti-babies and anti-life.

42 8,000 per year times ten years equals 80,000 dead babies. Over twenty years, this means 160,000 dead babies. Over thirty years, it means 240,000 dead babies. **Now we need a real "pro-life" movement. And it's called ImmorTalism.**

Case Study III. 4.5 Million Preventable Deaths in Black Americans

43 From 1979 to 1998, the Black-White ratio of age-adjusted, gender-specific mortality increased for all but one of the nine

major causes of death which accounts for over 80% of US mortality.

44 From 1980 to 1998, the average numbers of "excess deaths" every day among African-Americans compared to whites increased by a mind-boggling 20%.

45 **From 1940 to 1999, African Americans suffered 4.3 to 4.5 million "premature deaths" relative to White Americans.**

46 This averages out to *over 76,000 annual deaths* **suffered by Black Americans as a result of Systemic Homicide**.

47 Deep Recession which is a Great Depression for the Black community, the trend for black:white age-adjusted, all-cause mortality and white:black life expectancy is inexorably toward greater disparities and inequalities.

48 What has Barack Obama, the first African-American President, done about this? Where are the voices of the other Black politicians on this life-and-death issues? Why aren't the pulpits of Black churches ringing with denunciations on this? Where are the defenders of Black civil rights?

49 It is a testament to The Mortalist Paradigm that it has convinced Black Americans that such egregious inequality between white-black mortality rate and life expectancies are not political issues. To be accepted as basically "acts of God." Even by black activists and politicians and ministers who would be greatly and rightly aroused over police brutality. But shouldn't they be a million times more riled up over 76,000 deaths a year? More up in arms over 4.5 million deaths?

50 This not by any stretch of the imagination a complete count of the American Death Society's Systemic Homicides. Among other things, we have not included the Systemic Homicides due to the fatal inequality in ALE, between Poor, Middle-Class and Rich Americans. Nor have we included the extremely high infant mortality rate among African Americans which is worse than many Third World nations.

51 Neither have we counted the **Deaths from Smoking in the U.S. — over 400,000 annually.** These must be at the very least partially attributed to the U.S. Death Society. After all, American Presidents, Congresses, and Courts have allowed the nicotine drug cartel free rein. For decades brazen TV advertising and full-page ads claiming there's no proof smoking causes cancer were allowed.

52 Even now, the U.S. Commerce Department is still pushing Third World countries to open wide their markets to U.S. cigarettes. "Free Trade"! "Open Markets"! So the U.S. must be held accountable for a significant part of the tobacco deaths in the rest of the world.

53 Last but not least, we have not counted the premature preventable **"excess" deaths which can be calculated from the U.S. Average Life Expectancy which lags lethally behind Japan by 4.4 years, and 2.7 years behind Sweden and Spain.**

54 Have you heard of the above facts and statistics before? Were there blazing headlines, outpouring of outrage, Congressional hearings, and late night emergency meetings at the White House?

55 No. There were none. It is not news in the U.S. Death Society. Nor was it news in the human-rights organizations. Where are the condemnations and the Hague trials for these Crimes Against Humanity? Let's hear them. Let's call the court to order.

56 Whereas some dirt-poor Third World country might be able to plead poverty as to lack of universal health care, high mortality rate, low life expectancy, high infant mortality, the U.S. has no such excuses to avail of. It has been one of the wealthiest nations on the planet since the start of the twentieth century. This makes its denial of universal health care (a fundamental human right) even more egregious and damning.. And it makes its lower life expectancy, higher infant mortality so much more scandalous and outrageous.

57 Until the U.S. fulfills its obligations on Article 25 of the Universal Declaration of Human Rights and give the American people the health care, employment, and life security guaranteed in the EU, until then the U.S. has no moral right or credibility to pontificate on human rights against any nation.

Case Study IV. **Every 8 Years India Suffers 33 Million Excess Deaths — More than China in 1958 to 1961 Crop Failures**

58 This is the conclusion pointed out by Indian-born Nobel Laureate in Economics Amartya Sen. He wrote: "Finally, it is important to note that *despite the gigantic size of excess mortality in the Chinese famine (of 1958-1961), the extra mortality in India from regular deprivation in normal times vastly overshadows the former.* Comparing India's death rate of 12 per thousand with China's of 7 per thousand, and applying that difference to the Indian population of 781 million in 1986, we get an estimate of *excess normal mortality in India of 3.9 million per year.... (E)very eight years or so more people die in India because of its higher regular death rate than died in China in the gigantic famine of 1958-61.* India seems to manage to fill its cupboard with more skeletons every eight years than China put there in its years of shame." ("The Amartya Sen & Jean Dréze Omnibus," pp. 214-215, Oxford University Press. Italics added.)

59 3.9 million annual excess deaths caused by India's economic-political system from 1950 to 1976 means that India's capitalism and "democracy" caused over 101 million preventable, premature deaths. In other words, in roughly a quarter of a century, Systemic Homicide in India killed over 101 million people.

60 Remember this 101 million death toll from Capitalism is just in one country. In a mere quarter of a century. It does not include the First and Second World Wars. The battles between Capitalist Empires.

61 Noam Chomsky, the MIT professor who is one of the most trenchant analysts of U.S. Capitalism and its empire, has rightly juxtaposed this irrefutable 101 million death toll (from India's Capitalism alone in a mere 26 years) alongside the very inflated Cold-War allegation that the total death toll caused by 20th century Communism was 100 million.

62 Even if we were to accept this Cold-War smear in all our naiveté, it would still pale besides the fact that in just one Capitalist country (India) and in a mere 26 years, the toll of Capitalism was 101 million deaths.

63 This 101 million fact is documented by the Indian government itself, and therefore beyond dispute. And the source which soberly highlights it is impeccable: an Indian-born Nobel Laureate who has taught at Oxford, Cambridge and Harvard. The source for Communism's alleged death toll is rather suspect: some of Capitalism's most vociferous and brazen propagandists.

64 If we go from twenty six to thirty years, it gets worse. From 1950 to 1980, the Systemic Homicide toll in India was an absolutely mind-boggling and unforgivable 117 million deaths.

65 You would think that this would be huge headlines and round-the-clock news in the U.S. and Western Media. But it most assuredly is not. It does not even register a blip on its radar. Even though these facts are fully documented by official Indian government statistics. Even though the damning conclusion above by Professor Sen is to be found in a book published by Oxford University Press, in writings published in prestigious mainstream academic journals. And last but not least, although these facts are presented by no less than an acclaimed winner of the Nobel Prize in Economics.

66 A devastating drought and floods destroyed crops and were the major cause of the Chinese famine of 1958 to 1961. There is more reason to blame Capitalism for the Great Irish Famine (1845-1848), which killed roughly 1 million out of a popula-

tion of 8 million, a much higher proportion than the Chinese famine of 1958-61.

67   Droughts have historically resulted in millions of deaths — some as recently as during the U.S.-supported Chiang Kai Shek regime in wartime Honan (1943-1944), which caused an estimated 5 million deaths. From 1876 to 1879, a famine in Northern China killed 13 million. (The Bengal Famine of 1943 when India was under the British saw 3 million Indians perish.)

68   Anti-communists have tried to pin the entire blame of the famine on Mao's communist policies. But they cannot explain why when there were no catastrophic droughts and floodings, Maoist China managed to grow rice and corn and food to feed the world's largest population — a monumental achievement that China's robber-baron capitalism and dictatorship lauded by the U.S. in the 1920s to 1940s never came close to.

69   At the very time of the Chinese famine, the U.S. continued its ruthless economic embargo on China. This U.S. economic embargo included food. The U.S. was flushed with excess wheat and food and its agriculture was perfectly capable saving every hungry Chinese. The U.S. government knew exactly what was happening in China. But instead of offering to help for humanitarian reasons, it gloated over the Chinese agricultural collapse, and hoped it will lead to the fall of the Communist government. Through its economic embargo, the U.S. refused to sell or give any food to the Chinese people while throwing away and wasting so much food every day. It used food as a political weapon. This modus operandi is used again against North Korea. Under the Geneva Convention definition of culpability for Genocide or War Crimes, this makes the U.S. regime culpable for the millions of excess Chinese deaths caused by famine. The U.S. knew there were millions of hungry or starving Chinese. It had the power to save every single one of them. By offering to sell or give the Chinese government food. Instead, it refused to loosen its deadly economic embargo which included banning any export of food to China. This meant that the U.S. govern-

ment shared with China the culpability for every single Chinese who went hungry or died as a result of lack of food from 1958 to 1961.

70 The Cold-War argument that it is not Nature but Communist policies that caused the Famine of 1958 to 1961 is belied by the fact that except for these three years, China under Maoism managed for the first time in centuries to be self-sufficient in food production.

71 Since China has much less arable land compared to the U.S. and many other countries, and since it has the world's largest number of mouths to feed (at that time one out of every four mouths in the world), this was an awesome accomplishment for Maoist China, second only to its feat of greatly and quickly raising Average Life Expectancy.

72 We have so far accepted uncritically the claim that millions of excess deaths occurred as a result of the historic drought, floods and crop failures between 1958 and 1961. But Professor Wim Wertheim, a respected European China scholar who taught at the University of Amsterdam, had made a very persuasive case that the alleged millions of excess deaths from the crop failures of 1958 to 1961 never happened.

73 Wertheim explained: **"My conclusion is that the claim that in the 1960s a number between 17 [million] and 29 million people was 'missing' is worthless if there was never any certainty about the 600 million Chinese in 1953. Most probably these 'missing people' did not starve in the calamity years 1960-61, but in fact have never existed."** (Bold added)

74 Professor Wertheim pointed out that these extrapolations of "excess deaths" of 14 to 33 million from 1958-61 are based on the disputed 1953 census, which claimed that China's population suddenly grew 150 million people in a mere six years, from 450 million to 600 million.

75 In the next censuses, released by Deng only in the 1980s, there seemed to be tens of millions of Chinese missing. Aha! the an-

ti-Communists and anti-Maoists screamed in glee and unison, this must be the excess deaths from Mao's Great Leap Forward.

76 But the highly-disputed 1953 census claimed the number of Chinese zoomed 33% in a mere six years. This would mean that in six years, China's population supposedly increased by half the size of the current U.S. and E.U. populations!

77 These six years spanned 1947 to 1953, a period which included the bloody last two years of the Chinese Civil War and the entire Korean War where China fought the U.S. These were extremely turbulent, unstable years of revolutionary struggle in which people would usually not feel safe enough about their future to be having unprecedented number of babies.

78 A150 million jump in population in six years has never happened even in the most peaceful and stable periods in Chinese history. And to the best of our knowledge, such a miraculous jump in population has never happened anywhere else or at any time in human history, period. But it is on the cross of this apocryphal 150 million that anti-Maoists have tried to crucify Mao and Communism.

79 Extraordinary claims require extraordinary evidence. Here there is no evidence that can stand up in any court of law that is not of the ideological lynching variety. On the contrary, there is much evidence that this is a Cold-War lie more breathtaking than the U.S. claim that Saddam Hussein's Iraq had weapons of mass destruction.

80 The Japanese invasion and occupation of China in the Second World War was ruthless. It bombed Chinese cities. It used all the weapons of modern war — planes, tanks, artillery, bullets — on the most massive scale with intent to inflict the most damage on the Chinese population. Yet eight years of this systematic, brutal, deliberate carnage could "only" inflict 14 to 20 million deaths. And that stirred Chinese to heroic resistance. But somehow Mao's communist government allegedly inflicted 14 to 33 million deaths in three years and there was

not a whiff of unrest or a flicker of resistance. And, incredibly, word of this never got out until the 1980s.

81 If Professor Wertheim is right, it makes Indian capitalism's systemic homicide of more than 33 million excess deaths every eight years a million times more egregious and damnable. It stands alone. But even if Wertheim is somehow entirely or partially wrong, Nobel Laureate Amartya Sen has already conclusively shown that India's Systemic Homicide every eight years far exceeds whatever deaths occurred in China's years of tribulation, a one-time disaster which has never happened again under Mao or his successors.

CHAPTER 5
Global Heating's Apocalypse Now

1   There's a fly in the ointment.

2   Unlike the Pseudo-ImmorTalists, who believe we are inevitably zooming towards "The Singularity" (whatever that mantra means), we Scientific ImmorTalists, the Real ImmorTalists, do not have our heads in the sand.

3   The data coming in is ominous. The worst-case-scenarios in the Intergovernmental Panel on Climate Change (IPCC) Report (which won the Nobel Peace Prize with Al Gore) turn out to be too optimistic by far.

4   Contrary to the Global-Warming Denialists' smears, the "sin" of the IPCC is not that it is alarmist, or that its science and data about global warming and its effects are disputed or doctored. Rather, the "sin" of the IPCC Reports is that they were not allowed to be as candid, as clear, or as forceful (as the scientific data justifies) in their projections and conclusions about the consequences of global warming. Especially on how soon these negative effects will arrive at our doorsteps.

5   Why is this so? This is because the IPCC Reports were politically negotiated documents, subject to objections and hagglings from the United States, Saudi Arabia, China, or any other nation-state.

6   As the *New York Times* point out, "Even though the (IPCC final) synthesis report is more alarming than its predecessors, some researchers believe that it still understates the trajectory of global warming and its impact." Why? This is because "(t)he IPCC's scientific process, which takes five years of study

and writing from start to finish, cannot take into account the very latest data on climate change or economic trends, which show larger than predicted development and energy...." (*New York Times*, "U.N. Report Describes Risks of Inaction on Climate Change," Nov. 17, 2007)

7   Instead of catastrophe a hundred years from now, we are staring at catastrophe *now*.

8   The IPCC Report projected a 1 to 4 degree C rise in temperature by the end of the twenty-first century. But according to the U.S. own International Energy Agency report, due to the unexpected spike in global emissions, **"if current policies were not changed the world would warm six degrees by 2030, a disastrous increase far higher than the (IPCC) panel's estimates of one to four degrees (rise) by the end of the century."** (New York Times, "U.N. Report Describes Risks of Inaction on Climate Change," Nov. 17, 2007)

9   *What would a 6 degrees C rise mean?*

Dr. James Lovelock, the British climate scientist who formulated The Gaia Theory that the earth's biosphere is like a self-regulating organism, explains that "if global temperatures rise by more than 2.7 degrees C the Greenland glacier will no longer be stable and it will continue melting until most of it is gone..." He continues, "a rise in temperature globally of 4 degrees C is enough to destabilize the tropical rain forests and cause them, like the Greenland ice, to melt away and be replaced by scrub or desert." (p. 51, "The Revenge of Gaia" Lovelock cites Jonathon Gregory et al at Reading University and Hadley Centre's Richard Betts and Peter Cox)

10   *"The world is already at or above the worst case scenarios* in terms of (world carbon) emissions," warns Gernot Klepper of the Kiel Institute for World Economy in Germany. "In terms of emissions, we are moving past the most pessimistic estimates of the I.P.C.C. and by some estimates we are above that red line." (Ibid, NY Times, Nov. 17, 2007, italics added)

11 Dr. James Lovelock is one of England's most respected scientists and one of the world's top public intellectuals. He has an unrivaled record when it comes to warnings about global warming. In the early 1960s, Lovelock already predicted that the number one problem facing the world by the year 2000 would be The Climate.

12 In his latest book, *The Revenge of Gaia*, Dr. Lovelock forecasts that **extreme weather patterns will be the norm by 2020. By 2040, most of Europe would have turned into desert. And major cities like New York and London will be submerged by rising sea waters.**

13 According to a 2008 *Guardian* interview, "Lovelock believes global warming is now irreversible, and that nothing can prevent **large parts of the planet (from) becoming too hot to inhabit, or sinking underwater, resulting in mass migration, famine and epidemics.**"

14 As a result of this, Dr. Lovelock predicts "about **80% of the world's population to be wiped out by 2100.**" And **civilization will collapse**.

15 "Prophets have been foretelling Armaggedon since time began," he says. "But this is the real thing."

16 In the Preface of his book, Dr. Lovelock warns us that "The climate centers around the world, which are the equivalent of pathology labs in hospitals, have reported the Earth's physical condition...as seriously ill and soon to pass into a morbid fever..."

17 "I have to tell you," he continues, "....civilization is in grave danger."

18 "(B)efore this century is over, billions of us will die..."

19 Once we pass the tipping points (as more and more climatologists think we are approaching or have passed) and plunge into the hell that is The Scorched Earth Era, how long will it last before the biosphere returns to "normalcy"?

20 Based on what we know to have happened fifty-five million years ago, during the Eocene Era, Dr. Lovelock estimates that this Morbidly Fevered Earth would last at least **100,000 years.**

21 As alarmist as that may have sounded just ten years ago, it now sounds entirely, terrifyingly, possible. Consider these developments:

- The **Pine Island Glacier** in West Antarctica, which holds about 10% of the Antarctic Ice Sheet, is showing "dramatically large" changes. In other words, it is becoming unstable. Robert Bindschadler, NASA's leading expert in the dynamics of glaciers and ice sheets, is very worried. Why? "If you were to ask what the collapse of a marine-based ice sheet would look like, our answer would be accelerating (ice) flow, thinning ice, and retreating margins. And this is exactly what we're seeing in Pine Island Glacier. When you put the two together, you think, 'My goodness! Could this be the initial chapter of the collapse of the West Antarctic Ice Sheet?'"

22 In February 2008, British scientists in Antarctica discovered a new "sensational finding:" the Pine Island Glacier which caused concern in the 1990s for accelerating 1% a year into the ocean is now accelerating 7% in a single season, dumping so much more of its ice into the ocean. The BBC reported the scientists' conclusion: "if the trend continues…it could lead to a significant rise in global sea level."

23 How serious is this? The BBC reported that the British Antarctic Survey's David Vaughan now "believes that the risk of a major collapse of this section of the West Antarctic ice sheet should be taken seriously." This is shocking. Not too long ago, scientists expected these glaciers to last at least centuries, if not millennia.

24 And what would a collapse of the Pine Island glacier – one third of the West Antarctic Ice Sheet – mean? It would mean a worldwide sea level rise of 1.5 meters. Or 4 and 1/2 feet.

25 If the other two-thirds of the West Antarctic Ice Sheet collapses? Dr. Robert Bindschadler, NASA's distinguished expert on glaciers, has the answer for us. "(T)he latest study… came up with about 3.5 meters of sea level rise." That's three and a half meters. Or 11 and a half feet. (Jan 6, 2010 Interview in International Polar Foundation. Underline added)

26 1.5 meters in sea level rise would be disastrous, but 3.5 meters would be apocalyptic. And what's mind-boggling: it could happen anytime now.

40 Feet Rise in Sea Waters?

27 In its fourth and final "Synthesis," the Intergovernmental Panel on Climate Change (IPCC) for the first time lists some of the "extreme" scenarios which are "less likely." This includes the total melting of the ice sheets in Greeland and West Antarctica. The IPCC's scientists confess that their computer models are poor at predicting such an event. They did not predict the unexpectedly torrid melting that scientists at the frontline have recently witnessed in, for example, the Pine Island Glacier. The IPCC Synthesis Report also did not anticipate that instead of global temperature spiking by at most 4 degrees Celsius by 2100 that we would be on track to rack up a temperature rise of 6 degrees Celsius by 2030. Which if our best studies are correct would melt the ice sheets in Greeland and Western Antarctica completely.

28 As the *New York Times* noted gingerly, and almost at the tail end of its article, **"If these areas melt entirely, seas would rise 40 feet,** scientists said." ("U.N. Report Describes Risks of Inaction on Climate Change," *New York Times,* Nov. 17, 2007)

Thermosphere Shrinks 30%

29 The Thermosphere, the upper layer of earth's atmosphere, has shrank by a stunning 30% in only two years. From 2007 to 2009. What can cause the Thermosphere's contraction? Aside from the sun's activity, contraction can be caused by an increase in carbon dioxide, which has a cooling effect at such a high altitude. Why is this Thermasphere important? It protects us from harmful ultraviolet rays by blocking it like a good pair of sunglasses. So now when Planet Earth is zapped by ultraviolet rays, it will be at least 30% less shielded which makes us mortals that much more exposed and at risk for melanoma (a type of skin cancer). In the past decades, we have witnessed a sharp rise in skin cancer. Expect this lethal trend to greatly worsen.

Note: The CNN report ignores this obvious danger. It claims "Changes in thermosphere won't affect life on the surface but can affect satellites." All the U.S. Death Society can fret about is the threat to its military spy satellites.

30 Disaster is beckoning. And it is not in the distant future. Not a hundred years from now, which would still be a blink in evolutionary time. We're talking about catastrophe which could happen any day now. And come as swiftly as Hurricane Katrina hit New Orleans.

31 We're talking Apocalypse. And Apocalype Now.

It's impossible for a real ImmorTalist
not to care about Global Warming.

Just as it's impossible for a real ImmorTalist not to be in
solidarity with mortals struggling with cancer, heart
disease, stroke, and all the other major killer-diseases.

CHAPTER 6
Short-Lived Capitalist Mortals Destroy Planet in 200 Years

1   It's come to this. We are facing the most serious threat to our civilization and to the survival of our species.

2   And the response of most governments in the world thus far? See no evil. Hear no evil. And do nothing.

3   But first, we must ask *how did we come to this point?* What brought us to the edge of the abyss?

4   *We must pinpoint the source of the problem if we are to arrive at an effective solution.* If we don't, we will keep repeating the cause of the problem and adding injury to grievous injury upon the biosphere which is heating up to a boil against us.

Capitalist Industrialization Destroys Planet in 200 Years

5   In a mere two centuries, Capitalist Industrialization (Capitalism plus Industrialization) has succeeded in doing what no other economic system ever came close to doing. It has stirred up human-made Global Warming (heating!) to such an extent that it threatens not only civilization as we know it, but also the existence of our very species Homo Sapiens, as well as 70% or more of all other living species.

6   This fact is irrefutable. It is not just humanity or civilization that is causing Global Warming. It is Capitalist Industrializa-

tion. All humans are not equally culpable for Global Warming. Neither are nations equally culpable. And neither are economic systems and their industrializations equally culpable for Global Warming.

7   The carbon emissions statistics cannot be more clear and clearcut. It is not the poor Third World countries which have done it. It is not emerging China and India who have done it. It is not the Soviet Union which did it. It is surely not the Africans, North Koreans, Vietnamese or the Cubans. For at least the past two hundred years, and especially in the Pax Americana of the past 65 years, the Capitalist Western Industrialized states have been disproportionately to blame for most of the carbon emissions which has now led to the emergency crisis point we are staring at. China, with 20% of the world's population, after centuries is now catching up finally in total carbon emissions to the U.S., with 5% of the world's population. This does not transfer the guilt to China, but in fact spotlights where the guilt lies squarely.

8   Therefore, we use the term "Capitalist Industrialization" to distinguish it from other forms of Industrialization. For example, the rapid industrialization of the Soviet Union was achieved under another model. It was successful enough to enable the Soviets to decimate Hitler's armed forces during World War II much more than either the U.S. or Great Britain did.

9   The initial Industrialization of China — from 1949 to 1976 — was achieved under the Maoist model of self-reliance and without foreign capital or investments. Before their deaths, Mao and Zhou En Lai started in motion a 25-Year-Plan to transform China into a first-rank industrialized state by the year 2000. Maoist industrialization laid a strong foundation for today's 21st century China. This is the persuasive conclusion of Professor Maurice Meisner in his authoritative book "Mao's China and After," which *Foreign Affairs* magazine, published by the Council on Foreign Relations, concluded is

one of the few books on contemporary China which will stand the test of time.

10 During the Cold War, the U.S. routinely bragged about how much more advanced its industrialization was and derided the Soviet and Chinese industrializations as primitive.

11 **But whatever shortcomings or however "laggardly" the Soviet, Chinese Maoist, Iranian Islamist, or Castroite Cuban model for industrialization may be as compared to the U.S. model, one fact is crystal clear: all the other industrializations contributed much less to the world's carbon emissions than has the United States.**

12 Therefore, Socialist Industrialization and Islamic industrialization were much less culpable for Global Warming than the Capitalist Industrializations which occurred in the U.S., Great Britain, France, Germany, the Netherlands, and other Western nations.

13 This may be quite jarring for the values and beliefs many of us hold, but there is no denying this. And when the worst of global warming has kicked in, how will history judge the other non-capitalist models of industrialization? Probably much more benignly that it will judge the Western Capitalist model.

Capitalism's "Dominion" Theology

14 Judaeo-Christianity has programmed Western industrialized nations with the belief from the book of Genesis that God has given the chosen "dominion" over the planet. To plunder and pillage as they wish.

14A "And God blessed them, and God said to them, 'Be fruitful and multiply, and fill the earth and *subdue* it; and have **dominion** over the fish of the sea and over the birds of the air and over every living thing that moves upon the earth." — Genesis 1.28

15 "Dominion" theology is not merely the core belief of Reconstructionist Fundamentalist Christianity which aims to turn the U.S. into a theocracy ruled by Old Testament laws. It is also a core belief and teaching of triumphalist Capitalism. And what is U.S. Capitalism but a secular version of this dominion theology?

16 Capitalism has invoked and executed this "divine" license and "order" as if it were issued yesterday by Yahweh at the New York Stock Exchange.

17 In less than three centuries, Capitalism has truly taken dominion over the Planet, not to mention subdue it. Since its triumph in the Second World War, **the Grey Goo of U.S.-style Capitalism** has spread like the most virulent of viruses. And since the collapse of the Soviet Union, Pax Americana's New World Order of Globalization has been virtually unchallenged. Intensifying its global carbon emissions as though there's no tomorrow.

18 And the result? Global Heating. Biodiversity Collapse. The Sixth Great Mass Extinction of species. All these are the current horror flicks of Mortalist capitalism which insists on cancerous growth and profits even if it means Death.

19 Since 1977, Big Oil and the Republican Party have been pushing to drill for oil in the Arctic National Wildlife Refuge (ANWR), the largest protected wilderness in the United States. This is a most glaring example of Capitalism's Dominion Theology. It is also a million times more idiotic and short-sighted than the Genesis story of Esau giving up his inheritance for a bowl of pottage as he was temporarily hungry. This is the only Arctic refuge that 300 million plus Americans will need when global warming starts making large chunks of the U.S. unbearably hot.

Why Capitalism Cannot Solve Global Warming

20 During the Cold War, the U.S. government and its media mocked the 5 Year Plans of the Soviet Union and China as "centralized economic planning" which it claimed did not work. It touted as a virtue the fact that it had no such government longterm economic planning. And true enough, Capitalism is an economic System which cares only about the next Quarterly Earnings Reports. Its political system's office-chasers and office-holders can only think as far as the next election, and their myopic vision extends only two years, four years, at most five or six years down the road.

21 But what is Global Heating loudly telling us? That we need governments and societies capable of making and implementing not merely 5 year plans, but 100-year-plans. If the human species is to have any viable future on this Earth.

22 But at present, there are no governments which make plans for more than a few years. If there were, we would have taken effective worldwide measures since the 1960s and would not be in such dire straits. But no government did. So we are in serious harm's way, hurtling towards a global heat stroke which we have stoked, and which could linger for 100,000 years.

23 *This is the curse of Mortalist states run by short-lived or aged mortals. They cannot see any further than the next election, the next quarterly profits reports, the next employment statistics, the next GDP figures.*

24 We need ImmorTalist States and Societies if we are to beat Global Heating and cure Disease, Old Age & Death. It is the myopia of short-lived mortals which threatens to kill off our species. And most other species.

25 But we also need a Civilization which is not schizophrenic about Death. We need a Civilization which is for Life and against Death, period.

26 For example, if starting in the 1960s, the U.S. government decided to discourage fossil-fueled private cars by taxing them and gasoline heavily, if it had encouraged public transportation by subsidizing it heavily and making it faster, omnipresent, more convenient, and dirt-cheap, that might have made a big difference.

27 Instead, the U.S. government opted for Detroit's cars and eternal bondage to fossil fuel. Washington decided to build a great highway system starting in the 1920s. To get every American to own a car. And then to get every American family to own two cars. The U.S. then advertised and exported this idea of two cars per family to the rest of the world. It was "the American way of life." The Good Life. And now that too many of the 1.3 billion Chinese have bought into this lifestyle, the U.S. is now denouncing China for catching up to the U.S. on carbon emissions. How dastardly indeed! Suddenly the U.S. is all pious about how China's path is unsustainable and will lead to disaster.

28 **So the U.S. has finally admitted that if China, India, and the rest of the world mimic the so-called "American way of life" of two cars per family, a big house using enough electricity to light an Indian village, overconsumption of food (burgers, steaks, red meat) — if the whole world buys into the American (<u>capitalist</u>) way of life, then the nightmare scenario of global heating's rise by 6 degrees would be upon us by 2030. And Civilization as we know it would be drowned or heat-stroked. Now the U.S. tells us!**

29 The U.S. system prided itself on a laissez-faire economy, allowing capitalists and capital free rein with as little government regulation or planning as possible.

30 We can easily see now how such a System gets us into this Global Scorching mess. But how, pray tell, can such a System possibly get us out of our dire straits?

31 Capitalism's primary motivation is Profit. To put it bluntly, Greed. "Greed is Good," as the Gordon Gekko character preached in the movie "Wall Street." And as the U.S. and its TV "news" networks, its advertising and its movies still evangelize 24 hours a day in every corner of the globe. The Capitalist belief is: Everyone being greedy somehow inevitably ends up in everyone's best interest. Go figure. It's as unfathomable as The Trinity or Trickle-Down Economics.

32 Profit is the most powerful incentive, the greatest motivator, according to Capitalism. It is the best way to get anything done. The best way to get anyone to do anything.

33 Capitalist states and capitalists would like to pay the poor to die for them. And of course the poor in each Mortalist state are the cannon fodder of choice. But they do so more for love of country than for love of money.

34 Can money get people to die for an Empire and its wars? From Korea to Vietnam to Iraq to Afghanistan, we see that U.S. soldiers, among the best paid in the world, are none too eager to die for their country. This is progress. And this encouraging life-loving phenomenon is seen even more in other Western nations. Even the Germans and the Japanese, who were all too eager to immolate themselves in the last war. (But then the Germans died for Hitler, and the Japanese died for Emperor, not for filthy lucre.)

35 Today, even the most "patriotic" of Rambos demand to be outfitted in bullet-proof vests. They emerge from their bunkers only in heavily-armored vehicles. And they travel only in convoys. And even in the daytime, they never are foolish enough to venture out alone like Rambo. On the other hand, the Communists, the Iraqi resistance, and the Taliban seem to have an endless supply of young fighters who were or are willing to sacrifice their lives for little or no money at all. So the record clearly contradicts the Capitalist Dogma: money is not enough to get people to die for the U.S. in its wars.

36 The evidence is overwhelming and undeniable that most of the carbon emissions dumped into the atmosphere which created the global heating was spewed out by the U.S. first and foremost, followed by other Western capitalist industrialized nations.

37 So how does Capitalism and Profit solve the planet-threatening problem of global heating when it created the problem in the first place?

38 Capitalism's insatiable need for a never-ending increase in productivity, profits and markets, its dread and punishment of any slowdown in profits, its lust for profits, its belief that when an economy stops growing or contracts it must be in a bad way, in a "recession," worse, a "depression." This is the economic and political system which has fueled the most carbon emissions in all of human history.

39 Constant growth is demanded by Capitalism. Constant replication of its products, its services, its markets, its economy. But just as cancer is basically runaway replication of cells, so too capitalism's insatiable lust for growth and replication has turned out to be cancerous and toxic for our biosphere, for humans, and for most other species on our planet. The symptom of this cancer is Global Warming and its portents.

40 To insist that Capitalism which created the problem is also the solution is like admitting that gluttony causes morbid obesity, but insisting it's also the cure. But even those in the U.S. who readily admit to global warming and recognize the lopsided role played by the U.S., even they often fall for this dogmatic delusion that the mystical all-knowing all-powerful "market" with its "profit motive" can somehow solve global warming. No, it can't!

41 The second reason why we've come to this point: *Mortals with an average lifespan of eighty or less make very bad environmentalists.*

42 Short-lived mortals claim to care what happens to the earth after they are dead. But of course they don't. Because they don't expect to be around. In other words, they don't have long enough life expectancy to care about humans on Earth a year after they are dead, much less to worry that it could take up to 100,000 years for the biosphere to recover from its global-warming-induced fever.

43 This may be especially true and dangerously so in the case of someone like Dick Cheney, former Vice President under Bush Jr. A Dr. Strangelove clone.

44 Aside from being an oil man (CEO of Halliburton), Cheney was, is also a marked man, stalked by a long history of serious heart attacks. Cheney most probably does not expect to be around in the year 2040, or even 2020. So how can we trust someone who's a discredited retread from the Ford administration (1974-76), who presided over the fleeing of U.S. forces from Vietnam, to care about solving our global warming problem? Another case in point: Ronald Reagan when he was President, in his seventies, inching towards the average life expectancy, how could we expect him to be worried about global warming? He was more interested in the fundamentalist belief in the Second Coming of Christ so that he could cheat Death and be taken straight to the pearly gates. Subconsciously, these ailing or aged leaders probably feel if they have to go, then why should we stay and tarry?

45 The reality is: most humans care about their toothache today more than about global warming which could destroy civilization thirty years from now. They care more about their own retirement than that Homo Sapiens and other species might face extinction.

46. They may insist otherwise, but their behavior speaks louder than their words. Would people who really care about Planet Earth even twenty years from now have done what they have done to it?

CHAPTER 7
Expropriate The Denialists
LIMBAUGH, BECK & O'REILLY

1 The Global Warming Denialists are worse than the Holocaust Deniers. A million times worse!

2 History will never forget: the biggest Global-Heating Denier was the U.S. government under Bush-Cheney. It denied global warming existed almost up to its bitter final days in office.

3 History will also never forget nor forgive The Deniers. Nor will it ever forget or forgive *their Appeasers*.

4 The feckless or demagogic politicians, profiles in cowardice, who kowtowed to the Denialists, they will go down in history with more infamy than the appeasers of The Third Reich.

5 The U.S. and Western media is deeply complicit. By not taking the Bush-Cheney regime to task for its denial of global warming, for its refusal to sign the Kyoto Accord. For not asking the tough questions at each White House press conference. For following the lead of *Fox "News"* (the U.S. answer to Pravda). For following *The Drudge Report*, *The Sunday Telegraph* and Murdoch's *Times of London* without exercising its good judgment and discretion.

6 **It's worse than yelling Fire in a crowded theater. It's like announcing "No fire. Relax. Stay in your seats." In a soothing authoritative voice over the public address system. When a deadly fire smolders behind the thick velvet curtains and prepares to leap on its falsely-reassured victims.**

7 Is this Free Speech? Or is it the most heinous Crime Against Humanity?

8 As the *New York Times* and *Washington Post* with their cache of Pulitzer-Prizes should have known, the so-called "Climate-Gate" was all a brazenly-scripted Big Lie. Courtesy of *The Times of London* (owned by Rupert Murdoch) and *The Sunday Telegraph* (the "house newspaper of the Conservative Party").

9 Yet all the mainstream U.S. and European media played along, bestowing credence and obscenely generous print space and air time. It would be like they gave equal time to the Holocaust Deniers. Now that's an idea? Presumably this thought has never crossed their minds. And rightly so!

10 Doesn't Big Media have any good judgment or power of discretion left?

10A A smokescreen and smear trumpeted by Rupert Murdoch's Fox "News" and its ilk just before the Copenhagen Talks. What obvious timing. And now that such a transparent ploy was allowed to help destroy the Copenhagen Talks — our last chance? — there is no apology even after the clearing of the libelled scientists by an objective independent scientific review panel. Such is the wretched world we live in today.

11 When Pine Island Glacier collapses, and the sea waters swallow our trophy cities and densest population centers, The Elixxir Society shall hunt down the criminal Denialists. We the People shall try them for Crimes Against Humanity and Crimes Against the Planet. And we shall expropriate their properties as compensation for the incalculable and lethal damage they have conspired to wreak on our species and our planet. Not to mention countless millions of human lives lost.

- **Yes, Elixxir Society will use "Asset Forfeiture" laws against the ill-gotten gains of Rush Limbaugh, Glenn Beck, O'Reilly (who are against the Kyoto Accord), and all the other Major Denialists.** They are not journalists. They are propagandists who are outrageously paid to make sure nothing is done about Global Heating. **We shall put them <u>and their Puppeteers and Paymasters</u> on the dock at The Hague for the biggest of Crimes Against Humanity. And for commission of Crimes against the Planet.**

(Note: The U.S., U.K. and Ireland all have laws allowing the state to indulge in the practice of "asset forfeitures" (i.e. confiscation of property). This was supposed to be used in criminal dope prosecutions which presumably the likes of Rush Limbaugh, Glenn Beck and O'Reilly heartily approve. But "asset forfeiture" is actually, shockingly, used more often in civil cases. In the Texas town of Tenaha, for example, police have used the state forfeiture law to seize property from innocent motorists (mostly Blacks and Latinos of course). Even though not charged with any crime, their confiscated property or cash were never returned. We shall not stoop to such abuses worthy of a repressive Death Society. No, an ImmorTalist state will only use "Asset Forfeiture" for Crimes against Humanity and Crimes against the Planet.)

12 But we must each take individual responsibility too. If the ordinary Germans in Hitler's Third Reich are to be blamed because they knew or should have known about the concentration camps, then how much more blameable are we? The glaciers, the Alps, the Himalayas have been melting for decades. The Pine Island Glacier is starting to collapse before our eyes! How can we not have seen or heard of it?

13 Al Gore and the IPCC (Intergovernmental Panel on Climate Change) have gotten their Nobel Peace Prize quite a few years ago. Hurricanes like Katrinas are unleashed with more and more fury and frequency across the globe. The earth's temperature has been going up for more than a century.

14 How could we possibly not know? Our descendants, eking out a subsistence life on a wretched stir-fried planet, would rain down condemnation on us if we don't do something effective, soon.

15 *Just as ignorance of the law is no excuse, even more so ignorance of global heating is no excuse.* Especially since the ice
and glaciers everywhere, especially in the Antarctic, is melting before our very eyes.

16 The ordinary Germans in the Third Reich claimed they did
not know. Well, concentration camps were more hidden than
glaciers melting and less reported. So if one's excuse is one
was confused by the foxy propaganda of Limbaugh, Beck
& O'Reilly, that won't do. The Germans in the Third Reich
could have claimed they were bamboozled by the propaganda
of Herr Hitler and Goebbels too. But Anglo-Saxon historians
claimed, and rightly so, that that was untenable.

Let's Play Extreme Russian Roulette

17 The Denialists' argument is that we should not do anything
about global warming until we are 100% sure that there is
global warming and that it is created by human activity.

18 If this argument has a familiar ring, it is because the U.S. Tobacco Industry employed a similar and very successful argument for decades insisting that there was no scientific proof
that smoking causes cancer, and that until we are 100% certain of that, there should be no government regulation on the
advertising, sale, or distribution of cigarettes.

19 Yes, the Global Warming Denialists are using exactly the same
modus operandi that the U.S. Tobacco Industry used. To lure
countless young people to take up smoking or the older to
continue smoking. Despite overwhelming scientific evidence
and medical warnings.

20 Since the 1990s, we know from the the tobacco industry's in-
house research and memos that it knew from the 1960s just
how big a health hazard tobacco was. And yet despite this, it
went on confusing the public about how there's no clear evidence and how it is a matter of choice and freedom.

21 The people in the 1960s who fell for the argument that they must have 100% certainty that smoking causes cancer or heart disease before they will give it up…well, they are dead or mostly dead. And that is precisely what will happen to us should we be so foolish as to fall for the Denialists' devilish argument.

22 The same bad result will happen if we insist on doing something only if and when there is 100% certainty of Global Warming's consequences. By then that our coastal cities will be flooded. Severe weather like Hurricane Katrina will become the norm. Sea waters will rise a couple of feet or meters. Tsunamis will multiply. Large parts of Europe will become Saharan. The only way we can be 100% sure of these disastrous consequences is to wait until they happen.

23 Through their grip on Washington and by rejecting the Kyoto Accord, by wrecking The Copenhagen Summit, by getting the U.S. Senate to kill the Climate bill, *The Denialists are forcing us, the human species, to play Russian Roulette on Global Warming.*

24 In Russian Roulette, there are six cylinders in the gun, and *only* one bullet. But a sane person who somewhat values his or her life and is neither depressed nor drunk would usually say No, thanks. The odds may be only one in six, but since the risk is total catastrophe (blowing brains out), he or she will pass.

25 But the Global Warming Denialists' game of Russian Roulette is even more egregious. Instead of the one-out-of-six odds that you will blow your brains, in the case of global warming, the odds are more like five-out-of-six that you will spill brains. It's like loading five bullets in that gun, and only one cylinder is empty, only one cylinder has no bullet. And you are to bet your dear life on that one cylinder.

26 Would you take such odds when your life is at stake? Of course not. And yet on Global Warming, we are accepting much worse than 5 out of 6 odds. Amazingly, we are surrendering

to such odds when not only our lives and future, but that of the entire human species, and the entire planet, are at stake.

27 Why are the odds worse than five out of six in this Global Warming Russian Roulette? Because the scientific evidence that there is global warming and it is human-made is overwhelming. As Al Gore pointed out there were 928 peer-reviewed articles on climate change published in scientific journals in the decade before his book came out. And out of this 928, the percentage of articles doubting the human cause of global warming was zero. ("An Inconvenient Truth," p. 262)

28 The only question is how catastrophic and how probable and how soon are its consequences. There is near-total scientific unanimity among climate scientists that the consequences would be very serious indeed. The probability that they will happen is at least 90% or more. And sooner than we expect.

29 So these are totally unacceptable risks for any human, much less an ImmorTalist.

30 In fact, these would be normally, legally, unacceptable risks even in most Western affluent Mortalist states.

31 As Sir Martin Rees, the Royal Society Professor at Cambridge University, a Fellow of King's College, and England's Astronomer Royal, points out in his recent book "Our Final Hour":

32 "UK government guidelines on radiation hazards deem it unacceptable that even the limited group of workers in a nuclear station should risk more than *one chance in one hundred thousand* per year of dying through the effects of radiation exposure." (italics added) ("Our Final Hour," by Martin Rees, p. 129, Basic Books, 2003)

33 On Global Warming, you and I and our loved ones are forced to accept risk of over 90% probability of life-threatening civilization-collapsing apocalypse which kill not only us, but billions of humans worldwide. There is no Russian Roulette game so unacceptable or so unwinnable.

∞

Elixxir Society will use "Asset Forfeiture" Laws against the ill-gotten gains of Rush Limbaugh, Glenn Beck, and all the other Major Global-Warming Denialists.

We shall put them *and their Puppeteers and Paymasters* in the dock at The Hague for the biggest of Crimes Against Humanity. And for *The* Crime against the Planet.

∞

CHAPTER 8

The Obvious Solution to Global Heating

Per Capita Carbon Emission? Never Heard!

1   Per Capita Carbon Emission and the Percentage Share of World Carbon Emissions are what's essential. They are the keys to apportioning responsibility and, yes, blame. To finding out who is more a cause of the problem, and who is less so.

2   Even *The New York Times*,*Washington Post* and *CNN* act as if they have never heard of per capita carbon emissions before. But ...

   • The U.S. Department of Energy's Energy Information Agency compiles Per Capita Carbon Emissions data. And its 2008 data reveals that **the Per Capita Emissions of the U.S. is 19.18 Tons/Capita while China's Per Capita Emissions is an extremely low 4.91.**

   • The **U.S.** with 5% of the world's population is culpable for **20% of the world's total carbon emissions.** This is nothing new. It has spewed out a disproportionate percentage of the world's total carbon emissions since the end of the Second World War. And even before that. **China, with 20% of world's population, is now for the first time ever culpable for 22% of the world's carbon emissions.** (Source: U.S. Dept of Energy, Carbon Dioxide Information Analysis Center)

   • **India** is castigated along with China by the U.S. and its media. But India has a rock-bottom **Per Capita Emissions of 1.31**, one of the lowest in the world. Even though

India is 17% of the world population, it is culpable for only 5.5% of the world's total carbon emissions. No wonder India was furious at being so unfairly accused.

3   These are not Chinese "Communist" doctored data mind you. They are the official data compiled by the U.S. government's Department of Energy and widely available on the Internet to any print or TV or new media journalist — including Fox, Rush Limbaugh, or Glenn Beck — with the click of a mouse.

4   The only thing the U.S. has been more than eager to do is to blame China and India, which have ridiculously low per capita carbon emissions and percentage share of world carbon emissions compared to the U.S. This is geopolitics on a sinking Titanic.

5   As **Al Gore**, the former U.S. Vice President who won the Nobel Peace Prize for publicizing global warming, pointed out in his book "An Inconvenient Truth."

"If you compare the per capita carbon emissions in China, India, Africa, Japan, the EU, and Russia to those in the United States, it is obvious...that we are way, way above everyone else."

6   If Gore understands what per capita carbon emissions is, then certainly this basic concept is not beyond the grasp of the U.S. delegation to Copenhagen led by Obama.

7   Just as their Mortalist Governments *know*, so does the U.S. and Western Media. And history's judgment will be implacable indeed.

8 This game of scapegoating China and India for the lion's share of Global Warming is Machiavellian and Orwellian. Not to mention criminal because it poisons the negotiation table with distrust. So this Big Lie prevents nailing down where the biggest and most disproportionate sources of the problem lies.

9   Instead of making an emergency last-ditch effort to prevent the hellish nightmares of global warming, our so-called "lead-

ers" are playing the game of five-year-olds in telling mother "He did it!" "No, she did it!" "No, he did it more than I!"

10 Blest with blissful ignorance of Per Capita Carbon Emissions, the U.S. Media keeps on pretending that it is utterly fair to demand that China with over 4 times the U.S. population (1.3 billion people versus the U.S.' 300 million) — should be forced to restrict itself to the same carbon emissions spat out by the U.S.

Who Killed The Copenhagen Climate Summit?

11 The Chinese government and people see this demand as an all-too-transparent scheme to make sure China never catches up to the U.S. is somehow beyond the comprehension of the U.S. Big Media, despite all its Pulitzers.

12 China, India and the rest of the poor Third World saw the U.S. demands in Copenhagen to be in extreme bad faith, insolent, and completely unacceptable.

13 It is to Al Gore's credit that he had the guts and honesty to publicly denounce the U.S. for obstructing progress in Bali preparing for the Copenhagen Summit. Of course this was in December 2007, in the waning days of the Bush-Cheney regime. The *CNN* story's headline said "Gore: U.S. Blocking Climate Talks." The bone of contention? The Dec. 12, 2007 CNN story's summary points explained: "EU, developing nations favor specific target ranges for emissions; U.S. disagrees." In other words, the U.S. wanted and wants a toothless tiger.

14 Contrary to his promise of "transformation," to the discredit of his Nobel Peace Prize, Obama (as he has done in Iraq and Afghanistan) merely continues Bush Junior's ultra-cynical posturings, distractions, and scapegoatings on the Global Warming issue.

15 *Fronting for the U.S. Empire, Barack Obama went to Copen-hagen hyping an empty fraudulent offer and coupled it with outrageous demands. He knew full well that this unsavory combination would be totally unacceptable and would sink the last-hope summit. And it did.*

16 China, India and the Third World were totally unimpressed with Obama's offer. They knew he could not guarantee that the U.S. Congress, even though controlled in both houses by Democrats then, would pass any Global Warming legislation, no matter how watered down.

17 As it turned out, China, India and the Third World were totally vindicated in spurning Obama's fraudulent offer. Because as we know, the lame Global Warming bill died a very ignoble death in the then Democratic-controlled Senate. (See "Senate Democrats Abandon Comprehensive Climate Bill," *Washington Post*, July 22, 2010)

18 Make an insult-offer and couple it with egregious demands that you know would be deal-breakers. Then when the other side balks, blame them for breaking up the negotiations or for sinking the Copenhagen Summit. This is a well-known gambit. Anyone with any experience in negotiations has come across such cynical players.

19 Of course if the U.S. per capita emissions over the past 60 or so years is perfectly acceptable as a side effect of Capitalism's much-touted "American way of life," then China's eventually spewing out 4 times that amount must be perfectly acceptable too. After all, China is merely embracing "the American way of life" which the U.S. has exported to China and most of the world as a God-given right.

20 The U.S. and the West have been furiously dumping carbon emissions into our atmosphere over centuries of industrialization. Now Johnny-come-lately China, with fourfold the U.S. population, finally catches up since last year in Gross Carbon

Emissions, and the U.S. and Western Media cries "Aha! Foul! You're the devil!"

21 But Washington's Department of Energy reveals that actually China is still very much a laggard when it comes to Per Capita Carbon Emissions and Percentage Share of World Total Carbon Emissions.

22 But the U.S. wants to con the world into believing that overnight China and India are entirely to blame for all the global warming the U.S. and the West have seen fit to produce over many centuries of take-no-prisoner capitalist industrialization.

A Green China?

23 The truth is: much of China's carbon emissions is the result of products that it manufactures for the U.S. market. So that Americans can continue to enjoy cheap consumer goods and maintain their "living standards" despite wages which have stagnated since the 1970s.

24 China's industrialization is far greener than Western Industrialization at this stage of the game. Yes, it's true that many Chinese cities are so polluted in air, water, and many other ways. But so were London and New York at this stage. All you have to do is read Charles Dickens' novels.

25 At this point in their Industrializations, neither the British or the American Empire had implemented a 5-year Plan where the focus was to make its industrialization greener. China has already done so. With substantial results.

26 China is already the world's largest manufacturer of "green" equipments for saving energy, for cleaner, greener energy.

27 This includes Chinese cars!

28 In his book, Al Gore pointed out: "We're told that we have to protect our automobile companies from competition in places

like China where, it is said, their leaders don't care about the environment. In fact, Chinese (car) emissions standards have been raised and already far exceed our own. Ironically we cannot sell cars made in America to China because we don't meet their environmental standards." ("An Inconvenient Truth," page 272)

29 And that book came out in 2006. Perhaps that's one reason why the U.S. has such a deficit in its trade with China.

The Fair & Obvious Solution

30 Each country's Percentage Share of the world carbon emissions must be restricted to its Percentage Share of the world's population.

31 The United States is only 5% of the world's population, but it accounts for at least 20% of the world's carbon emission. This outsized share is not a recent phenomenon. The U.S. has been grabbing an extremely disproportionate share of the world's carbon emissions since after the Second World War.

32 For the last two centuries, the British Empire, the various European empires, and the new-world U.S. Empire were spitting out carbon emissions into the atmosphere as a by-product of their feverish "Industrial Revolution" and their affluent "First World" way of life.

33 China was, for most of this period, not a player at all in this game of carbon emissions. In fact, China's Industrial Revolution did not start in earnest until 1949, when the Communist Revolution finally triumphed.

∞

China's carbon emissions (which for the first time ever stands at 22% of the world's total) is about right for its share of the world's population (20%). It should stay there, or go down a point or two.

Since it is around 5% of the world's population, the U.S. must go down to 5% of the world's carbon emission, instead of its current piggish 20%. Or its prior higher levels since 1945.

∞

CHAPTER 9

How AIDS Got A Billion from Reagan (Why The ImmorTalist Movement)

So how do we get as much — no, more! — government funding than the Iraq and Afghanistan wars for a Real War Against The Real Terrors? To cure Heart Disease, Cancer, Stroke and the top-ten killers in the U.S., in Japan, in Germany, in France, in Scandinavia? And as our population ages, how do we solve its health problems by making anti-aging research a top national funding priority? Here's how from the pages of recent history.

ACT-UP & The Religious Right's Reagan

1   How did a few thousand gay activists force the Reagan regime to increase AIDS funding from zero to almost a billion dollars by the end of its reign in 1988? Yes, the same Reagan who doodled and waltzed while the bodies piled up in the first crucial years of the epidemic. The same regime whose electoral strategy was to bring the "fag"-hating Religious Right into the Republican tent. The same Reagan who refused to even use the word "AIDS" in any official speech in his first term.

2   By the time these pariah gay activists were through with Reagan, AIDS funding was, by 1988, already much bigger than the current total budget for the National Institute on Aging (NIA). Without their ACT UP movement, there may still be no AIDS cocktails saving and prolonging the lives of many millions.

3   But how was this "miracle" pulled off? We need to remember Ronald Reagan courted the Religious Right shamelessly and relentlessly in his presidential campaigns. It worked. The

disproportionate turnout of the fundamentalist "born again" Christian vote helped Reagan win the Southern states ("the Bible Belt"). Without the Religious Right, Reagan would not have gotten his White House gig. So once he got in, Reagan, the actor, was not dumb enough to annoy the Jerry Falwells, the Pat Robertsons and all the other TV evangelists who then played the same role now played by the likes of Rush Limbaugh and Glenn Beck.

4   The Religious Right was in the Reagan White House and in the halls of the U.S. Congress. It was litmus-testing Supreme Court nominees. In the Reagan White House, it not only had influence and access, it had raw power.

Silence Equals Death

5   When the AIDS epidemic erupted, the American public was not as tolerant of homosexuals as it is now. In fact, half the country was downright hostile and the other half went by the "don't ask, don't tell" philosophy. So the public was very susceptible to the Religious Right's incendiary argument that AIDS was God's punishment for homosexuality and its "promiscuity."

6   When AIDS first broke out in the West, it was labeled "the gay plague." TV evangelists and fundamentalist pulpits thundered across the U.S. that it was Almighty God's retribution for sexual "abominations" and "perversions." Just like what he allegedly did to Sodom and Gomorrah. Many Americans wondered if those "promiscuous" homosexuals were reaping what they sowed.

7   There was every reason to believe that AIDS would cause a severe backlash and set back the gay cause by decades. And that gays, shameful of AIDS, would crawl back into the closet.

8   And yet the opposite happened.

9 Instead of **going back into the closet to die quietly (as all mortals are supposed to)**, the most incredible and unforeseen thing happened: gays refused to die quietly.

10 Gay activists saw that **AIDS was not only a disease, it was — like all diseases — politics.**

11 Politics and politicians decide how much or how little to spend on a disease. On research to treat or cure. On caring for those who come down with it. On how much a prevention campaign gets. And politics decide on whether the disease is even to be mentioned at all in any political campaign or speeches.

12 Since the Reagan White House along with the Religious Right had decided that AIDS did not exist (except for gays who were being whipped by Yahweh), there was no need for the government to fund it, much less talk about it in presidential speeches or polite company.

13 **Silence was the official U.S. AIDS policy under Reagan, and silence is always the official policy on Death.**

14 Silence is not only official policy, it is The Death Society's *modus operandi*.

15 Compared to its fulminations about Pinko-Commies (then) and Uncle Osama and his Al Qaeda (now), The Death Society is deafeningly silent about your heart attack, your cancer, your stroke, your Alzheimer's, and all the other killers most likely to kill you.

16 **Not only is The Death Society silent on what will kill you, it expects, nay it demands, that you be silent too. And that you go quietly into that dark night.**

17 Way before the Reagan-Religious-Right's passive pogrom against gays, there was the Third Reich's active one against Jews.

18 Jews in the Third Reich were expected to (and did) go quietly to their camps and their gas chambers. Reagan expected condemnation — official, religious, vicious — would be more than enough to get gays with AIDS to sneak back into their closets, and stay there.

19 But **for the first time in history, a group of garden-variety mortals refused to accept a Disease that was killing them as "natural." They refused to bow to this as an "Act of God."**

20 Yes, there had been the March of Dimes to cure polio. But that was created by Franklin D. Roosevelt, the brahmin U.S. president, to cure the disease he had. And of course the NIH's cancer institute was pretty much the lobbying of ladies-who-do-lunch types like Mary W. Lasker who also doled out the Lasker Awards, and Florence Mahoney.

21 But ACT UP was a totally different animal. It was not noblesse oblige, not establishment, not respectable, not genteel. ACT UP was instinct for self-preservation, anti-establishment, pariah, and downright rude.

22 To the shock of the Reaganites, the Religious Right, the Vatican, and the Mortalist powers that be, **gay boomers not only refused to go guietly, they made a huge fucking scene.**

23 ACT UP raided headquarters of pharmaceutical giants and chained themselves to the lobby with TV cameras filming away. They interrupted trading on the New York Stock Exchange. They went on national TV and accused President Reagan, New York's mayor, the NIH of mass murder. They delayed the opening of the Montreal International AIDS conference. They denounced the *New York Times* for its AIDS coverage and demanded its obituaries state AIDS as the cause of death, and recognize the gay partner. They held raucous rageful community meetings. They "desecrated" the New York Cardinal's Holy Communion service. Instead of back into closet, they came out proudly to parents, families,

friends, and enlisted them in their fight. Larry Kramer outed those in the closet in print and on national TV. They marched, they screamed, and most of all they organized a potent, loud, effective movement.

24   Amazingly, ACT UP was at most a few thousand, mostly young gay people. In October of 1987, at its height, founder Larry Kramer estimated ACT UP at **"almost a thousand" strong.** But what this teaches us is how few it takes to change things.

25   **What a thousand fearless fighters for Life can achieve! Where are the thousand young or not-so-young Immor-Talists?** Just a thousand people, willing to go anywhere, at their own expense, at the drop of a hat, to protest and be uncivil and disobedient. It takes only a thousand to have the Reagan Regime and the Catholic Church in retreat, even running scared.

26   AIDS activists, many of whom had earlier fought for gay liberation, were too politically savvy and smart to think that just having fundraisers in bars would be enough to fund research good enough and fast enough to control or conquer AIDS. So although they passed the hat too, most of all they pushed and pulled for U.S. government funding where they knew the big bucks were.

27   They saw that it was a project that only the NIH and its army of top scientists were equipped for, and that only the U.S. Congress could fund research on such a scale as to tackle a major epidemic.

28   So they learned how to become lobbyists, or hired excellent ones. They figured out where the levers of power were, and who and what committee controlled the purse strings. And they went after them.

29   Gays were not the first to politicize Disease, but they were one of the first to see that it was politicized. And to do something about it.

30 **In The Death Society, all "good" mortals are expected to die quietly ("peacefully"). And 99% of all mortals do as expected.**

31 So we see that the political environment then could not have been more hostile to gays. Yet, because of a new radical gay movement called ACT UP, founded only in March of 1987, **funding for AIDS research rose to almost one billion dollars in less than two years, by the end of the Reagan regime.** An incredible feat, since the Reagan regime was no friend of gay people.

32 In addition, ACT UP has an enduring legacy benefitting all sufferers of all diseases. ACT UP forced the speeding up of the process for approval of new drugs at the FDA (Food & Drug Administration). As the *New York Times* noted "Perhaps ACT-UP's clearest imprint has been its role in speeding the dissemination of new drugs, a change that may affect treatment of many diseases in addition to AIDS."

33 **But the NIA (National Institute on Aging) was established way back in 1974. It has been almost four decades, and the NIA's budget is still at the same level that the AIDS research budget was in 1988! Adusted for inflation, it's much less!**

34 How passive, docile, we have been. Aging is the biological condition which affects us all, and has so far killed everyone. Allowing the NIA to stagnate and languish is simply a scandal and an atrocity. And it will kill us all, unless we correct it now, and in a big way.

35 **Fact: In Fiscal Year 2004, AIDS research at the NIH got $2.85 billion from the Bush regime and Republican Congress. Like Reagan, neither the Bush White House nor the Republican Congress are gays' buddies. But this shows what could be done and it also shows how absolutely horrendous it is that the budget now for the NIA is still at around $1 billion (the same as AIDS research budget in 1988).**

36 What's more, **the NIA budget, outrageously small and stagnant, is being axed at this very moment.** Dr. Richard J. Hodes, M.D., the NIA's director, recently posted an open letter on its website acknowledging the "increasing concern about the reduced pay line and (reduced) success rates (in applying) for aging research at the National Institute on Aging (NIA)." "I recognize the impact that the situation is having on established researchers as well as on the development of younger scientists for the field (of anti-aging research), " Dr. Hodes admits in his open letter of October 25, 2010.

37 The National Institute on Aging (NIA) should be the crown jewel of the National Institutes on Health (NIH). After all, the NIA is the institute chartered to tackle the master disease, the master syndrome, of which cancer, heart disease, stroke, Alzheimer's, diabetes, osteoporosis, and obesity are all symptoms. But instead the NIA is the poor neglected stepchild. An ImmorTalist Movement must rectify this unacceptable situation now or we are doomed.

Pseudo-ImmorTalists Blame The Masses

38 Pseudo-Immortalism's so-called "leaders" have got it all wrong. Aubrey de Grey is one of their leading lights.

39 Mr. de Grey claims that the public is in an "pro-aging trance." (Tell this to the multi-billion-dollar cosmetics, plastic surgery, diet and fashion industries!)

40 Despite all the facts and analysis presented to him in Elixxir's open letter, de Grey insists: "Thus, of the four communities that might make a difference to the pace of the relevant (anti-aging) research, the one which there is *no point whatever* in directly lobbying is the government." (italics added)

41 One doesn't know whether to laugh or cry. To be so cocksure that one is imperially right when one is so damnably wrong is no virtue. Especially for a "leader." Only a moribund move-

ment with no future would accept someone like Aubrey de Grey as one of its leading lights and talking heads. It makes for very dim lighting and wits indeed.

42 Aubrey de Grey — who claims to be an immortalist, who dares to dream the biggest dream of immortality — cannot even imagine that the so-called "pro-aging trance" of society could possibly be altered. What kind of immortalist is Aubrey de Grey? What kind of "leader" is he?

43 Aubrey de Grey does not get it. **It is the mission of a political movement to challenge, subvert, overturn, and transform the most established, the most accepted, the most inviolable public opinions, social traditions and mores.**

44 If de Grey has read any current history, he would have seen that a viable movement *can* fundamentally transform public consciousness in an amazingly short time.

45 *Has Mr. de Grey ever heard of the Abolitionist, Labor, Suffragette, Feminist, or Civil Rights movements? How about Gandhi's civil disobedience movement against the British Empire? The list goes on and on and on. Every social or political leap has been achieved through a mass movement.*

46 The fact that Aubrey de Grey is ignorant of this disqualifies him as leader and spokesperson of any political movement with any future or hope of success. And so de Grey is where he is — "leader," "spokesperson" and poseur par excellence of Pseudo-Immortalism. That's where he belongs.

47 Can de Grey's much-hyped Methuselah Prize really hope to match billionaire Michael Milken's $350 million in private foundation money?

48 Isn't Aubrey's goal of 10,000 years (so sensationalistic it destroys all credibility and stirs outrage and backlash) so much more ambitious than Michael Milken's goal of simply curing prostate cancer? And if so, how can we possibly believe even for a moment that Aubrey's quaint little prize (though a good

fundraising gig for him) could possibly have any chance of succeeding without massive state funding on a scale as big at least as the Iraq or Afghanistan wars, year in and year out, over decades if needs be?

49 To solve the mystery of human biological aging is a thousand times more ambitious and complex a goal than to cure one of its symptoms like breast or prostate cancer which even with signficant state funding over decades has so far failed to produce any victory.

50 So how can we believe we are going to conquer Aging on the cheap? Yes, $20 million is a farce. $100 million would be a pittance. Even a billion here and there would be crumbs and not anywhere enough, as the history of the NIA (National Institute on Aging) has amply warned and proven.

51 After over half a century of Pseudo-immortalism's so-called "movement," with very few takers, there is no longer any right or excuse on their part to blame the public for its "pro-aging trance." What a relative handful of gay activists, swimming against officially-sanctioned bigotry, were able to achieve on AIDS funding, tells us the problem is not with the "unwashed masses" being in an "pro-aging trance," the problem is with the Pseudo-immortalists and their monumental incompetence.

52 If people fighting life-threatening diseases have little or no time or patience for Pseudo-ImmorTalists like Aubrey de Grey, we Scientific ImmorTalists understand their impatience and contempt completely. While seriously ailing mortals are hoping for a few more years or even a few more months, de Grey and his band of Pseudo-immortalists are yakking about how they will live 10,000 years.

53 We the true ImmorTalists cast our lot with people battling cancer, heart disease, stroke and other terror-diseases. Just as the public, we have zero interest in de Grey's fundraising scheme to award the scientist who can hatch the longest-lived lab mice. De Grey's far-fetched scenario is that such a long-lived

mouse would arouse the voters to such orgasmic excitement that they would then force their politicians to fund anti-aging research with a vengeance. This is what counts as "political analysis" and "political strategy" in these rarefied hermetic pseudo-immortalist circles.

54 The fact is there had been many "Methuselah" mice bred before, all the way back to Dr. Clive McCay's Cornell lab in the 1930s. And nothing happened. Not one of these Methuselah mice resulted in any Mortalist regime opening wide its spigot of public funding for anti-aging research. And we know for a fact that not one of those Methuselah mice aroused the masses to demand of their government to fund anti-aging research.

55 **No long-lived mouse in the annals of history has ever spawned a mass movement, but a stay-young human could.** *The masses will be much more excited over a stay-young human than over an overstaying mouse. Rest assured.*

56 *What a mouse cannot do, a political movement can.*

57 To cure aging is not a pet project for a small foundation. At least if the desired end is success and not a quixotic venture tilting against a real dragon.

58 **It's time to speak out against this amateurism and this deadly delusional "strategy." Too long we real ImmorTalists have been silent. But here too Silence Equals Death.**

59. The notion that we are all in this big immortalist tent where someone like Aubrey de Grey should have license to go on plying his lethal circus-barker act without worrying about any deserving criticism is not only wrong, it is deadly, not just for individuals, but for the movement.

60 First of all, there is no big tent; at this point there is hardly a tent. So it's a hundred times more important to make sure real immortalists, not pseudo-immortalists, are in it. Secondly, de Grey and his ilk are confusing the public about what Immor-

Talism is truly about. And the media loves to have him play the immortalist devil in their freak-show hour.

61 By his disastrous media-whorings and relentless fundraising, people like de Grey are sucking the air, not to mention the money, out of any embryonic fledging thing that could grow into a truly potent immortalist movement. And that is why there is no viable immortalist movement until now.

Strategies Matter. The Wrong Strategies Kill.

62 We speak out against Aubrey de Grey because his naive un-founded ridiculous "strategy" will surely lead his followers not to eternity, but to their doom.

63 To get big bucks for anti-aging research, which could lead to cures for cancer, heart disease, stroke, Alzheimer's, os-teoporosis, we need a mass movement to push for it. To get a great increase in funding for research to cure the top killer-diseases, when the Mortalist regimes are claiming they have to ax research, we must have a powerful orga-nized movement. This fact has been proven not just by gay activists on AIDS recently, but by many other movements from the 1960s and 1970s.

Breast & Prostate Cancer Activists Increase Funding

64 Unlike Pseudo-Immortalists, Breast Cancer and Prostate can-cer activists have learned from Gays on AIDS.

65 Women with breast cancer organized themselves into groups like the National Coalition for Breast Cancer. In just a few years they forced Washington to increase funding for breast cancer research 800 percent. In Fiscal Year 2009, the NCI funded breast cancer research to the tune of $685 million.

66 Prostate cancer activists have forced the U.S. budget for prostate cancer research to increase by at least 20 times. In Fiscal
Year 2009, the National Cancer Institute funded $341 million
on prostate cancer research.

66A Comparison: **NIA (National Institute on Aging) budget is
still stuck at just over 1 billion dollars. Where AIDS research funding was in 1988.**

Movements Change Public Opinion

67 How did the modern civil rights movement in the 1960s compel a Southerner from Texas, President Lyndon B. Johnson, to
push through a landmark Civil Rights Act in 1964?

68 By transforming the political and racial consciousness of a
majority of Americans on the segregation issue. And that's
the job of a new political movement.

69 This is why pseudo-immortalists are politically clueless or in
self-serving denial. They try to justify their inability to churn
up a viable movement that could win bigtime anti-aging funding by resorting to the excuse that the masses are in an "pro-
aging trance."

70 **If indeed the public is in an "pro-aging trance," then it is
their job and that of a mass movement to change that into
a pro-anti-aging-research trance!**

71 Civil rights for blacks, integrated schools and housing, and
busing in the 1950s and 1960s in the South were vote-losers.
Yet the civil rights movement and its allies got a good number
of officeholders and politicians to support them because of a
perceived shift in public opinion on the race issue.

72 If that's not a hard enough task for a movement, then how
about protections for the ultimate lepers in the U.S. till recently? Yes, homosexuals. Especially in the Southern states,
the "Bible Belt."

73 What daunting hurdles of hostile public opinion faced the handful of American gay activists and their fledging movement which started in the United States of the 1950s

74 Remember anti-sodomy laws are still on the books in something like half the U.S. states and as many U.S. states have *recently* passed anti-gay-marriage laws.

75 *Did the gays whine about how public opinion was so irrevocably homophobic after over two thousand years of Judaeo-Christianity that it was futile and foolish to even try to change it? Did they resign themselves to the "fact" that government will never fund anything related to gays because it is sure to stir controversy and lose votes?*

76 No! Unlike pseudo-immortalists, gays are not whiners and not losers.

77 Gays and AIDS activists understood and understand it is precisely the need to overturn entrenched, Judaeo-Christianity-sanctioned, and overwhelmingly accepted public condemnation of their very existence and core nature, which made it absolutely imperative to create a Gay Liberation movement.

78 If society were totally fair to workers, women, blacks and gays, why would there be any need at all for a labor movement, a feminist movement, a civil rights movement, or a gay movement? How is it possible that something so basic is beyond the grasp of pseudo-immortalism's "sages"?

79 To solve the mystery of human biological aging is a thousand times more ambitious and complex a goal than to cure one of its symptoms like breast or prostate cancer, which even with significant government funding, science has so far failed to conquer.

$378 Million Not Enough to Prevent Death at 61

80 Michael Milken, the billionaire ex-junk-bond-master, has spent $350 million through his foundation on prostate cancer research. In addition, Milken has lobbied Congress and the White House to gain the greatly-increased federal funding for prostate cancer. In spite of all this, this year, seventeen years after his foundation was set up, almost 218,000 Americans will be diagnosed with prostate cancer, and over 32,000 Americans will still die from prostate cancer. There is still no cure for prostate cancer.

81 So should we bet our lives on Aubrey de Grey's (or any pseudo-immortalist's) little foundation and believe that it will snatch us the biggest of all prizes, the one that mortals have been dreaming of since the dawn of the species?

82 So maybe a foundation won't make the grade. But how about the all-knowing all-powerful Market of Capitalism? Capitalism will come up with the Cures and the Breakthroughs to conquer aging and its myriad disease manifestations, right? That's what _____ _____ bet on. And if anyone could pull it off, it was him. He raised $378 milion for a venture capital fund devoted to health. Well, more specifically for "How to defeat aging and death." To his credit, Mr. _____ was an out-of-the-closet immortalist.

83 The *New York Times* described his Healthcare Investment Corporation as "the largest venture capital fund devoted to health care." As the lengthy *Times* profile pointed out, "Mr. _____ truly believes that scientists are close to unlocking the secret of eternal life. And he truly believes he may be one of the first recipients of this largess."

84 Elixxir told Mr. _____ that he should hedge his bets and practice The Elixxir Program and buy more time while waiting for his high-tech salvation. But Mr. _____ was

cocky: he didn't need The Elixxir Program. He just needed venture-capital Capitalism. The Market will provide. As the *Times* reported, "He is looking for the right scientists to start a company devoted solely to turning back the biological clock."

84A Elixxir still remembers that beautiful summer day in July, 1995 that he opened his *New York Times* and saw another article on our great venture capitalist. The title was "_____ **Dies at 61**: Backed Health Care Ventures." It was the obituary page. Our venture capitalist didn't live forever after all. And his **$378 million venture capital fund**, quite a bit of money in the 1980s and early 1990s, was apparently not quite enough to save him. (We intentionally did not tell you his name assuming you must have heard or known of him. You've forgotten? Or you have never heard?! It shows how our rich man has already faded into oblivion. And they all will, unless ImmorTalism saves them.)

85 Alas, this is the fate of every billionaire or wealthy mortal who is so unwise as to bet his salvation solely on Capitalism's "omnipotent" Market. Bet on The ImmorTalist Movement and Party. Bet on The Elixxir Society and The Elixxir Program. They are your best bets. For what does it profit you if you should gain the world, but lose your own life?

86 How can we delude ourselves into believing we can conquer human biological aging on the cheap? Yes, $10 million, $50, Milken's $350 million or a $378 million venture capital fund were and will be lethally inadequate.

Why a Movement is Not Enough (The Limits of Acting Up)

87 ACT-Up, though successful and effective for a few years, died out. Its fate teaches us another most important lesson: **Spontaneous Revolts, spontaneous movements, do not last.**

88 **So why did ACT UP die out? As much as we admire what it has accomplished, we must also critique its weaknesses and mistakes to make sure we — the ImmorTalist Movement — don't repeat them.**

89 Let's go to ACT UP's New Members Introduction. Here we see its Achilles' heel and why it was a given that it would lose steam and self-destruct.

   "...because of the immensity of the task of ending the AIDS crisis, ACT UP felt there was a need to make *every member a leader, rather than having a few members holding the power. That is why there is no president or Board of Directors in ACT UP.* It is no wonder then that ACT UP is run as openly and democratically as it is. *ACT UP has no paid staff; everyone is a volunteer.* The membership in attendance every week at Monday Night meetings, the floor, has the final say on all of the organization's business. Because of this, the meetings can run very long and become heated and emotional. They can also be tedious and frustrating. It can be extremely confusing and overwhelming for new members and even old members. Just remember that we run things this way because we care about what you have to say. While we ask members to wait until their third meeting to vote, you have as much right to speak and to be heard (from your first attendance) as anyone else in the room."

90 What kind of movement can survive when any loudmouth who's high or free-floatingly hostile, someone who's never joined any ACT UP protest before, has the right to just crash into its Monday meetings and hijack the floor. And if he can scream the loudest, he could heckle or even tongue-lash the group's veteran most effective activists or even its founder as if he were the Master of ACT UP?

91 And this is precisely what the New Members Intro Sheet admitted to. Of course, ACT UP rationalized that this needless weekly mayhem and self-bloodletting was "democracy" in action. It was not. It was anarchism. Political amateurism.

92 It must have been amusing to the gendarme and the FBI infiltrator. They didn't have to do anything really. The group, in its heyday, basically self-destructed. When it could have gone on to contribute even more to the AIDS issue and save even more lives. But even the most committed could only take so many of those meetings' exhausting, demoralizing screamfests. People stopped going, dropped out, burned out. ACT UP disintegrated.

93 That there was no staff, no board of directors, no organization after the first year was not only juvenile, it was criminal. ACT UP was facing the most organized and hierarchical of foes — the Mortalist State itself, not to mention the Catholic Church, and the "evangelical" fundamentalist churches, the NIH bureaucracy, and yes, the staffs and bureaucrats of Congress and the White House itself. What chance does any group or movement have against this array of Mortalist forces?

94 It was **a tragic repeat of the 1960s and its romantic anarchism**. It was a failure in the 1960s, and 1970s, and again with ACT UP in the 1980s. *There is not one instance in all of history in which anarchism has ever prevailed against the organization and hierarchies of the State. None. And there will never be.*

95 Our ImmorTalist Movement must grasp this hard-won lesson and refuse to have to learn it again and suffer its bitter consequences. To mount an ImmorTalist Movement with the same anarchistic romanticism is to ensure its defeat and to guarantee our collective and individual deaths. We true ImmorTalists shall not be a party to any such amateurish and doomed efforts.

Why ImmorTalist Organization Will Save Us

96 Organization, organization, organization. Staff of Professional ImmorTalists. Yes, we need hierarchies and specializations. Because we must confront enemies who are super-organized,

with hierarchies and specializations. And we don't wish to go down like the Incas, the indigenous people before the organization, hierarchy and specialization of the Conquistadors.

97 When Global Heating and its apocalyptic scenarios kick in, the only thing that can save us is organization, hierarchy, specialization. When something like Katrina happens to New York, Miami, London, Shanghai, or an earthquake as catastrophic as the one that hit China before the Olympics, you can be certain that the cry will not be for "Less Government" or "Small Government," but rather the demand will be "More Government" and "Big Government." And the shrillest cries will be from the most fervent believers of "small government" and the evangelists of how private sector and individualism can do it all. When their beachfront properties are drowned as a result of rising seas, governments will hear their ear-piercing skull-busting screams.

98 The ImmorTalist Movement urgently needs real leadership. Not the Pseudo-ImmorTalists' so-called "leaders." Pseudo-Immortalism started in the early 1960s. It cannot claim the media ignored it. It had more than its fifteen minutes. Even landing on *Life* magazine. But it squandered all this opportunity by its inept "leadership" which is worse than no leadership at all.

99 The Civil Rights Movement, the Women's Movement, the Environmental Movement, the Gay movement, even the Religious Right movement — all these movements which started in the sixties or seventies have long since gone on to secure influence, respect, power. They have grabbed permanent seats at the funding table. And they have embedded themselves into the agenda of either the Democratic or Republican Party. All except the Pseudo-ImmorTalist "movement."

100 Now remember, the Gay Liberation Movement did not happen until Stonewall which was in 1969. And there was no group in the U.S. which was more socially ostracized than homosexuals. The Religious Right movement began in earnest

only when Jerry Falwell mounted an anti-gay campaign with Anita Bryant in Dade County, Florida in 1977.

101 Robert Ettinger's book and Cryonics started way back in 1962. The Gay and Religious Right movements did not start till 1969 and 1977. The Gay movement came seven years after Pseudo-Immortalism's birth. The Religious Right didn't even start until fifteen years after Pseudo-Immortalism.

102 Just compare the Gay, Religious Right, Feminist, Civil Rights movements to Ettinger and de Grey's so-called "movement." There is no comparison. All the other movements have thrived. They demand and get respect and they have varying degrees of real, even raw, power. They get funding for what they want.

103 And how about Pseudo-ImmorTalism? Nothing! After almost half a century, we know beyond the shadow of a doubt that Pseudo-Immortalism is not the Immortalist movement we have been waiting for. That horse won't run. The key to success is to ride a good horse. That horse will never win the Kentucky Derby.

104 We need an ImmorTalist Movement. And more!

105 AIDS funding has stalled. AIDS is not a big issue in the media anymore. Even though, and maybe because, it is less a white disease now, and more a Black and Hispanic disease.

106 There is still no vaccine. The big drug companies are simply not interested. A vaccine is not as profitable as the HIV drug cocktails which every HIV person needs to take for the rest of his or her life.

107 Insolvent U.S. states are beginning to cut back on financial aid for access to prohibitive AIDS cocktails. And it is not even an issue. No more ACT UP. No more rage.

108 So yes, we need an ImmorTalist Mass movement. But we need more than that to fulfill humanity's most ancient dream and win the biggest Prize.

109 As for our mass movement, there is no better-qualified demographic to create it than baby boomers. After all, the boomers have spawned all the other great movements since the 1960s. Including the Civil Rights, Feminist, Anti-Vietnam-War, Gay and Countercultural movements.

110 Boomers are qualified, having learned from past mistakes, to ignite a new ImmorTalist movement to save themselves and the planet.

111 This time around, boomers are in positions of power. They are in charge. So will they act like all the previous generations?

112 Or will they be the generation once more to break all rules. To go against the conventional wisdom that people become more conservative and reactionary as they grow older.

113 The clock is ticking. This time it's personal.

114 **Boomers — in fact all mortals — must act as if they are threatened with Death every single minute of every day. Because they are.**

115 But aside from self-preservation (a natural instinct**), it may be the boomer's destiny to birth an ImmorTalist movement which will finally *save all mortals for all time from Disease, Old Age and Death.***

116 **And if they are too mortgage-ridden and bent to heed destiny's call, then their children, the younger generation, must do so.**

117 **Better still, an ImmorTalist movement which combines the expertise, experience and resources of boomers with the younger generations' idealism and energy.**

118 To accomplish this most worthy of missions, we need the *greatest* movement of all time. To save ourselves and the Planet.

> (S)ince power never falls to those who will not reach for it
> and since government is power,
> it followed by the laws of nature that political parties
> would develop to grab for the power.
>
> — Theodore White, *America in Search of Itself*

CHAPTER 10
Why The ImmorTalist Party

1 On July 20, 1992, the eighth international conference on AIDS opened with an urgent plea from its chairperson for the creation of a political party dedicated to AIDS and other health-care issues. This new party would be to Disease what the established Green Parties in Europe are to the Environment.

2 A radical idea from some crackpot? It could not have come from a more respected, credentialed, establishment voice. This idea was floated by none other than Dr. Jonathan Mann, who happened to be the former head of the World Health Organization (WHO) Global Program on AIDS, and a distinguished professor and pillar at the Harvard School of Public Health.

3 The *New York Times* ran an article the next day on Dr. Mann's speech. "Although world leaders express concern about health, it receives second-class political treatment in almost every country," Dr. Mann pointed out.

4 "Why has no government and no society been called to account for failures in health? Why do governments tremble when the inflation rate rises, yet no elections are lost over health issues like AIDS or infant mortality,'" the *New York Times* quoted Dr. Mann.

5 Dr. Mann's work on AIDS broke his heart but opened his eyes
and raised his political consciousness. He came to realize that
AIDS, like all diseases, epidemics, pandemics, is not only a
scientific or medical problem, it is also a political problem.

6 AIDS is not only a disease, it is also politics. And politics is all
about the allocation of society's resources, which are always
limited no matter how rich the society is. So politicians decide on how important a disease AIDS is, and how much it
should get in government funding.

The Green Party Got It —
Even the Vatican Got It

7 The insight that you need a political party or at least a political
movement if you have needs and objectives which can only
be attained by gaining political power and control of government is nothing new.

8 The environmental movement got it since the early 1970s in
Europe. The Green Party is an established party in Euro-
pean parliaments everywhere from Germany to France to
Sweden. In fact, in Germany, The Green Party was even
the junior partner in a ruling coalition under the Social
Democratic Party.

9 The Labor movements got it in Europe since at least the 18th
century. Social Democratic Parties sprouted all over Europe.
That party began as the party of the working class. And organized labor.

10 The Vatican, unfortunately, got it too. And quite a while ago.
To counter the Social Democratic and other progressive parties, the Catholic Church, in its reaction, spawned the so-
called "Christian Democratic Party." Sad to say, this political
franchise still exists in most of the EU.

11 The Soka Gakkai religious movement created the Komeito Party. Its own political party to protect its own interest at the table. In a short time, it became the junior partner in a ruling coalition in Japan.

12 Even **Gandhi,** a "saint," understood he needed an organized political party, not just a movement, to get rid of the British Empire in India. And Gandhi's party is still the ruling party in India.

13 So there! Everyone gets it but Pseudo-Immortalists. But of course they cannot even imagine an ImmorTalist movement. And that's why we say they're no Immortalists.

NO PARTY = DEATH

14 But what happened to Dr. Mann's call for a political party devoted to health issues? Nothing.

15 Six years after his speech, on September 2, 1998, tragedy befell Dr. Jonathan Mann. Swissair Flight 111 crashed off Nova Scotia. He and his wife, AIDS researcher Mary Lou Clements-Mann, sitting next to each other, perished in it. Dr. Mann was only 51.

16 It is now 18 years after Dr. Mann's stirring and incisive speech calling for the creation of political parties worldwide devoted to health issues like disease and death. 25 million people worldwide have died of AIDS so far, and over 30 million more are living with AIDS. In the U.S. alone, over half a million Americans have died of AIDS.

17 It's time to take up Dr. Mann's call. But not just on AIDS. We need to take the idea to its logical conclusion. The idea of a political party has occurred to Elixxir long before Dr. Mann's speech in 1992. But just like Dr. Mann, Elixxir has been waiting for someone to do the idea. Mann's untimely demise is a cautionary tale for all of us.

Life-and-Death Questions

18 Is a real potent ImmorTalist movement enough to get us the cures for cancer, heart disease, stroke? Is a movement, no matter how effective, sufficient to win that Ultimate Prize – the conquest of Aging and Death?

19 NO. A sweeping ImmorTalist movement is a prerequisite. But it can only get us halfway to the Promised Land. The Mortalist parties are in agreement that there should be cuts in cancer, heart disease, stroke research at the NIH. They are already axing the NIA budget for anti-aging research, the only hope for countless millions of baby boomers around the world.

20 The Mortalist parties are coming at you wielding axes, and swinging at your head. Should you trust ax-wielders? NO.

21 Is there hope that the parties in power will somehow tackle the Global Warming issue in time to save us from its civilization-collapsing consequences? Is there hope for the Mortalist parties controlling the Death Societies around the world to agree on a plan of action to forestall the worst of Biodiversity Collapse and The Sixth Great Mass Species Extinction already happening?

22 Again the answer is NO.

23 If there's hope in the Mortalist parties, we would not be in such mortal danger now. The National Institute on Aging (NIA) would be the best funded of all the institutes at the NIH. 79 million baby boomers should already be benefitting from one or two NIA anti-aging life-extension breakthroughs with a couple more coming down the research pipeline. But instead, nothing.

24 On Global Warming, if any deliverance could possibly be expected from the two ruling U.S. parties, they would have taken effective measures starting in the 1960s. To prevent our ever getting to the tipping point that many scientists believe we are in now.

25 It's five minutes to midnight. Or is it one minute to midnight? The countdown is ticking mercilessly before planet-scorching tsunami-rising, biodiversity-collapsing, and civilization-destroying catastrophe strikes. Irrevocably. And send us into 100,000 years of endlessly broiled earth. Sending us back to the subsistence of the medieval Dark Age.

Why Only The ImmorTalist Party Can Save Us

26 The ImmorTalist Party is our only hope. Why? Because only an ImmorTalist Party has the breadth and sweep of vision to successfully confront Global Warming, Biodiversity Collapse, Asteroids, not to mention an all-out War Against Disease, Old Age & Death.

27 All our life-threatening planet-endangering problems require the farsighted vision, longterm planning, and total commitment to Life that only an ImmorTalist Party has.

28 The myopic vision, attention-deficit-disordered brains and Death-acceptance of Mortalist parties have brought us to the brink of species and planetary catastrophe. And if we bet on these same horses, we will get the same disastrous results.

29 A movement must attach its agenda to a political party which it can trust to fight for its agenda, and deliver on it when it comes to power. Or else a movement's agenda will lose steam, be a non-thriving orphan, and disappear.

30 The big problem is there are no Mortalist parties we can trust to deliver on dramatic increases in research to conquer Disease, Old Age & Death™. Our trust has been repeatedly violated by promises always reneged on after they get into office. We have been in a bad failed marriage where our partner is a pathological liar, a cheat and an abuser. But we have hoped against hope.

31. We have kept on voting for them, against our better judgment. But unless we are card-carrying masochists, there is a time to say "Enough is enough!" And the time is now. Because if we don't see how disastrous and destructive the parties have been to our lives, to our freedoms, to other species, and to civilization and the planet's future, then we are in absolute denial. And we shall never see the light in time.

Transformation is Fast, "Reforms" Take Forever

32 All attempts at reforms of the U.S. since the early sixties have failed. They have been ruthlessly crushed. Or co-opted. Or they ran out of steam or money. Or they've been rolled over by the Religious Right and its soul mate, the Extreme Secular Right, in the never-ending U.S. Cultural Revolution. ("Culture Wars.")

33 The hippies' Flower Power. "The Summer of Love" in Haight-Ashbury. John Lennon's "Imagine." Ginsburg's Om. Leary's Acid Psychedelic Trips. The Children's Crusades for Gene McCarthy, Robert Kennedy, Martin Luther King Jr. *They all came to naught, and much grief. They did not and could not have prevailed against the guns, the truncheons, the tear gas, and the organized repression-security apparatus of the FBI, the National Guard, the police, and the military.* This Empire, unlike the Soviet, wasn't, isn't going to go quietly.

34 Why was the American Spring of the 1960s so easily crushed? Why did the uprisings of the 1960s and early 1970s fail, and turn into disillusionment, apathy and political fatalism?

35 Why? Because **there were no real political leaders who grasped the essential need to create their own political party. A party with the organization, vision, discipline, know-how, and perseverance to present a credible alternative to the status quo.** One which can attract not merely

the young but their parents, grandparents, workers and middle-class, in a coalition that could win, that could take over, and that could run the government and transform society.

36 Abie Hoffman was a great media performance artist, but he was a dreadful political leader. He was a genius at media pranks (running a pig for President) and getting his father's generation riled up. But he was manic-depressive and did drugs. Allen Ginsberg was a great poet but had no inkling how to take on and change Empire except chanting Om. The Black Panther Party was political adventurism with no political hope whatsoever from the get-go.

37 The expectations of overnight systemic changes were totally naive. So if their Revolution did not take over Empire in a few short years, if their candidate (whether McCarthy, Kennedy, or McGovern) did not win or, worse, got shot, then they give up. Retreat into Yuppiedom and political resignation.

38 **The U.S. Mortalist Empire, with over 700 military bases outside its borders, plus over 4,800 bases inside its territory,** was surely in no mood to just cave in and die. <u>Empire was super-organized, ultra-hierarchical, armed to the teeth. As it is now. Yet the boomers refused organization, hierarchy and specialization.</u> Their movement failed to rally support beyond their demographics. It proved unable or unwilling to create basic institutions to provide foundation for movement and alternative to status quo.

39 Most of all, the American Spring of the 1960s was easily crushed because it failed to create the most essential vehicle required for any serious attempt at Regime or (even harder) System change: a new political party with the agenda, ambition and leadership to replace the discredited old Mortalist order.

40 We are not Puritans. But people who are high on drugs a significant part of the time are not viable or sustainable leaders. And definitely not revolutionists. For one thing, it is hard to exercise good sober judgment while on drugs. Bad judgment leads to bad decisions.

41 All the Sixties could muster was Abie Hoffman's joke-anar-
chist-party – the Yippies Party.

42 With no viable and visible alternative party to vote for, American voters felt they had "no choice" (and they don't) but to
keep on voting for the same two old bankrupt parties (an even
worse choice).

Immortalist Issues

43 *If death from AIDS is bad and must be fought and prevented,
if death from heart disease, cancer, stroke is bad, and must be
fought and prevented, then Death itself must be bad, and must
be fought and prevented with all our might.*

44 And that's exactly what an ImmorTalist Party and State vows
to do. Wage War Against Death.

45 If Aging is highly-correlated with and always ends in Decline
and Death, then Aging must be undesirable, and must be prevented.

46 And that's what an ImmorTalist Party and its ImmorTalist
State will do: fund the research to prevent, slow down or reverse the biological aging process.

ALE (Average Life Expectancy), NOT GDP

47 The U.S. average life expectancy (ALE) is at least four years
less than that of Sweden, and even lagging behind Cuba. So
why isn't this a burning issue? The ImmorTalist Party should
make it an overriding issue.

48 ALE (Average Life Expectancy) is a million times more important to the average person than GDP (Gross Domestic
Product). ALE is all about health, vitality, dying or not dying,
how you live, when you die, how you die, and whether you
have access to health care.

49 But all we hear about and all the politicians tremble at are the GDP, the stock market, inflation, deflation, interest rates. We need to change this. The ImmorTalist Party demands ever-more increases in ALE. Every year. We demand every government matches what China did from 1949 to 1976: increase ALE by 33 years.

50 **African-Americans have an ALE of only 72.9 years. Or 5.2 years less than White non-hispanic Americans.** African-Americans have as low an ALE as Nicaraguans and Colombians. So it's as if black Americans are citizens of a poor Third World nation. And they are.

51 Now that's a huge gap in life expectancy between whites and blacks in the U.S. And a lethal one which means millions of blacks are dying prematurely. An ImmorTalist Party must make this totally unacceptable, a political scandal. It must point out that life expectancy in the U.S. is highly correlated with income, education, health care access.

52 Which U.S. ruling party banned all federal funding of stem cell research? Answer: The Republican Party with Bush Junior in the White House. Which party in control of Congress banned all cloning, even therapeutic cloning (which could lead to treatments or cures for diseases)? Answer: The Republican Party. Which party did not (and still mostly does not) even recognize the existence of global warming? The Republican Party. Which party voted in lockstep to kill the Comprehensive Climate Bill in the U.S. Congress? The Republican Party.

53 How can an ImmorTalist possibly support such a party?

54 There is much reason and room for rage. The 2 million American deaths each and every year from Cancer, Heart Attacks, Heart Failures, Strokes, Alzheimer's, Obesity and all the other Aging-Related and Old-Age-induced chronic ailments or acute killers. Most of these deaths are needless, premature, and preventable.

Health Care is a Human Right

55 What makes Americans put up with no universal health care
    which is a basic right in the E.U.? Yes, the Republicans taking
    over Congress claim their mandate is to rescind Obama's pal-
    try health care "reform" which Big Business won't tolerate.
    How can they blabber about so-called "human rights" when
    they deprive the American people of such a basic human
    right? In every major European Union nation universal health
    care has been a reality and a very successful and welcomed
    one for at least half a century.

56 We ImmorTalists reject any claptrap about "human rights"
    which does not include the right to health care, housing, food.
    "Human rights" means nothing without the right to see a med-
    ical doctor when ill. These are the most basic human rights,
    which are sorely lacking in the U.S.

57 If you don't have health care, the chances are quite good that
    you do not have a prayer to even live to the miserly U.S. av-
    erage life expectancy. And if you don't have health care, it
    is futile to dream about living long, much less immortality.
    And if you don't have health care, then cancer, heart disease,
    stroke become financially-catastrophic illnesses.

58 This is why The ImmorTalist Party is absolutely for univer-
    sal health care. And an ImmorTalist Society will guarantee
    universal health care coverage. And <u>we will make sure that
    all those Republican Senators and Congresspersons who are
    against universal health care will be stripped of the excellent
    government-funded health care coverage they enjoy.</u>

59 Demand every Republican House member and Senator who
    wants to rescind the health care law give up their "Social-
    ist" one-payer health care system that every Senator and Con-
    gressperson enjoys. Demand they give the same universal
    health care coverage they enjoy in Congress and the White
    House to the American people.

A New Kind of Politics

60 No more settling for crumbs from the Mortalist funding table. Let's take over the table and sit at its head.

61 No more squandering priceless Time trying to rearrange the deck chairs on the Titanic. The Mortalist regimes and parties are beyond salvaging.

62 No more playing the Mortalist game with its lethal rules and the same endgame in which we get sick, grow old, die.

63 Let's wise up and play another game, our game. The Immor-Talist Game. In which we have a real shot at The Grand Prize of Life.

64 **Let's create a new kind of Politics. ImmorTalist Politics. The politics of Life and Bliss. No to the politics of Blood, Sweat and Tears! No to the Politics of Sacrifice! No to appeasement of the Mortalist gods.**

65 **Our campaigns and our candidates believe in the Politics of Bliss. Your happiness is our agenda. And we know you can never truly be happy until you are liberated from the specter of Disease, Old Age & Death (D.O.D.™).**

66 **Anyone who cannot love should be disqualified from public office. Anyone who claims not to like sex is either a liar or a pervert.**

67 **Yes, our ImmorTalist candidates can love, can make love, while they are campaigning. We practice the politics of joy.**

68 **Don't you get it? Never support any Mortalist politician. Because they are people who worship Blood, Sweat and Tears, and so have no qualms in demanding that of you.**

69 We refuse to play their game. We will invent and play our own.

70 The ImmorTalist Party rejects the Mortalist rulebook. It will play by its own rulebook. It refuses to follow their demonic

pace, their deadlines. We shall march to our own drummer, and go by our own clock.

71 Their Game, their rules, their pace, their "productivity" have brought us to the edge of the abyss. So we need to invent a whole new game of politics: ImmorTalist politics.

72 If we play their rigged game, we lose of course. So we play our game in which they lose and we win.

73 <u>We will communicate directly with the people. We will create our own ImmorTalist Media. We refuse to be filtered and vetted by their Media.</u>

74 <u>With the brave new world of the Internet, which allows for cheap and fast dissemination of ideas and recruitment of cadres, an ImmorTalist movement and party could establish the first ImmorTalist State in record time.</u>

Covenant Between Government and People

75 We believe that <u>the major covenants between the government and the people are legally-binding contracts. When the government violates its primary covenants with the people, it should be punished just like someone who breaches a legal contract.</u>

76 A politician or political party which promises one thing in running for office and once in office does the exact opposite is a con man, a perpetrator of fraud, a criminal. And they should be prosecuted for racketeering, fraud, and breach of contract.

Down with the "Character" Issue

77 To hell with the so-called "Character" Issue. That's a red herring. A bogus issue. Designed by the Religious Right to distract us from life-and-death issues.

78 What do we really care about the so-called "character" issue? We know by now our politicians are free of conscience and character, and quite capable of doing the unconscionable and the characterless.

79 Baby boomers, those born after the Second World War, are 79 million voters strong in the U.S. They are still the biggest bloc of voters in the U.S. and in most other countries too.

80 *Boomers are the "scandal" generation. Boomers broke and abolished all the old taboos. Sex before marriage. Sex with no marriage. Sex with both genders.Sex with our gender. Divorce on demand. Open marriage. The Summer of Love.Free Sex.*

81 So does the majority of boomers really care that Bill Clinton might have inhaled? Or that he got a "gift" from Intern Monica?

82. Do we really care if a politican is committing "adultery"? Or if he or she is gay or bi or panesexual or asexual?

83 Are we really shocked to know that our politicians use profanities and four-letter words?

84 These may be issues to Religious Right nuts. But they are not to the majority of boomers. And certainly not to the majority of American voters who are very "secular" when compared to the Religious Right partisans.

85 So let's have the ImmorTalist Party take aim at this farce. This fake "character" issue. Let's show once and for all that the voters in the U.S. and in most other countries (except the theocratic states) do not really care for a religious litmus test for public office masquerading as "the character issue." Let's prove that we are no longer in the dark age of the Inquisition.

86 Let's field the first slate of candidates who are immune to blackmail by the Mortalist Regime's spy agencies. We know how J. Edgar Hoover, the FBI's lifelong director, managed to skirt the mandatory retirement age which applied to every-

one else. Hoover had a dossier on all the Presidents. In other words, he blackmailed them. We can safely assume the CIA and every spy or police agency worth its name in every Mortalist State is doing the same.

87 Perhaps this explains why no U.S. President could say no to the military and its budget "requests". It has all the dirt on them.

88 **Our ImmorTalist candidates, being completely transparent about everything, including their personal lives, stand proudly for personal freedoms – including sexual liberation**. So we will be the only candidates who are not "national security risks." We are immune to blackmail by the spy or repression security apparatus of either our own country or that of other countries.

89 *All the Mortalist candidates are at risk for blackmail by the FBI or the CIA or by other countries' spy agencies. They are huge national security risks. If blackmailed by the FBI or CIA, it means they will not do what they promised to do or were voted to do. If blackmailed by other countries' spy agencies, it means they might betray their own country. Only ImmorTalist candidates will be free to do what they say they would do.*

CHAPTER 11

Can an ImmorTalist Party Win?

1   Jimmy Carter ran for governor of Georgia when even his own top advisers advised him against it. They said the incumbent can't be defeated. They told Carter he should run for Lieutenant Governor first. Bla bla bla. Carter told his top aide "If I don't get but two votes, mine and yours, I'm going to run for governor."

2   How can we call ourselves "Immortalists" if we don't even have the Audacity and Will of that Southern Baptist Peanut Farmer?

3   But the naysayers and the nervous nellies will reply "But he's Jimmy Carter!" To which Elixxir shall reply "And we are ImmorTalists!"

4   Carter only wanted to be governor and President of a declining Empire. We want to conquer Disease, Old Age & Death. So which of us should have more daring and determination?

5   If we cannot even imagine our own ImmorTalist Party, with our own ImmorTalist candidates, standing for the cure of cancer, heart disease, stroke and all major killer-diseases, if we cannot see that for our species to survive we must have ImmorTalist Societies and ImmorTalist States, then we are no ImmorTalist. And we should not blaspheme against that sacred word by calling ourselves one.

6   But we are in luck, because the political situation is excellent for a new party and movement. A quick survey and analysis below will explain why.

Loss of Faith in Mortalist Regimes

7 **86% of Americans now see their government is " broken,"
according to a recent CNN poll.** So there is a political opening. It is possible for a third political force to emerge. But the
window for this to happen is short, and the path treacherous.

8 If there were such widespread and deep dissatisfaction with
any other regime in any other country, CNN would have been
quick to point out the situation is extremely unstable, volatile,
pre-revolutionary, or even revolutionary.

9 The so-called "Tea Party" Movement is a most current testimonial
to this political combustibility fueled by the American voter's
total disconnect to their rulers and their lack of faith in their dysfunctional money-greased political system. But such movements
tend to be hijacked or co-opted by one of the two ruling parties.

10 **American people and voters have lost faith in their Mortalist regime. The corollary: Americans believe fundamental
change is needed. And the same can be said for the people of
France, Germany, Spain, Greece, Ireland, Iceland, etc.**

Economic Meltdown + Political
Instability = Political Opening

11 The financial meltdown and the economic turmoil of the past
decade have opened the eyes of tens of millions. Awakened
from their zombied state. Breaking free of their programming.
The people see now that Mortalist Capitalism does not work.
It has failed. Just like the Soviets.

12 What people need now is a real, visible, compelling choice. An
ImmorTalist Party can and should give them a real alternative.
One which responds to their deepest needs. An ImmorTalist
Party which demands a Real War against the Real Terrors: Dis-
ease, Old Age, Death. A new party that is the standard bearer for
humanity's oldest dream: to vanquish Death, to liberate Life.

U.S. Instability since 1960s

13 The fact is the U.S. has been suffering political instability since the early 1960s. Kennedy won over Nixon by a squeaker in 1960. No mandate. The Cuban Missile Crisis, in which Kennedy and the U.S. proved quite willing to sacrifice the world in an all-out nuclear war with the Soviets. "Camelot" ended in President Kennedy's assassination. (Another attempt at Reagan almost succeeded. And an attempt at Ford. Yes, that's not only political instability, but political violence.)

14 Johnson took over after Kennedy was killed, won in a landslide over Goldwater (who led a Tea-Party-like movement). But then Johnson squandered his mandate on the Vietnam War debacle which plunged the nation into protests and turmoil. Counter-culture movements, civil rights, feminist, anti-war, gay movements raged all through sixties. Unpopularity over Vietnam forced Johnson to renounce running for a second term.

15 Nixon won by a thin victory in 1968. Again no mandate. The country bitterly split over Vietnam. Nixon won by a landslide in 1972 but less than two years later was facing impeachment over Watergate break-in which he covered up. Nixon became the first U.S. President to resign in disgrace. His Vice President Agnew went to jail. Then his handpick Gerald Ford was caretaker for two years before he was thrown out by the voters for his pardon of Nixon.

16 Then Jimmy Carter, the peanut famer-governor, won, waging an anti-Washington campaign. But Carter lasted only one term. Ronald Reagan, an aging B-movie actor, and Goldwater supporter, became President. But he got less than 51% of the popular vote.

17 **Reagan was a passive and senile front man who could never recognize the only black member of his Cabinet. The easier for Empire's power elite and handlers to control.** This modus operandi has been used in empires since the dawn of history. And it has now found favor in the American Em-

pire. Aside from Reagan, Bush Jr. obviously did not run the show.

18 Reaganism kowtowed to Wall Street and Big Business, justifying this by its "theory" of "trickle down" economics, which even Bush Senior called "voodoo economics." Reaganism started the the biggest peacetime military buildup in history, creating what was then the biggest government deficits, and still the biggest source of the U.S. deficit, the 800-pound gorilla which everyone pretends isn't even in the room. Reaganism bedded Wall-Street and busted Unions. Reagan won in the Southern Bible-Belt by getting the Republican Party into bed with the Religious Right, joining them in fag-bashing, race-baiting, law-and-ordering and Armaggedon-wishing.

19 Reagan insisted "Trees cause more pollution than automobiles do." He was the pioneer Global-Warming denialist. He invoked the doctrine of pre-emptive strikes before Bush Jr. (tried to assassinate Libya's Gaddafi by bombing him). While the epidemic raged, Reagan refused to even talk about AIDS until into his second term. Reaganism tried to get U.S. over trauma of Vietnam by cannot-fail desensitizing invasions; tiny Grenada was a dress rehearsal leading to the debacles in Iraq and Afghanistan.

20 As Paul Krugman, Nobel Laureate in Economics, points out, there's a direct line which leads from Ronald Reagan to George Bush Junior. Reagan's legacy includes huge budget deficits, out-of-control national debts, redistribution from middle class and poor to the very rich, tax giveaways to big business, reckless foreign and military policies and adventures, the gutting of safety-net social programs. The Great Cue-Card Reader's corrosive economic, social, and military policies continue to this day.

21 George Bush Senior succeeded Reagan, but was a failed one-termer. Bill Clinton beat Bush and became the first two-termer Democrat in a generation. But he failed to deliver on his pri-

mary campaign pledge of universal health care. In his first mid-term elections, his party lost control of Congress and he signed off on the dismantling of much of the U.S. social safety net.

22 In his second term, Clinton was impeached by a Republican House of Representatives over a blowjob by a fat intern. That was high crimes and misdemeanors, cried the Republicans. For rest of second term, Clinton was stalked by the Republican special persecutor like Ahab did the great white whale. Partisan vitriol and attacks reached a new peak during the Clinton years.

23 After Bill, Bush Junior restored the Bush dynasty by "winning" though he lost by half a million votes to Al Gore. Bush "won" a second term, again by dubious "winning" in Ohio over John Kerry. After the election, it was discovered that millions of votes were thrown away, not counted. (So there, American voter, you don't count.)

24 Angry over souring economy and Iraq and Afghanistian fiascoes, the country now after eight years of Bush and Republicans turned to an untested new Democratic Senator Barack Obama, who promised "transformation" and pullout from Iraq. The voters gave the Democrats control of both houses. Two years later, the voters ejected the Democrats from the House. And Obama is no longer popular with half the country. Plus, in elections, anywhere from 40 to 80 percent of voters choose not to vote. So most U.S. elections have no mandate or legitimacy.

25 If this is not political instability, what is? Politically, the U.S. is in chaos, and the situation for a new movement could not be better.

America's Great Cultural Revolution

26 All this time, the U.S. has been in the throes of a most vicious, unrelenting, paralyzing "Culture Wars" which makes the Maoist Cultural Revolution a tea party by comparison. In length China's Cultural Revolution lasted less than ten years.

The U.S. Culture Wars, on the other hand, has been raging since at least the McCarthy witch hunts of Communists starting in the late 1940s. The Culture Wars by no means began only in the 1960s. The American Cultural Revolution has been raging unabated for over six decades.

27 Every time you hear about the abortion or no-marriage-except-straights or prayer-in-school or "patriotism" (or lack thereof) issue, you are witnessing the U.S. Cultural Revolution. These issues have long been resolved in Europe, where the Inquisition, Christendom and their *theological* issues are no longer driving politics. But every time you see U.S. politicians attacking each other over such issues, ducking for cover, or rising or falling over them, you see the tremendous cost, paralysis and stalemate caused by this unremitting American Cultural Revolution. U.S. politics and its theological debates are more similar to Iran's theocratic state than to the E.U.

Two Nations Divisible?

28 What does the endless, intractable, unresolvable U.S. Cultural Revolution tell us? That **the United States is irretrievably split down the middle.** The cultural divide between the Bible Belt and the rest of the country is so deep and unbridgeable that the U.S. might as well be two countries. The difference in basic assumptions and beliefs between the Religious Right-dominant parts of the country and the rest of the U.S. is as big as the difference between Sweden and Franco's Spain.

29 The typical tourist to the U.S. visits only New York and Los Angeles and San Francisco. But were he or she to venture into the deep Bible Belt states, he or she would find it to be another country.

30 The split down the middle extends to U.S. politics as well. This is why the presidential elections are always so close, and so devoid of any clear mandate.

31 *This problem goes all the way back to the U.S. Civil War* in which the same Southern Bible-Belt states wanted to secede but were kept in the U.S. Empire by the war that killed over 620,000 Americans. More than all U.S. war casualties from its Revolutionary War to Vietnam. As the Religious Right and Tea-Party-ites show, it is not mere disagreement, it is hatred. The chasm is as wide and as explosive as ever. Will the U.S. Empire hold together?

The Empire in Rigor Mortis

32 No empire lasts forever. And great empires may decline *over a long period* before they disintegrate. For example, the Roman Empire declined over a period of hundreds of years before it collapsed. It was the same for China's Han Dynasty Empire.

33 So we should not be surprised that the U.S. Empire's decline began since the early sixties. Arguably as early as 1951. When in the Korean War, China, with no air force, and merely two years after Mao took over, was able to fight to a draw (i.e. defeat) McArthur's vastly superior U.S. forces. And dealt the U.S. Marines its worst rout ever.

34 Unlike an ImmorTalist Party in the E.U. which has a reasonable chance of getting into Parliament, the ImmorTalist Party in the U.S. does not. Except in the event of the Mortalist regime's total meltdown, economic and political.

35 *Such a meltdown is becoming more likely with each passing day as the U.S. (already insolvent, and, despite its crippling military budgets, refusing to let go of the Iraq or Afghanistan wars) is hurtling towards outright bankruptcy.*

36 In fact, **we predict that sooner or later, the meltdown and collapse of the U.S. Economy and Empire is unavoidable.** As soon as the world stops believing in the government's i.o.u's and the dollar bills the U.S. Federal Reserve is frantically printing, the meltdown could occur overnight and

with shocking force. <u>As Obama himself admitted on CNBC, "We're out of money now." And that was in 2009!</u>

37 But before the meltdown occurs, the U.S. ImmorTalist Party must come up with a way to transform the Mortalist system without engaging in quixotic campaigns. What Ross Perot and Ralph Nader have proved is that it is currently impossible to crack the totally-rigged and completely-closed two-party system.

38 *We demand an ImmorTalist Party that not only flails at the leaves and branches, but strikes at the root of the problem.*

39 We need an ImmorTalist Party so that we don't have to vote for the "lesser evil." We want to vote for our own party with a platform mirroring our deepest needs and desires. To be free from the scourge of Cancer, Heart Disease, Stroke et al killers. To strike at their source, at the Master Disease itself: The Aging Syndrome, of which all our ailments are nothing but symptoms.

40 We don't want to lose anymore when the con-artists from our "respectable" "established" parties win. What's the good of betting on a horse if when it wins you get nothing? Or worse, you lose?

41 In every election in every country, issues of life and death are not debated on the political agenda. Cancer, heart disease, stroke — we have been brainwashed into believing that these are not legitimate political issues. That they are "acts of God" or deaths by "natural causes." They are not.

∞

**We predict that sooner or later, the meltdown
and collapse of the U.S. Economy and
Empire will occur. It is unavoidable.**

∞

CHAPTER 12

U.S., E.U. or Scandinavia?
(Where is ImmorTalism's First Base?)

1 To win, The ImmorTalist Party needs different strategies for different nations.

2 Unlike the U.S., the political system in the E.U. and in Scandinavia especially is not totally rigged. It is not totally open either as the Mortalist parties in power of course do their best to create a system in their favor. But it is possible, though still difficult, for a new party to emerge.

3 The Parliamentary system in individual E.U. states and at the E.U. Parliament level is not a winner-take-all system like in the U.S. Here there is proportional representation. This means a new party does not have to either get the most number of votes or get nothing.

4 Proportional representation means that if a new party manages to get 4% of the votes, it will enter Parliament with 4 percent of its seats. So the votes of voters who choose to vote for new parties or minority parties are recognized and counted. Unlike in the U.S., where the system is intentionally designed to greatly discourage anyone from voting for any new party since their vote will be "wasted."

5 Exhibit A: While the Green Party has become an established party in E.U. states like Germany, France, and Sweden, the Green Party in the U.S. has gotten nowhere.

6 The Scandinavian countries have clean elections. Unlike the big-money-infested U.S. elections which usually go to the highest bids. In Sweden, for example, a new party, like the

Green Party was in the 1980s, did not have and did not need twenty million dollars to get into the Swedish Parliament. But the American pundit would argue that Sweden is a small country. Yes, but it is roughly the same population as New York City. And we know Multi-Billionaire Bloomberg spent $102 million of his own fortune to buy re-election. That came out to $174 per vote. And he barely "won". Swedish democracy is much more democratic. The last Parliamentary elections probably cost at most 10% of what Bloomberg spent.

7 So yes, it is possible for a new party to emerge and eventually get that threshold percentage of the vote (which probably hovers around 4%) to get into a national parliament. One must not underestimate the difficulty, but it is doable. An ImmorTalist Party must break into some parliament in the E.U. Whether it is in France, Germany, Spain, Ireland, Sweden, or Iceland. It should also aim to get into the E.U. Parliament which legislates for a population of 500 million people.

8   Can an ImmorTalist Party Win in the U.S.?

• Ross Perot, the billionaire who ran as an Independent presidential candidate, proved that the U.S. system is so rigged that even a billionaire like him who won over 19% of the popular vote lost 100%.

• When Steve Forbes, the publisher of Forbes magazine, was running for the Republican nomination for President, even he with his hundreds of millions was barred by the New York Republican Party from being on the ballot in its primary. He concluded that the New York Republican primary is as closed as anything in a Stalinist state.

• Ralph Nader, the most recent Third Party presidential candidate, was preceded by Eugene McCarthy and John Anderson. All worthy, all got nowhere.

9   The U.S. political system is rigged and its elections closed to any but the two official reigning parties. Even Thomas Fried-

man, the *New York Times* columnist, recently called the two-party system a "duopoly." Exactly the same charge leveled by Ralph Nader and Eugene McCarthy against the two parties.

10 Just as in its economy, its politics is "winner takes all". There is no such thing as proportional representation like in the European Parliamentary system.

11 The U.S. imposes extremely costly, crippling, and unconscionable demands on Third Parties and their candidates just to get on the ballot. They need to get thousands of signatures just to get on the ballot in each state or city. If they get all those signatures from their grassroots support, they still need to hire expensive lawyers to fend off court challenges to invalidate those signatures on arcane and technical grounds. By the time they get on the ballot (most don't), they have exhausted their funds and have little or no money to buy the election like the two parties can afford to.

12 It is no accident that all the periodic groundswell for Third Parties and their candidates in the United States have come up with a big zero. It is surely not a testament to either the Republican or Democratic Party's superiority or popularity. But rather to their ruthless and shameless imposition of basically insurmountable hurdles for a new party. On this duopolic rigging of elections, the two parties are in hearty agreement.

- When he was running for President, **Jerry Brown**, California's Governor third time around, pointed out that "$724 million was spent in 1994 to elect the 104th Congress, and most of it was intended to influence members of Congress in their official duties. That fits the classic definition of bribery. If Attorney General Janet Reno were actually defending the Constitution, she would indict the entire Congress as a criminal enterprise under the Racketeer Influenced and Corrupt Organizations Act (RICO)."

13 The U.S. political fundraising is nothing but **Legalized Corruption**. And Big Business and the wealthy are obviously not going to bet money on any Third Party since they want at least 50% chance of a big return. Like a billion-dollar tax break or tax-loophole.

14 What's "legal" campaign fundraising for U.S. Presidential, Congressional or Gubernatorial candidates would in most EU countries send the candidates not to Parliament but to jail.

15 The prevalence of legalized corruption explains why and how the U.S. regime could be bribed and gagged on such an earthshaking issue as Global Warming by its Oil Cartels and Big Business.

Run in Democratic or Republican Primaries?

16 It is possible to run ImmorTalist candidates of course in either the Democratic or Republican primaries or in both. Just to raise the flag, to ventilate the new ImmorTalist issues, to increase visibility and to prove we can win some voter support. It will be extremely difficult and thankless. Should ImmorTalist candidates in spite of the odds do well enough (though not win) in those primaries, it might get other Democratic or Republican candidates to try to co-opt their issues and positions at least in campaign speeches.

17 It is highly unlikely that either party would carry out the ImmorTalist agenda or platform after the election is over and it's back to business as usual. The most we can expect is a few more crumbs to be thrown our way, and the expectation that we would be most grateful. How can we be certain of this? By following the money. The two parties are financed by Big Business. The Republican Party a bit more than the Democratic Party.

18 **An ImmorTalist Party must change and challenge the Mortalist system in the U.S. not by playing by their rulebook,**

but by ours. To play by their rulebook is to lose. The only chance we have of winning is by creating our own rules for our own game. But we need to throw their own rulebook at them, and use it to create our own game.

Game-Change is our Strategy

19 How do we do it? That's the $64 million question.

20 Since the U.S. Empire is armed to the teeth and would not hesitate to crack our skulls, we must reject the reckless romantic adventurism of groups like the so-called Black Panther Party or the Weatherman in the sixties and seventies. They had no real constituency and were ignorant of the enormity of the "national security" apparatus they were facing. We reject similar groups in Europe, which in the 1960s and 1970s labored under the same political illusions and romanticism and came to naught and much grief. These sporadic juvenile stunts may be good for tabloid headlines and movies. But they do not result in any change or transformation.

21 In the U.S. Empire's plutocracy's big-money-fueled elections, we ImmorTalists should not drain ourselves and be bogged down in any kamikaze Third Party electoral campaigns which only demoralizes us and gets us nothing.

The Goal of an ImmorTalist Party?

22 The ImmorTalist Party's goal is not merely to make a point or to take a stand. It is not to feed at the trough like the Mortalist parties. It is not content at winning an election here or there. And not even a small minority slate in Congress or Parliament will satisfy it.

23 With two million people dying in the U.S. each year (not counting those dying in France, Germany, or Sweden, or the

rest of the world) it is simply not enough to merely increase the budget for the NIA (National Institute on Aging) or NIH (National Institutes on Health). Whether by two or ten times.

24 **The Goal of an ImmorTalist Party is to create an Immor-Talist State. The Elixxir Society.** *It is to win a state, as many significant states as possible, and turn them ImmorTalist. The purpose of The ImmorTalist State is 1) to cure Disease, Aging & Death, and 2) to save us from Global Warming, Biodiversity Collapse, and Mass Species Extinction.*

Important: We are not against Science and Technology. We are all for using Science and Technology to vanquish Disease, Old Age & Death. We are all for using Science and Technology to stave off the worst of Global Heating, Biodiversity Collapse, and Mass Species Extinction. We are for health-preserving life-extending Science, Medicine and Technology. Not dirty fossil-fuel-based technology. Green Technology. Clean Technology.

How the ImmorTalist Party Will Prevail over the Mortalist State

25 The Mortalist State is self-destructing. That's how ImmorTalism will win.

26 Lenin and the Bolshevik Party were the beneficiaries of the Russo-Japanese War. Lenin himself realized that the Bolshevik Party was not strong enough to push Tsardom aside. But he saw clearly that the humiliating and shocking defeat for the Tsar at the hands of the Japanese, and the disastrous Russian involvement in the First World War resulting in horrific casualties would be Tsarism's death knell

27 In the same way, the U.S. invasions and occupations of Iraq and Afghanistan and the financial and economic meltdown are bringing Mortalist Capitalism to its knees. And if these won't do it in, then Global Warming and its civilization-collapsing effects surely will.

People Will Turn to The ImmorTalist Party

28 When Gaia's wrath makes the sea surge and sweep away our great cities and coastal population centers, when global heating turns much of the earth into desert, when the tsunamis are upon us, then you can be sure that the mortals in The Death Society will turn away from Mortalism.

29 **The ImmorTalist Party shall be there. The only credible alternative. Like the British turned to Churchill, the people will turn to us since we would be the only party to have repeatedly warned of the coming apocalypse. And since we of all the parties have the courage to tell the voters what must be done to fend off disaster and catastrophe.**

30 *All the Mortalist parties are Appeasers of the Denialists. Only we would be free of the Appeasement taint. And so the people of the world shall see.*

31 The ImmorTalist Party will be the only party that will do whatever it takes to save *Homo Sapiens* and the Planet.

32 When the worst scenarios of global warming kick in and discredit all of the Mortalist parties and regimes for their denial, inaction, and bad actions, the people shall turn to us. Then they will have the will, born of desperation, to do what must be done to survive.

33 We shall be there. To lead the remnant. But it is our task to do everything possible to get the people to turn to us *before* the nightmare is upon us. While there is still time to prevent the worst.

34 We must salvage enough of civilization with enough science, medicine and technology to cure Disease, Old Age and Death.

35 Humanity's long march to conquer Disease, Old Age and Death is in its last mile. We must now gird up our loins, to make our audacious dash, to storm Mortalism's evil fortress. Or we shall have to face the unbearable possibility that The

Breakthroughs which can save us will come *after* we have expired.

36 What greater tragedy could there be? To miss The Breakthroughs by twenty-four hours is as bad as missing it by twenty-four centuries.

37 We see that Death will not give up easily. As we are ready to finally storm its lethal fortress with the new weapons of science, medicine and technology, Death materializes another daunting demon, a twin-headed one, that of Global Warming and Biodiversity Collapse, to make a last-ditch attempt to prevent us from seizing The Prize. We have no choice but to battle them all at once. Not only that, we have no option but total victory. For only in total victory will we preserve our lives, all Life, for all time.

38 If The ImmorTalist Party does not ascend to power and prevail, there can be no hope whatsoever for the human species. Extinction or virtual extinction will be our fate.

39 U.S.-style Mortalist Capitalism has conjured up the hellfires of a scorched Earth to engulf us. The Religious Right's wet dream is to turn its doomsday prophecies into our boiling reality.

40 If we don't prevail, humanity shall regress to a Stone Age existence on a fevered planet for the next 100,000 years. An eternity in hell of our own making.

41 So now we have a choice. A real choice. A stark choice.

42 It's between Life and Death. Heaven on Earth or Hell on Earth. For ever and ever.

43 We shall not fail because we can't afford to. The future of our species and the Planet itself depends on our winning.

CHAPTER 13
The ImmorTalist Party Platform

1 $888 BILLION for a U.S. WAR AGAINST DISEASE, OLD AGE & DEATH (D.O.D.) — <u>Save 2 Million Americans who die from Cancer, Heart Disease, Stroke etc. killers each and every year.</u> ($888 billion is only the same amount as The Wall Street Bailout & Car Industry Bailout. Alternatively, the amount should be as big as a country's annual Military Budget.)

2 BAIL OUT PEOPLE FIGHTING CANCER, HEART DISEASE, STROKE and other Life-Threatening Diseases from Financial Hardships

3 DRAMATICALLY INCREASE RESEARCH FUNDING FOR CANCER, HEART DISEASE, STROKE, OBESITY, DIABETES, ALZHEIMER'S, OSTEOPOROSIS, COPD, PARKINSON'S, SPINAL CORD INJURIES, AIDS & all other major killers.

4 MAKE ANTI-AGING RESEARCH A TOP FUNDING PRIORITY to save 79 million baby boomers in the U.S. and many billions more in the rest of the world

5 FUND PROVEN DIETARY OR LIFESTYLE INTERVENTIONS TO PREVENT OBESITY, HEART DISEASE, CANCER, STROKE, DIABETES, HYPERTENSION, OSTEOPOROSIS & ALZHEIMER'S.

6 GUARANTEE EMPLOYMENT, HEALTH CARE, HOUSING, RETIREMENT SECURITY & EARLY RETIREMENT AS HUMAN RIGHTS

7   PAID SABBATICALS – 1 year off for every 10 years of work

8   EARLY RETIREMENT – to lower high & persistent unemployment & decrease carbon emissions

9   INCREASE ALE (AVERAGE LIFE EXPECTANCY) BY 30 YEARS (China did it so it's possible!)

10 MAKE U.S. CATCH UP TO CUBA in ALE (AVERAGE LIFE EXPECTANCY)

11 SAVE 45,000 AMERICANS WHO DIE EACH YEAR FROM LACK OF HEALTH CARE by providing Universal Health Care

12 SAVE 8,000 U.S. BABIES FROM DEATH EACH YEAR by slashing the murderously high U.S. Infant Mortality Rate

13 TO PAY FOR ABOVE IMMORTALIST PROGRAMS, MAKE RICH CORPORATIONS PAY Their Fair Share of TAXES. STOP TAX BREAKS & WELFARE FOR MULTINATIONALS & THE RICH. SHUT DOWN THE RUINOUS & LOST WARS IN IRAQ & AFGHANISTAN WHICH ARE TURNING THE U.S. AND ITS ALLIES INTO MAGNETS FOR ATTACKS.

14 PREVENT NIGHTMARE SCENARIOS of GLOBAL WARMING, BIODIVERSITY COLLAPSE & MASS SPECIES EXTINCTION.

I. $888 BILLION for a U.S. WAR AGAINST DISEASE, OLD AGE & DEATH (D.O.D.) (or an amount as big as a country's annual Military Budget)

1   A Real War Against The Real Terrors: Heart Disease, Cancer, Stroke, Alzheimer's, Diabetes, Osteoporosis, AIDS, Obesity, and all the top killers.

2   9/11 killed around 3,000 people. These killer-diseases kill 2 million Americans each year. And countless millions around the world.

3   We must save as many of those who will otherwise be soon killed by HEART DISEASE, CANCER, STROKE, EMPHYSEMA, ALZHEIMER'S, DIABETES, PNEUMO- NIA, KIDNEY & LIVER DISEASES, OSTEOPOROSIS, AIDS, PARKINSON'S, PNEUMONIA, SPINAL CORD INJURY, SEPTICEMIA, OBESITY. An ImmorTalist gov- ernment will do so.

4   With genome mapping, stem cells, genetic engineering, scientists say <u>we are on the brink of major breakthroughs and cures</u> for cancer, heart disease, stroke, diabetes, Parkin- son's, spinal cord injuries and other top killers. It is *criminal* that the Mortalist regimes are not dramatically increasing research funding now but instead are axing such funding. Such life-saving research is essential to saving you, your loved ones, and the countless billions who will die of such diseases in the future. The ImmorTalist Party stands for im- mediate correction of this lethal Mortalist policy.

5   <u>If the number of deaths from cancer, heart disease, stroke were the result of foreign attacks or wars, it would no doubt force any government to make the prevention or decrease of such casualties its Number One Funding Priority.</u>

6   We say every death from heart disease, cancer and stroke etc is just as unacceptable as those from 9/11 or wars. Because every death from disease is *preventable, premature or treatable or cur- able*.

7   Your chances of dying from another 9/11 attack are nil. But your chances of dying from heart disease, cancer, stroke, or any one of the other killer-diseases are excellent. So we de- mand The Death Society correct its grossly-misplaced priori- ties to protect us from the real threats you face every day. An ImmorTalist government vows to do this.

II. BAILOUT People Fighting Life-Threatening Diseases (and their families) from financial hardship or bankruptcy.

1   The Mortalist regimes scurried to bailout Wall Street, Investment Banks, Hedge Funds, The Car Industry, and throw tax cuts and tax-loopholes at billionaires. The ImmorTalist Party demands that it should have at least the decency to bailout the real heroes: people struggling with cancer, heart disease, stroke, diabetes, Alzheimer's, etc, as well as their longsuffering families. The ImmorTalist Party stands for this and vows to make it a top priority in an ImmorTalist government.

2   **EMERGENCY FINANCIAL ASSISTANCE** for unemployment, paid leaves of absence, disability, rehabilitation, health care & prescription medicine coverage, nursing care (short or long term), Medicare eligibility before 65, early retirement option, access to promising new treatments or clinical trials, dietary counseling or interventions which could prevent, alleviate or reverse heart disease, hypertension, diabetes, cancer, stroke, Alzheimer's, osteoporosis, etc.

III. INCREASE DISEASE RESEARCH FUNDING DRAMATICALLY

1   Discover New and Better Preventions, Treatments & Cures for Heart Disease, Cancer, Stroke, Obesity, Diabetes, Alzheimer's, Osteoporosis, AIDS and all major killers. In time to save you and your loved ones. And to make sure that the scourge of Disease is eradicated from human existence. (**Make sure you sign Our Demand** at the beginning of this manifesto.)

IV. MAKE ANTI-AGING RESEARCH A TOP PRIORITY

1   **Anti-aging research is the path to revolutionary treatments or cures for aging-related diseases like heart disease, cancer, stroke.** If cancer, heart disease, stroke, Alzheimer's, osteoporosis, obesity etc are Aging-Related and Aging-Correlated diseases, as Science and Medicine agree

they are, then Anti-Aging Research which sees them as *symptoms* of a master disease syndrome (The Aging Syndrome) will lead us to life-saving treatments or cures faster and more cheaply.

A) In addition to the traditional research strategy, we need to fund a *new paradigm* which sees that heart disease, cancer, stroke, diabetes, osteoporosis are heavily-correlated with our biological aging, and therefore are *symptoms* of our biological aging. This paradigm is in line with the mission of the National Institute on Aging (NIA) as stated in the 1974 Act of Congress creating it.

B) Anti-Aging Research is urgently needed to ensure that those born after the Second World War, the biggest population group, will remain healthy. So as not to unduly burden the health care system. To remain productive and continue to contribute to society. In the U.S., boomers are 79 million strong.

2   *The graying demographics is the biggest threat to most affluent nations. Whether it be the U.S., Japan, Germany, U.K., France, or Scandinavian nations like Sweden, Norway, Denmark, Finland.*

3   The ImmorTalist Party says that a graying population obviously demands anti-aging research. It promises that an ImmorTalist government will make anti-aging research one of its highest priorities.

V. DIETARY/LIFESTYLE INTERVENTIONS TO PREVENT OBESITY, HEART DISEASE, CANCER, STROKE, DIABETES, HYPERTENSION, OSTEOPOROSIS & ALZHEIMER'S

1 Fund, create, or invest in *scientific* dietary and lifestyle intervention programs which are proven to prevent or slash our risk for diseases of aging like cancer, heart disease, stroke, obesity, hypertension, diabetes, Alzheimer's, osteoporosis.

2   Such a scientifically proven dietary intervention already exists. It has been repeatedly proven in prestigious laboratories and published in peer-reviewed scientific journals over
decades. In addition to slashing our risks for heart disease,
cancer, stroke, obesity, diabetes, Alzheimer's, osteoporosis,
it also slows down our biological aging by up to 50%. It may
also extend our maximum human lifespan of 120 significantly. The Elixxir Program is an adaptation of this anti-cancer,
anti-heart-disease, anti-stroke, anti-aging diet. It is designed
to make it possible for more people to enjoy its life-saving
benefits. If there are other practical, doable adaptations, they
will be explored and funded too in the ImmorTalist state.

3   The ImmorTalist Party will do everything possible to educate
voters and the public on proven and potent scientific dietary
or lifestyle interventions. Compared to triple-bypass surgery,
stroke rehabilitation, chemotherapy, surgery to staple stom-
achs for morbid obesity, dietary interventions are very inexpensive and not saddled with serious side effects as many expensive drugs are.

4   The Elixxir Society and State shall do everything in its power
to invest in or fund programs to teach the population how
to use diet and nutrition to greatly decrease the incidence of
expensive chronic diseases like cancer, stroke, heart failure,
Alzheimer's, and as an effective way to cut costs for its health
care system and maintain its long term viability.

VI. GUARANTEED EMPLOYMENT, HEALTH CARE, HOUSING, RETIREMENT SECURITY & EARLY RETIREMENT

1   The ImmorTalist Party stands for everyone working less, getting paid more, and retiring earlier and enjoying paid sabbaticals before retirement. This is the only way to avoid the
catastrophic scenarios of Global Warming by greatly lowering society's carbon emissions. It is also the best way to lower
the high and persistent unemployment rate in many countries.

2   *The baby boomers* — those born after the Second World War whether in the U.S., E.U. or Japan — *have paid their dues.* Their spending has been responsible for the longest economic "boom" in U.S. and E.U. history. Society must now honor its covenant with the boomers to guarantee their retirement security on a livable pension. To solve the high unemployment and to make way for the younger generations, we will encourage early retirement at 58 or 60 by making it financially possible to do so and still maintain a good quality of life.

3   ***The ImmorTalist Party denounces the new "law" rammed through the French Parliament, without allowing for adequate debate, refusing to defer to the people's sovereign will.*** The ImmorTalist Party opposes this new "law" to raise the French retirement age from 60 to 62. It condemns all similar retroactive illegal "laws." **Elect ImmorTalist Party candidates to the French Parliament and we shall work tirelessly and ceaselessly to rescind and overturn this illegal outrage and to <u>lower the retirement age to 58.</u>**

4   We condemn this as a shameful betrayal of the state's explicit covenant with an entire French generation about to retire. French President Sarkozy claims there is no money, but there is money to give himself a salary raise of 140% — from 101,000 Euros to 240,000 Euros annually.

5   **This so-called new Sarkozy "law" is illegal and unconscionable because it brazenly tears up the State's written explicit contract with the French people and puts in a new contract without the French People's assent.** Such a regime must fall. The ImmorTalist Party therefore supports continued relentless opposition by the French workers and people to the Sarkovsky regime on this. It is a template which other Mortalist states in the EU will try to follow to increase their retirement age and to attack their Retirement Pension Security package for Big Business.

- The ImmorTalist Party stands for the immediate over-turning and rescinding of this and all such "legislation." When an ImmorTalist state comes to power, we shall not only restore the retirement age to 60, but <u>lower it to 58 years in France and throughout the EU</u>, to lower unemployment and make way for the younger genera-tion in jobs.

6   Immortalism vows to break the yoke of repression imposed by Mortalist Capitalism's regimen of "blood, sweat and tears." ImmorTalism stands for Life.And its Party's mission is to free up as much of Life as possible for you. This is why, unlike the Mortalist state which supports a return to 18th cen-tury capitalist serfdom, The ImmorTalist Party supports Early Retirement and full Retirement Security.

7   This is a top and "holy" priority for The ImmorTalist Party and any ImmorTalist Government.

- **<u>The ImmorTalist Party stands for the constitu-tional enshrining of Retirement Security and Early Retirement as part of the basic, inalienable, and guaranteed Human Rights so that no Mortalist re-gime can tamper with it.</u>**

8   *This is one reason why it is imperative to elect as many Im-morTalist Party candidates to the EU Parliament as quickly as possible.*

WARNING: The Sarkozy regime and similar ones in Europe are taking orders from the IMF and Big Business to *regress* the EU to a Reaganist 18th century Jungle Capitalism. <u>They are trying to ape the U.S. model in Europe even though the U.S. model is mired in the most serious financial crisis since the Great Depression of the 1930s!</u> And even though the U.S. is insolvent and on the verge of bankruptcy. Such is their ide-ological blindness and idiocy that they do not deserve to hold one single seat in any Parliament. What the rightwing par-ties stand for is the equivalent of following the Third Reich Model in its last days in 1944.

VII. PAID SABBATICALS: ONE YEAR OFF EVERY TEN

1   After the first ten years of work, a person is entitled to one
     paid year off. This is a paid one-year "sabbatical." Or mini-
     early-retirement. Which can be used by younger workers to
     recharge their batteries, indulge in their hobby, or take a long
     dream vacation around the world.

VIII. DO WHATEVER IT TAKES to Alleviate GLOBAL WARM-ING, BIODIVERSITY COLLAPSE & MASS SPECIES EXTINCTION.

1   Unlike in The Death Society, global warming, biodiversity
     collapse, and mass species extinctions will be urgent top pri-
     orities for The ImmorTalist Movement, Party and Society.
     This must be backed up by serious government budgets and
     commitments to cut carbon emissions by whatever it takes to
     fend off the nightmare scenarios of global warming, biodi-
     versity collapse and mass species extinction which threatens
     our very civilization. It means signing and implementation
     of the Convention on Biological Diversity (CBD). It means
     emergency funding for rapid creation of nature preserves and
     oceanic sanctuaries around the world to minimize the mass
     species extinction already happening.

2   Unlike the Mortalist parties and regimes which are capable only
     of short-term planning and focus (the next election, the next
     quarterly earnings reports), ImmorTalist Parties and ImmorTalist
     Governments — by their nature and because of their ultimate
     goal — care deeply about our immediate and long term future, as
     well as the planet's future. We shall do everything in our power
     to preserve the planet and its species for the long term future.
     Unlike the Mortalist Capitalist parties, we fully grasp that Global
     Warming has the serious potential to not merely wreak havoc
     with hurricanes and tsunamis and heat waves, its worst case sce-
     narios can destroy Civilization itself. Since the window of op-
     portunity to still do something is almost closing, we must act at
     once, and effectively, to prevent a nightmare future.

3   Anyone who wants to cure cancer, heart disease, stroke, diabetes, Alzheimer's, AIDS, osteoporosis, spinal cord injuries, Parkinson's IN TIME TO SAVE US should support the ImmorTalist Movement and The ImmorTalist Party.

4   You don't have to wish to live forever to support us.

5   No ImmorTalist Party or State is going to require anyone to live one day longer than he or she wish. Rest assured. It is the Mortalist Parties and State that are denying you the choice of more life. **The Death Society is robbing you of the opportunity to live to 120 (your maximum life span) in youthful vigor.**

6   To continue supporting the Mortalist parties — in which curing Cancer, Heart Disease, Stroke, and other killers are at the bottom of their agenda and priorities — is to vote for your own Death.

7   For the first time in human history, we are on the brink of revolutionary new treatments and cures. But the Mortalist State and Parties refuse to do anything but throw crumbs at such research. They even ban them.

8   The $64 million question is: are the life-saving cures and breakthroughs going to come in time to save you and your loved ones?

9   **The ImmorTalist Movement, The ImmorTalist Party, and The Elixxir Society are 100% committed to doing everything in our power to make The Breakthrough Treatments and Cures arrive in time to save you and your loved ones.**

10 **But we need your help and support** to make history. You have the choice: to fight back and support us, or to go quietly into that dark night.

11 **You have nothing to lose but Disease, Old Age & Death. Nothing to lose but a life of endless, meaningless, life-robbing toil under Mortalist Capitalism.**

Mortals of the World Unite!

CHAPTER 14
Join The Elixxir Society
(The Twelve ImmorTalists)

1 So where have you been all this time? Elixxir has been waiting for you. And you've been waiting for him.

2 Get Elixxir 12 good ImmorTalists and we shall overturn Mortalism. And transform The Death Society into The Elixxir Society.

3 **Evolutionary Destiny has already created the 12 Great
ImmorTalists. They are already out there. If you are, or
you believe you are, one of the twelve, then it is your duty
to identify and offer yourself. There is much to be done,
and so little time to do it in.**

4 Yes, you should come and visit Elixxir in Europe. In Scandinavia. Near the Arctic Circle. *Come join The Elixxir Society.
Before it's too late.*

5 As Dr. James Lovelock, the eminent British climate scientist points out, once Global Heating kicks in, only the areas
around the Arctic Circle would be tolerable and habitable.
And this is where the remnants of collapsed Mortalist Civilization will retreat to build a new civilization.

6 Sweden, Norway, Finland, Greenland (Denmark), Russia,
Canada and Alaska (U.S.) all have land surrounding the Arc-
tic Circle (also known as "the Arctic Basin"). When Global
Heating makes most of the planet too hot to live, the areas
around the Arctic Circle will be the cradle of our new Immor-
Talist Civilization.

7 Why wait until catastrophe has struck to make the pilgrimage to the North? You might as well do it now. Better now than later.

8 We must build a new ImmorTalist Civilization. One that is free from Mortalism, its ideology of Death, its Mortalist Regimes, and its Death Societies.

9 Our ImmorTalist Civilization will be totally dedicated to Life. There will be no ambivalence about Life or Death. We are *for* Life and *against* Death. We are Pro-Life all the way. Life with no limits. Life liberated from Disease, Old Age and Death.

10 Only such a civilization, an ImmorTalist Civilization, can survive. Because only it will refuse to repeat the self-annihilations of Mortalist Civilization. Only it will refuse to glory in Death as Mortalism does in its endless wars, its "acceptance of Death," its Cult of Human Sacrifice.

11 **Only mortals who love Life enough to demand Immortality will care enough to save the planet. Only the long-lived wannabes — and the long-lived — have a stake in the planet's future.**

12 Elixxir is already here. In Europe. Near the Arctic Circle. If you are a serious ImmorTalist, or serious about staying alive, then you need to be here too.

20 Years to Save the World

13 Former U.S. Vice President and Nobel Peace Laureate Al Gore reportedly warned before the 2009 Copenhagen Climate Summit that many top climate scientists believe that we have at most five years to prevent the nightmare scenarios from becoming our daily reality. But since the U.S. and the Climate-Warming Denialists have succeeded in demolishing what may be our last hope at Copenhagen, what happens to those five years?

14 Dr. James Lovelock, the eminent British climate scientist who came up with the "Gaia" theory, fears it is already too late. That all we can hope for is **a remnant living around The Arctic Circle to try to rebuild a collapsed civilization.**

15 Lovelock recently estimated that **if we're "lucky**," "it's going to be **20 years before it hits the fan."** (Bold added)

16 We need to take seriously Lovelock's best estimate that we have a mere 20 years before shit hits the fan. No Mortalist state would, but an ImmorTalist State would. And before our state arrives, all real ImmorTalists, The ImmorTalist Movement and The ImmorTalist Party must take this 20 years' last chance of rescue most seriously.

17 Because there are other climate scientists who have come to a similar conclusion but are not at liberty to publicize it. Lovelock has been an independent scientist and he can say what he pleases. At 91, he is not worried they're going to take his "medals" away.

18 **20 years may be all the time that an ImmorTalist movement is given to do whatever it takes to i) prevent the apocalyptic scenarios of Global Warming from devastating our civilization, and/or ii) create the Remnant to replace the Mortalist Civilization which is collapsing from its economic financial meltdown and whose fate will be sealed when the full brunt of global heating and biodiversity collapse hits.**

19 So at the same time we joust with the unholy trinity of Disease, Old Age & Death, we must also fend off the looming specter of Global-Heating-induced disaster which could melt down civilization and extinguish most of the human species.

20 **Let's listen to Dr. James Lovelock: "Before this century is over, billions of us will die, and the few breeding pairs of people that survive will be in *the arctic region*, where the climate remains tolerable."**

21 Location, location, location. Elixxir already has gained a foothold near the Arctic Circle. He can get to the Arctic Circle anytime he wishes should the need arise.

21A How about you? Are you joining Elixxir? If you are destined to be a member of The Remnant, step forward and be counted now. There is no time to lose.

Why Live a Wretched Life?

22 Why are young people living like Third World coolies in New York City? Paying 500 to 800 dollars for tiny cramped coolie rooms. 6 1/2 by 8 1/2 feet. A cubicle really. Some living in dangerous neighborhoods. Three or four or even five packed like sardines into an apartment. With mice and bugs as company.

23 **What kind of life is that?** To be in New York? Doing what? Learning how to be a Mortalist serf the rest of your life?

23A **Why are you putting up with such a moiling, wretched life? You are not happy. Elixxir *knows* you are not happy**.

24 You can come to Europe and live for three months with no need for a visa if you have a U.S. Passport. Why don't you take advantage of that while it lasts? Come and help Elixxir hatch The Elixxir Society. And have a hundred times more fun, more meaning, and more purpose in your life.

25 Come join The Elixxir Society!

26 There's *la dolce vita* to be had here in Europe. In Scandinavia. In Stockholm. It's enchanting here in spring, summer, and fall. For the winter, we can either stand our ground like a Viking or go like the birds to warmer climes. Provence, Tuscany, Madrid, Barcelona, the Canary Islands are easily within grasp. If we hunger for huge cities, then we can hop on a plane and go to Berlin, London, or Paris.

27 It's *not* a shabby life. Why live like a coolie drudging on $40,000 or more a year in Manhattan when you can live very nicely on that here?

28 Bars, restaurants, clubs. You will find some of the most fabulous in Stockholm and in Scandinavia. Sweden has produced not merely Stieg Larsson, Abba or Ikea but also Bergman, Garbo and Strindberg.

29 As Andy Warhol observed, there are more beauties here of either gender than you will ever find in New York City. Why do you think the scouts for the modeling agencies all flock here like vultures?

30 People have a much higher quality of life in most of Europe compared to the U.S. It's a fact. Come and see for yourself.

31 But most importantly, you can be part of a movement to eliminate Disease, Old Age & Death (D.O.D.). A movement to save the planet from Global Heating and Biodiversity Collapse.

32. Isn't that a better use of your life than being an unpaid intern for some company that's bloodsucking you? An internship which has no real possibility of ending in a permanent position, especially one with a livable wage. Not to mention no good health care coverage and no retirement benefits.

What Shall We Do in The Elixxir Society?

33 **Elixxir will, first and foremost, teach you The Elixxir Program.** So that you will stay young. So that obesity and diabetes and all the Symptoms of Aging won't creep up on you. Or if you are no longer young, The Elixxir Program can slow down your biological aging as much as possible — based on the only anti-aging intervention known to 21st century science and medicine.

34 If you are really an ImmorTalist, or want to be one, you must show it by your lifestyle, your eating and your meals.

35 It's like when all those eager new recruits went to India to join Gandhi's movement. The first thing he told them was not to organize a rally or make a speech or write an article. The first thing he taught them was how to use the spinning wheel to make their own clothing from Indian cotton.

36 When you join Elixxir and his Elixxir Society, the first thing he will teach you is The Elixxir Program.

37 And The Elixxir Program is not free. It is priceless. If it were free, you would not take it seriously. Therefore you would not benefit from its life-saving age-retarding life-extending power.

38 The Elixxir Program tuition and fees for "room and board" will help Elixxir seed and sustain The Movement and Party. If Judaeo-Christianity still sells its "Bible" to help sustain itself after thousands of years, then we, The ImmorTalist Movement and Party, are lucky to have The Elixxir Program serving the same function. What's more, The Elixxir Program, unlike the Judeo-Christian Book, is scientific, and can keep you from growing old, fat, sick, and ugly. Not to mention dead.

Match The Mormons

39 180 years after its founding, The Mormon Church (Glenn Beck and Presidential Candidate Mitt Romney are Mormonites) still "expects" its single adult youth to serve **two years** of **fulltime missionary service**. And the Mormon youths do as expected.

40 These two years of missionary service are totally unpaid. And this is required of every rank-and-file member. To pay for these two years, young missionary volunteers and their families must save up money for years to pay for those two years' living expenses which cost around $10,000. They have to pay for everything including roundtrip airfare, room and board for two years. So they raise this money from their parents, their friends, their church members.

41 As if that's not demanding enough, Mormon missionaries do not have any choice as to where they serve. After they turn in their mission papers to church headquarters, they are issued a "mission call" by the church's presidency.

42 Missionaries proselytize for 12 hours every day, from 9:30 a.m. to 9:30 p.m. They knock on doors (known as "tracting") which is more daunting than the salesperson's "cold calling." They chat up people on the street. Remember, these are 19 year olds whose peers would think it is the height of "uncool" to do such things. And yet the Mormon Church has no problem getting millions of its youths to do all these "uncool" things.

43 A strict schedule dictates what time they come home at night and when they get up in the morning. During these two years (when they are usually 19 to early 20s), there's no dating, no television, no movies, no Internet surfing, no personal phone calls! They may write home once a week and are allowed to call home twice a year.

44 Male missionaries must wear suit, white shirt, and tie, and be clean-shaven. Female missionaries must wear only full-length modest dresses or skirts. And they address each other as "Elder" (for the guys) and "Sister" (for the gals).

45 The Marines sounds like more fun!

46 And yet, by 2007, the Mormon church had dispatched its one-millionth volunteer missionary into the world. In 2008 alone, over 52,000 full-time Mormon missionaries were serving around the globe.

47 Is it any wonder that the Mormon Church is one of the fastest growing churches in the world?

48 But it's not just the Mormons. To join a Catholic order, any Catholic order, you need to give up all your possessions still. It is not only the so-called "cults" which make this demand.

49 If we cannot match their fanaticism with our commitment, then we are no ImmorTalist, and we shall perish. It's that simple.

Where's our Trotsky? Our St. Paul?

50 It is so easy now to get a cheap flight to anywhere in Europe to meet Elixxir. But it was not so easy for 23-year-old Trotsky when he wanted to meet Lenin and offer his services. Lenin was in London, and Trotsky was in exile in Siberia.

51 To meet Lenin, Trotsky had to leave his wife and two children and escape their Siberian exile. Penniless, Trotsky managed to make his way across Europe. And crossed the English Channel. One early morning, there was a knock on the humble London abode of Lenin. Lenin's wife answered the door, and saw Trotsky on their doorstep.

52 The Chinese Communist movement started its Long March of 8,000 miles to escape U.S. supported dictator Chiang Kai Shek. Of the 100,000 communists who began the march, only 8,000 made it to Yan'an where they regrouped and rebuilt the movement. Extremely inaccessible, rural, and poor, Yan'an did not deter thousands of Chinese from all parts of China making their way to its caves to join the Communist movement. During the brutal Japanese occupation of China, thousands more Chinese made the treacherous pilgrimage to Yan'an to offer their services, and often their very lives.

Raise Your Own Salary in Six Months

53 The biggest fundamentalist church in the world is probably South Korea's Yoido Full Gospel Central Church in Seoul. Since 1958, it has metastasized into one million members, all proudly organized in tens of thousands of Maoist-style cell groups. Its founding pastor boasted that when he sent out his pastors to plant a new church, within six months they succeed in getting their new congregation to pay their own salaries. Within six months!

54 You think of course you're smarter than those holy rollers. Well, if you're so smart, prove to Elixxir that you can do what those pastors still peddling real estate in heaven can do in six months.

55 *Elixxir challenges you.* Do what they do, and our ImmorTalist Movement will be fully staffed with the best and the brightest on the planet in no time at all.

56 If these prosperity-gospel peddlers can create a church of a million members in roughly the same time that the Pseudo-Immortalist sect has existed, it shows you how dead as a door-nail Pseudo-Immortalism is.

57 **The real ImmorTalist Movement and The Elixxir Society must not only match but exceed the feat of these Korean pentecostalists and in a much shorter time. If we are to save our individual, societal, and planetary futures.**

58 *Ex-pentecostalist, ex-Mormon, ex-Marine, ex-Jehovah's Witness, ex-fundamentalist, or ex-military are welcome to join us. We need your self-discipline, your seeing that there's a need for organization and leadership, and your capacity for 100% commitment to the greatest cause.*

59 In the beginning they will dismiss us, even laugh at us. But what else is new? Didn't they laugh at Noah's Ark? Didn't they laugh at all the new political movements and parties until they succeeded? But that's why we need ImmorTalists strong enough to defy Mortalist public opinion and the Mortalist media. We shall have the last laugh. Rest assured.

60 **We need ImmorTalist Warriors.**

61 Are those Mormons and Pentecostals "fanatics"? Yes, and The ImmorTalist Movement could use a million of them to triumph over Disease, Aging and Death, and to save The Planet.

Our Golden Egg: The Elixxir Program

62 Their holy book is 2,000 to 4,000 years old. They have to sell ancient illusions and delusions. They sell real estate in heaven. And still they make a thriving trade out of it. What excuses do we have?

63 Come, you can exploit Elixxir and The Elixxir Program. If we cannot sell an anti-aging guru who's actually stayed young, who can pass for 29 in his fifties, then we can't convince the masses of anything. But Elixxir knows you can.

64 If Estée Lauder can make a billion-dollar business out of selling hope with her kitchen potions, we surely can do better with <u>The Elixxir Program, based on the only scientific anti-aging program. The only game in town if you want to greatly retard your aging and have a real shot at extending the maximum human lifespan of 122 by up to 50%.</u> There is one person reading this manifesto out there right now who can turn The Elixxir Program into a billion-dollar business so that ImmorTalism will have some spare change to send it into orbit.

65 Unless we ImmorTalists have the same level of total commitment to our cause as the Mormons, the Bolsheviks, the Long March partisans, we will not achieve our goals of curing cancer, heart disease, stroke. And we won't find a cure for Aging. And we will surely die.

What Will You Be Doing If You Join Elixxir?

66 *We are incubating The Elixxir Society! The alternative to The Death Society. We are creating a new way of life.* Not just a new paradigm, but a new Life-Style. The Elixxir LifeStyle™. In opposition to Mortalism's DeathStyle™.

67 Just like missionaries, we must plant ImmorTalist Movements and Parties all across the E.U. And in the U.S., Canada and Japan.

68 But **unlike Mormon missionaries, and unlike Death Society's Blood, Sweat and Tears, we are at the same time
training on The Elixxir Program, eating fabulous meals,
sipping the best wines, uncorking the finest bottles of
champagne, marauding through the international play-
grounds, living each day as if it were our last, savoring
the midnight sun, and learning the immortalist politics of
bliss and love by living it.**

69 **Let's model and materialize The Elixxir Society. The alternative, the replacement, for The Death Society.**

70 **Let's create The ImmorTalist Movement and The Immor-
Talist Party and win ourselves an ImmorTalist State. Not
just one, but a whole bunch of ImmorTalist States.**

71 **Toward our goals, we write and publish books. Make movies for ourselves and for the world. Do performance art,
stage demonstrations, recruit and duplicate. And organize, organize, organize.**

72 Life in Europe — especially in Scandinavia — is very fine
indeed. Sweden, Norway and Finland regularly rank near or
at the top of countries with the best Quality of Life. Compared
to the average American "middle class" existence, life here is
amazingly nice, gentle, and secure.

Are You One of the Twelve?

73 **There are twelve kinds of talents that Elixxir is urgently
looking for. Elixxir needs a filmmaker or film producer,
an editor, a publisher, an organizer, a promoter, a wiz fundraiser, a great publicist, a direct marketeer, a webmaster
and web designer. And of course a billionaire or two. And
a Chief of Staff.**

74 Give Elixxir these and we shall have The ImmorTalist Movement and The ImmorTalist Party that we desperately need. In

less time than you imagine, we can take over a Mortalist state and turn it ImmorTalist.

75 If you are one of the above, please answer the call.

76 There is no pay in the beginning. Not even for Elixxir at this point. It's an Unpaid Internship or Apprenticeship to begin with. If you are really good, then you or we should be able to get you a salary in six months to a year. Just like the South Korean church.

77 We need to put our professional ImmorTalist talents to the best use, and not waste their time. Yes, we need *Professional* ImmorTalists. We are tired of the Pseudo-ImmorTalist amateurs.

78 We demand Immortalists who know how to do things, how to run things, how to organize political campaigns, how to promote a fundraiser-concert, how to turn Elixxir, the only anti-aging guru and philosopher, into a movie, a movie franchise, a book, a series of bestselling books. That shouldn't be hard if you are someone who knows how to do it. If you are in a position to make those things happen.

79 If we can only get people who demand pay at the going rate to help us, then we are not going to make it as a movement. And if we don't make it as a movement, we won't make it, period. The Ancient Mortalist Religions are still demanding "martyrdom" of their believers. And still getting it.

80 ImmorTalism is the only movement which does not demand your martyrdom. *ImmorTalism does not want you to die for it; ImmorTalism wants you to live for it.*

80A So here in more detail are the Twelve ImmorTalists we need for The ImmorTalist Movement:

1. Chief of Staff – You can help Elixxir find all the others below. And organize his time, schedule him, be his gatekeeper.

2. Majordomo – You can run Elixxir's household and put the Pope's majordomo to shame.

3. Filmmaker/Film Producer – You can make an epic movie franchise out of Elixxir.

4. Editors, Publishers – You can edit and publish Elixxir and ImmorTalist books.

5. Book Agents, Talent Agents – You can turn Elixxir into a bestselling series that rivals Tolkien and Harry Potter. After all, an intimate peek into the life of "the only anti-aging guru who has actually stayed young" (Investor's Business Daily) should sell at least a few million copies.

6. Online List Builders, Social Networking consultants, Webmasters, Web designers – Come and help. We should have as many subscribers as Facebook.

7. Organizers – You know how to get us the millions suffering from life-threatening diseases and their loved ones. You know how to or could learn how to organize everything from a benefit concert to a march on Washington.

8. Fundraisers – You know how to raise money for The ImmorTalist Movement and The ImmorTalist Parties.

9. Publicists – You know how to get us media buzz. And you know how to handle all the Mortalist smears and attacks coming our way.

10. Direct Marketer – You know direct marketing cold. Direct mail. Internet direct marketing. We've got lots of work for you.

11. Attorneys & Accountants – Yes, we need you too.

12. ImmorTalist Multimillionaires/Billionaires – You can help support the ImmorTalist Movement and its Parties. We need your help. And you need us to stay alive.

The Young ImmorTalists

81 If you are not any of the above, but you are absolutely convinced you should be *one of us*, and that you could contribute to The Elixxir Movement, Party, and Society, then by all means let Elixxir know. He will be happy to stand corrected.

82 Experience is not always needed. Gary Hart was a 34 year old new lawyer who had never run a significant political campaign. McGovern recruited him and Hart became the general of a guerilla political campaign which won McGovern the nomination against all odds. Pat Caddell was a 21 year old Harvard senior who became McGovern's whiz pollster.

83 The same can be said for many of the top assistants, aides, and operatives on the other side. From the Goldwater campaign to the inner sanctum of the Religious Right. It is always the young and the fearless who get things done, who shake things up, who, yes, change the world. The young don't know it couldn't be done, so they go ahead and do it.

The Boomer ImmorTalists

84 Ah, my dear Baby Boomers. You are the greatest generation. You ended racial segregation. You put a stop to an unjust and genocidal war. You freed women and gays. And you created the environmental movement.

85 But now the question is: are you going to go quietly, and bitterly, into that dark night? Like all the generations before you. Or are you going to use all your experience, expertise, and hard lessons, and this time go all the way to fulfill your utmost potential.

86 Your dream of eternal youth and saving the planet was, and is, right on. Now it's time to put the foundation under it. And in the process procure for all mortals The Cure for Cancer, Heart Disease, Stroke, and conquer the Master Disease of Aging.

So that humanity can finally say in victory "O Death, where is thy sting?"

What Could be More Important?

87 If you are in the U.S., it's easy to come to Europe or Scandinavia. If you are already in Europe — France, Germany, the United Kingdom or in Scandinavia — then it's even easier. Take the first step. E-mail.

88 Step forward and identify yourself and put yourself in the service of Immortalism. To Cure Disease, Old Age, Death. To save the planet and species from Global Warming and Biodiversity Collapse. That is our mission.

89 Remember, only ImmorTalism which totally embraces Life and absolutely rejects Death can save us from the gathering storm. Only The Elixxir Society ready to do *whatever it takes* can turn back the Armaggedon clock, which is one minute to midnight.

90 Is there anything more important than this? So what are you waiting for? Come visit Elixxir and join The Elixxir Society. He needs your help.

immortalism.com

ElixxirSociety.com

∞

Twenty years may be all the time The ImmorTalist Movement is given to do whatever it takes to cure Disease, Old Age & Death, to fend off the nightmare scenarios of Global Warming, and to create a new ImmorTalist Civilization.

∞

To Do List...
to
Conquer Disease, Old Age & Death™
And
SAVE THE PLANET

Don't forget to

1 **Sign Our Demand!**

Go to immortalism.com to join Americans and world citizens in signing The Demand for a War to Cure Disease, Old Age & Death.

2 **Recruit at least 10 others to Sign Our Demand**

Ask your family, friends, associates — through your e mail to sign and join Our Demand. (Our Demand is in the front of this book.) The more the better!

3 **Support** The ImmorTalist Party Platform. (Go to immortalism.com to sign.)

4 **Visit Our Websites** and **Subscribe** to our Lists to Cure Disease, Old Age & Death. And return often to find Latest News, Analysis & Offers you won't find elsewhere. Get on our Lists. We need to show The Death Society's powers that be that we are legion.

5 **Offer your services, your skills, your talents! We know you're out there. And we need you.** Enlist in our War against Cancer, Heart Disease, Stroke, Diabetes, Alzheimer's, Osteoporosis, and Obesity etc killers *now.*

6   **If you believe you qualify as one of the 12 ImmorTalists that Elixxir is searching for, then step forward. Elixxir's been waiting for you. Together we will build The Elixxir Society.**

7   **Help Elixxir jumpstart and fund The ImmorTalist Movement. No foundation or fatcat is funding our movement. We need to do it ourselves. And time is running out.**

8   Organize your ImmorTalist Cell/Study/Action Group and <u>buy at least 10 copies of this book "Cure Disease, Old Age & Death: The ImmorTalist Manifesto."</u> If the fundamentalist Christians and Mormons know how to organize and sell books, surely you can too.

9   Your Group should <u>Get On The Elixxir Program.</u> It might be easier to organize around The Elixxir Program. A 100% scientific eating program which can dramatically retard your aging and prevent cancer, heart disease, stroke, hypertension, Alzheimer's, osteoporosis, and obesity. All with one proven delicious fabulous eating program.

10 Organize your Study/Action group and **buy 10 sets of "How to Look 20-Something at Past 50: The Elixxir Program Executive Report." You can get it at wholesale price and make a profit too. Inquire about Wholesale Orders** at orders@foreveryoungbooks.com

Your life — and your loved ones' lives — may depend on your taking action now.

If Christians can still make Bible-selling a billion-dollar business, why can't we sell The Elixxir Program? If Estée Lauder could parlay her potions of "hope" into a billion-dollar business, why aren't we smart enough to sell the only scientific anti-aging program?

If there's a multimillionaire or billionaire looking for a challenge, here it is. It could even save your life. The only game that matters.

You don't have to be a billionaire. Anyone who's a decent salesperson should be able to make a living and sustain herself or himself in six months by selling The Elixxir Program. And then you can make staff. We urgently need staff and organization.

Elixxir will contribute a significant part of the proceeds from your buying and selling of The Elixxir Program books or coaching into our movement-building. He is already doing that.

http://www.Immortalism.com

http://www.Elixxirprogram.com

http://www.NoMoreDying.com

P.S. FREE $99 Lifesaving Elixxir Newsletter subscription with this book. Don't forget to get yours with your receipt now. Just go to **http://www.ImmorTalism.com, http://www.ElixxirProgram.com, http://www.ElixxirSociety.com,** or **http://www.NoMoreDying.com**. Do it NOW so you won't forget!

Elixxir...The Only Anti-Aging Guru who has Actually Stayed Young

(Investor's Business Daily, Marilyn Much)

Reveals

How To Look 20-Something At Past 50!

1. Slash your Risk for Cancer, Heart Disease, Stroke, Diabetes, Osteoporosis, Alzheimer's

2. Lose Weight by Staying Young

3. Reverse 70% of your Age-Related Changes in Gene Expression in a Few Weeks

4. Look Years Younger in 72 Hours

Plus — a $500 gift

Imagine living to 120...with youthful vigor, free of disease... Elixxir is living proof — **Life Extension Magazine**

Elixxir is Most Amazingly Youthful...He is his own best argument — **Dr. David Weeks, BBC** Broadcaster, Bestselling Author, Expert on the SuperYoung & **Jamie James,** former **New Yorker** magazine art critic

Seeing is Believing! — **Marilyn Much, Investor's Business Daily**

Dear Friend,

My classmates and childhood friends have all grown old, fat, and ugly. I can still **pass for 20-something at past 50.**

I'm still getting carded. Still chased by suitors half my age. I've stayed as slim as in senior high. I make love with the potency and stamina of a young man. No Viagra.

And I just love family and class reunions!

My name is Elixxir. I've been on the only scientific anti-aging program for a third of a century.

Want to learn how I've stayed young and how you can too?

You can in my executive report

How to Look 20-Something at Past 50!
The Elixxir Program Executive Report

Science knows of <u>only one way</u> to dramatically retard your aging and greatly extend your maximum lifespan potential of 120 years by up to 50%.

The **New York Times, Wall Street Journal, AP** etc. have all reported this scientific fact. Proven repeatedly in prestigious laboratories around the world.

Life Extension Foundation calls it **"the only method proven to slow aging and extend lifespan in mammals."**

The Elixxir Program is *based on* the landmark anti-aging disease-preventing life-extending discovery by **Dr. Clive McCay, M.D.**at **Cornell Medical School.**

Still our *only scientific* anti-aging breakthrough!

So powerful it can *reverse* up to 70% — yes, 70%! — of **age-related changes in your gene expression** *in a few weeks.*
(Proc Natl Acad Sciences, Sept. 4, 2002, Stephen Spindler, Ph.D.)

Even in old rats. Great News for those of us who weren't born yesterday.

Dr. Stephen R. Spindler, Ph.D., who led this University of California research team said **"Older people may be able to benefit rapidly from switching (to such a program).**

You want to put the brakes on your aging and extend your lifespan? The **New York Times** concludes the scientific foundation of The Elixxir Program is **"the best—in fact the only bet."**

TO ORDER with our 60-Day Money-Back Guarantee, just go to http://www.Elixxir.com

Even **Dr. Atkins** admitted it is **"the best researched and most generously documented** (of all anti-aging programs)."

Barry Sears, Ph.D. calls it **"the Holy Grail of anti-aging."**

But amazingly most people still don't know about it. Or if they do, they've been told it's "too difficult."

Well, what if they're wrong? Dead wrong?

For three decades, I've tackled this challenge and transformed this scientific anti-aging regimen into *la dolce vita* **(The Sweet Life)**. I call this eating program The Elixxir Program™.

The result? After seeing Elixxir in person, the senior reporter of *Investor's Business Daily* crowned Elixxir as.........

"The <u>only</u> anti-aging guru who has <u>actually</u> stayed young."

Yes, probably like you, this veteran reporter has had enough of so-called "anti-aging gurus" who look *older* than their age.

Why model yourself after failure?

Dr. David Weeks, BBC Broadcaster, known for his long-running study of those who look at least 10 years younger than their age, raves...

**"Elixxir is Most Amazingly Youthful ...
He is his own best argument"**

Seeing is Believing

- My face is **wrinkle-free**. My skin **glows**. It's **baby smooth**.

- My body is virtually **fat-free**.

- A 26 inch waist. My BMI (body mass index) is that of a **teenager**.

- **Cellulite-free tight**, **smooth buns**, **Fat-free abs** Without Gym Torture.

- **A full head of <u>hair, still black</u>. <u>No liver spots, no turtle neck</u>.**

- **Watch your <u>Excess Weight & Ugly Fat</u> Melt Away on The Elixxir Program**

- **And *Keep them Away for Life—Without Gym Slavery.***

Too good to be true?

Just look at my most recent pictures. Elixxir is Baby Boomer but could pass for Generation X.

This is why Investor's Business Daily's Marilyn Much exclaims after meeting Elixxir, *"Seeing is believing!"*

Your Best Insurance against <u>Heart Attack</u>, <u>Cancer</u>, <u>Stroke</u> & Major Killer Diseases

Staying young is the best disease-prevention. The Elixxir Program not only dramatically slows down your aging, it also **slashes your risk for** Heart Disease, Cancer, Stroke, Diabetes, Hypertension, Osteoporosis & Alzheimer's.

At the same time you're staying young, slim, and beautiful. Only the Elixxir Program can achieve both for you.

Order with Mastercard, Visa, PayPal. It's easy!
Just click or go to http://www.Elixxir.com

See your Blood Pressure, Bad Cholesterol, and Blood Sugar Plunge...and Your Immune System Supercharge....Within a few weeks to a few months on The Elixxir Program.

The Sweet Life *(la dolce vita)*

On The Elixxir Program. Here's why...

Eat Anything
No ban on carbs or meat. Don't have to give up pasta or rice like on Atkins. You don't have to become almost vegetarian like on Pritikin or Ornish.

Champagne Is Fine
So is fine wine, Cognac and Calvados. A toast to the Forever Young Life!

No Hunger
Never feel hungry or deprived—ever again!

Safeguard Your #1 Asset
Legendary financier Sir Nathan Meyer Rothschild declared "I've got to keep breathing. It'll be my worst business mistake if I don't."

What is your most valuable asset? Your health and life. Without that, you have nothing.

Can You *Afford* to Grow Old & Die?

On her deathbed, **Queen Victoria** desperately offered *"My kingdom for a moment of time."* Don't wait until a heart attack, stroke or cancer strikes to 'get it.' You don't have time to reinvent the wheel. Can't afford to nickel and dime yourself. Or do trial and error.

As *"the anti-aging guru to the pampered set" (Investor's Business Daily),* retaining Elixxir as your coach will cost you. Perhaps a million dollars.

Limited-Time Offer

But for a short time only, Elixxir's Executive Report **How to Look 20-Something at Past 50!: The Elixxir Program is yours for only $99 + $15 shipping & handling* (total US $114).**

Learn about <u>Elixxir's Million-Dollar Anti-Aging Program</u> for only $99 (plus S&H). You don't get value like this every day.

Risk-Free 60-Day
Money-Back Guarantee

If *for any reason* you are not fully satisfied,
just return Elixxir's Executive Report in
60 days (2 months), you will get your $99 back.

No Questions Asked. Hassle-Free Refunds.

(Shipping & Handling not refundable)

So what do you have to lose?
Disease, Old Age & Death?

Order with Mastercard, Visa, American Express, Discover

or PayPal. It's easy! Just go to http://www.Elixxir.com

Gift #1 if you order now

$500 Value Credit Voucher towards personal coaching by Elixxir & Associates and a personal invitation to join Elixxir and his beauties in one of their international playgrounds. (Credit Voucher not exchangeable for cash)

Gift #2 if you order now

Elixxir reveals, in a short personal memo, the easy way to

"Look Years Younger in 72 Hours!"

Your spouse, loved ones, friends will <u>notice at once</u>. And wonder what you did. The value of an excellent facelift.

Order Now Risk-Free
with Mastercard, Visa, American Express, Discover or PayPal.

It's easy! Takes just a Minute!

You have Nothing to lose...
Everything to Gain.

TO ORDER with our 60-Day RISK-FREE Money-Back Guarantee, just go to **http://www.Elixxir.com**

Note: Our Bonus Gifts of 1) $500 value Credit Voucher towards personal coaching by Elixxir & Associates, and 2) Elixxir's memo on "Look Years Younger in 72 Hours!" may be revoked at any time. So order now to make sure you claim your bonus gifts.

12 ImmorTalist Warriors
Elixxir Wants You

"Before this century is over, billions of us will die, and the few breeding pairs of people that survive will be in *the arctic region*, where the climate remains tolerable." — *Dr. James Lovelock, Eminent Climate Scientist*

We have only a few years left to prevent the apocalyptic scenarios of Global Warming from destroying civilization. The U.N. Panel on Climate Change. NASA scientists. Al Gore. The U.N. Secretary-General. Climate Change Scientists Worldwide. They all agree on this.

Elixxir is searching the four corners of the earth to find The 12 ImmorTalist Warriors.

Where have you been? Elixxir's been waiting for you.

If you've read this book, and agree with even just 50% of it, what are you doing there? Running The Rat Race? Playing their rigged game where you end up loser?

What happened to all your dreams of great deeds? Your talents? Your idealism?

If you've had your wake-up call from Cancer, a Heart Attack, a Mini-Stroke, why haven't you awakened yet?

Doing more of the same will only get you more of the same.

Step Forward and Offer Yourself. There is no time to lose.

Conquer Cancer, Heart Disease, Stroke. And all the other major killers. Including the master disease — The Aging Syndrome.

The Twelve will join Elixxir's mission. Are you one of the Twelve?

Then you are one of the chosen. To help humanity conquer Disease, Old Age & Death. To save the Planet. And you will learn from Elixxir how to stay young on The Elixxir Program.

The Death Society wants you to be all alone. Demoralized. Exhausted. Afraid.

They want us to do politics with no community, with no support system. Like a Don Quixote tilting at windmills.

Alone you are impotent and easily discouraged. As part of The Elixxir Society, you are powerful and you will persevere till victory.

If fishermen can create a new faith with a carpenter's son, if they can make the Roman Empire fall to its knees, why can't you?

When Disease, Old Age and Death are looming, when Global Warming's apocalypse is descending on us, saving yourself and the planet is **the only sane and rational thing to devote your life to.**

To apply and get more details, write an e mail — 500 words maximum — to Elixxir on why you believe you are one of the twelve, what you can bring to the table, and why you would like to stay young on The Elixxir Progran and save the planet.

Send e mail to **12immortalists@gmail.com**
or go to **http://www.immortalism.com** or
http://www.ElixxirSociety.com and follow instructions.

Index

ORDER FORM

Special Quantity Pricing for bulk purchases for Support/Study Groups, Classes, Advocacy Organizations, Libraries, or Bookstores are available. Inquire with e mail to **orders@foreveryoungbooks.com**

NUMBER OF COPIES _____

SUPPORT/STUDY GROUP _____ ADVOCACY GROUP _____

Name _____

Address _____

City _____ State _____ Zip _____

Phone/Mobile _____

Fax _____

E mail Address _____

Website or Blog (if any) _____

Please send more information about

____ Your Other Books

____   The Elixxir Program

____   The Elixxir Society

____   The Elixxir Newsletter & Any Other Relevant Similar Info

Thank you! We will send you the info on a bulk purchase discount as soon as possible.

Reminder: If you like the book, please go to Amazon.com etc online booksellers to post a review. You don't have to agree 100% to post a positive fair interesting review. Don't let the Mortalists overwhelm us or silence us!

FREE $99 Lifesaving Elixxir Newsletter subscription with this book. Don't forget to get yours with your receipt now. Just go to **http://www.ImmorTalism. com, http://www.ElixxirProgram.com, http://www.ElixxirSociety.com**, or **http://www.NoMoreDying.com**. Do it NOW so you won't forget!

www.ingramcontent.com/pod-product-compliance
Lightning Source LLC
Chambersburg PA
CBHW051721260326
41914CB00031B/1675/J